CLUB STAFF - WHO'S W

Hon Life President
Mr Brian Bowman

Hon Vice President
Mr Andy Burnham MP

Hon Life Members
Mr Brian Bowman
Mr Tommy Coleman
Dr M Doublet-Stewart
Mr Michael Latham
Mr John Massey
Mr Fred Parkinson
Mr Alan Platt
Mr Allan Rowley
Mr Frank Taylor
Mr John Woods

Board of Directors
Mr Derek Beaumont *(Owner)*
Mr Michael Norris *(Chairman)*
Mr Matthew Chantler *(CEO)*
Mr Jason Huyton *(Commercial)*
Mr Michael Latham
(Media and Communications)
Mr Steve Openshaw *(Operations)*

Commercial Manager
Mrs Amanda Lee

Business Development Manager
Mr Neil Barker

Retail Outlet Manager
Mrs Gillian Jolley

Finance Manager
Ms Jane Smith

IT Manager
Mr Andrew Parkinson

Lottery Manager
Mrs Christine Brown

Assistant Lottery Manager
Mr Jonathan Simpkin

Social Media Manager
Mr Darren Lilly

Official Club Photographer
Mr Paul McCarthy

Leigh Centurions TV
Production: Mr Drew Darbyshire,
Mr Robert Lee, Mr Keiran Makin,
Mr Chris Stott, Mr Joe Wood

Club Ambassador
Mr Alex Murphy OBE

FOOTBALL AND SUPPORT STAFF

Head Coach
Mr Neil Jukes

Assistant Coaches
Mr Paul Anderson
Mr Paul Cooke
Mr Kieron Purtill

Player Welfare Manager
Mr Ste Maden

Head of Performance Analysis
Mr Ste Mills

Statistician
Mr Cliff Sumner

Strength and Conditioning Coaches
Mr Nathan Pennington
Mr Paul Wood

Club Doctor
Dr John Morgan,
Bucket & Sponge Medical Services

Physiotherapists
Mr Jonathan Skinner
Miss Elizabeth Cunliffe

Masseur
Mr Robert Stewart

Training Assistant
Mr Thomas Wood

Kit Managers
Mr Sean Fairhurst
Mr Frank Taylor

CONTACT DETAILS

Leigh Centurions, Leigh Sports Village Stadium, Sale Way, Leigh WN7 4JY

Telephone: 01942 487887 **Commercial Sales:** 01942 48789
General Enquiries: enquiries@leighrl.co.uk
Commercial Sales: Amanda.Lee@leighrl.co.uk
Lottery: lottery@leighrl.co.uk **Press Enquiries:** Andrew@leighrl.co.uk

Facebook: facebook.com/leighcenturionsfanpage
Twitter: twitter.com/LeighCenturions or tweet us @LeighCenturions

Scratching
Shed
Publishing

Airdrie Print Services Ltd,
24-26 Flowerhill Street,
Airdrie, North Lanarkshire,
Scotland ML6 6BH.

2017 BETFRED SUPER LEAGUE FIXTURES

RD	DATE	HOME TEAM	AWAY TEAM	VENUE	KO
1	Friday Feb 10 (Sky)	Castleford Tigers	Leigh Centurions	The Mend-A-Hose Jungle	8pm
1	Saturday Feb 11 (Sky)	Catalans Dragons	Warrington Wolves	Stade Gilbert Brutus	6pm
1	Saturday Feb 11	Salford Red Devils	Wigan Warriors	AJ Bell Stadium	3pm
1	Thursday Feb 9 (Sky)	St Helens	Leeds Rhinos	Langtree Park	8pm
1	Sunday Feb 12	Wakefield Trinity	Hull FC	Rapid Solicitors Stadium	3pm
1	Friday Feb 10	Widnes Vikings	Huddersfield Giants	Select Security Stadium	8pm
11	Thursday Feb 16 (Sky)	Huddersfield Giants	Salford Red Devils	John Smiths Stadium	8pm
11	Friday Feb 17 (Sky)	Leigh Centurions	Leeds Rhinos	Leigh Sports Village	8pm
2	Friday Feb 24	Huddersfield Giants	Wakefield Trinity	John Smiths Stadium	8pm
2	Thursday Feb 23 (Sky)	Hull FC	Catalans Dragons	KCOM Stadium	8pm
2	Friday Feb 24	Leeds Rhinos	Salford Red Devils	Headingley Carnegie Stadium	8pm
2	Friday Feb 24	Leigh Centurions	St Helens	Leigh Sports Village	8pm
2	Friday Feb 24	Warrington Wolves	Castleford Tigers	Halliwell Jones Stadium	8pm
2	Friday Feb 24 (Sky)	Wigan Warriors	Widnes Vikings	DW Stadium	8pm
3	Thursday Mar 2 (Sky)	Castleford Tigers	Leeds Rhinos	The Mend-A-Hose Jungle	8pm
3	Saturday Mar 4 (Sky)	Catalans Dragons	Widnes Vikings	Stade Gilbert Brutus	6pm
3	Friday Mar 3	Huddersfield Giants	Hull FC	John Smiths Stadium	8pm
3	Saturday Mar 4	Salford Red Devils	Warrington Wolves	AJ Bell Stadium	3pm
3	Friday Mar 3 (Sky)	St Helens	Wakefield Trinity	Langtree Park	8pm
3	Friday Mar 3	Wigan Warriors	Leigh Centurions	DW Stadium	8pm
4	Friday Mar 10 (Sky)	Hull FC	St Helens	KCOM Stadium	8pm
4	Friday Mar 10	Leeds Rhinos	Catalans Dragons	Headingley Carnegie Stadium	8pm
4	Friday Mar 10	Leigh Centurions	Huddersfield Giants	Leigh Sports Village	8pm
4	Sunday Mar 12	Wakefield Trinity	Salford Red Devils	Rapid Solicitors Stadium	3pm
4	Thursday Mar 9 (Sky)	Warrington Wolves	Wigan Warriors	Halliwell Jones Stadium	8pm
4	Sunday Mar 12	Widnes Vikings	Castleford Tigers	Select Security Stadium	3pm
5	Saturday Mar 18 (Sky)	Catalans Dragons	St Helens	Stade Gilbert Brutus	6pm
5	Friday Mar 17	Hull FC	Widnes Vikings	KCOM Stadium	8pm
5	Friday Mar 17 (Sky)	Leeds Rhinos	Wakefield Trinity	Headingley Carnegie Stadium	8pm
5	Thursday Mar 16 (Sky)	Leigh Centurions	Warrington Wolves	Leigh Sports Village	8pm
5	Sunday 19th March	Salford Red Devils	Castleford Tigers	AJ Bell Stadium	3pm
5	Sunday Mar 19	Wigan Warriors	Huddersfield Giants	DW Stadium	3pm
6	Sunday Mar 26	Castleford Tigers	Catalans Dragons	The Mend-A-Hose Jungle	3.30pm
6	Friday Mar 24	Huddersfield Giants	Leeds Rhinos	John Smiths Stadium	8pm
6	Friday Mar 24 (Sky)	St Helens	Warrington Wolves	Langtree Park	8pm
6	Thursday Mar 23 (Sky)	Wakefield Trinity	Leigh Centurions	Rapid Solicitors Stadium	8pm
6	Friday Mar 24	Widnes Vikings	Salford Red Devils	Select Security Stadium	8pm
6	Friday Mar 24	Wigan Warriors	Hull FC	DW Stadium	8pm
7	Friday Mar 31	Castleford Tigers	Huddersfield Giants	The Mend-A-Hose Jungle	8pm
7	Saturday Apr 1 (Sky)	Catalans Dragons	Wakefield Trinity	Stade Gilbert Brutus	6pm
7	Friday Mar 31 (Sky)	Leeds Rhinos	Wigan Warriors	Headingley Carnegie Stadium	8pm
7	Saturday Apr 1	Leigh Centurions	Widnes Vikings	Leigh Sports Village	6pm
7	Thursday Mar 30 (Sky)	Salford Red Devils	St Helens	AJ Bell Stadium	8pm
7	Saturday Apr 1	Warrington Wolves	Hull FC	Halliwell Jones Stadium	3pm
8	Friday Apr 7	Hull FC	Salford Red Devils	KCOM Stadium	8pm
8	Friday Apr 7	Leigh Centurions	Catalans Dragons	Leigh Sports Village	8pm
8	Friday Apr 7	St Helens	Huddersfield Giants	Langtree Park	8pm
8	Friday Apr 7	Wakefield Trinity	Widnes Vikings	Rapid Solicitors Stadium	8pm
8	Friday Apr 7 (Sky)	Warrington Wolves	Leeds Rhinos	Halliwell Jones Stadium	8pm
8	Thursday Apr 6 (Sky)	Wigan Warriors	Castleford Tigers	DW Stadium	8pm

RD	DATE	HOME TEAM	AWAY TEAM	VENUE	KO
9	Friday Apr 14 (Sky)	Castleford Tigers	Wakefield Trinity	The Mend-A-Hose Jungle	TBC
9	Thursday Apr 13	Huddersfield Giants	Catalans Dragons	John Smiths Stadium	8pm
9	Friday Apr 14	Hull FC	Leeds Rhinos	KCOM Stadium	TBC
9	Friday Apr 14	Salford Red Devils	Leigh Centurions	AJ Bell Stadium	TBC
9	Thursday Apr 13 (Sky)	Widnes Vikings	Warrington Wolves	Select Security Stadium	8pm
9	Friday Apr 14 (Sky)	Wigan Warriors	St Helens	DW Stadium	TBC
10	Monday Apr 17 (Sky)	Catalans Dragons	Salford Red Devils	Stade Gilbert Brutus	TBC
10	Monday Apr 17	Leeds Rhinos	Widnes Vikings	Headingley Carnegie Stadium	TBC
10	Monday Apr 17	Leigh Centurions	Hull FC	Leigh Sports Village	3pm
10	Monday Apr 17	St Helens	Castleford Tigers	Langtree Park	3pm
10	Monday Apr 17 (Sky)	Wakefield Trinity	Wigan Warriors	Rapid Solicitors Stadium	TBC
10	Monday Apr 17	Warrington Wolves	Huddersfield Giants	Halliwell Jones Stadium	3pm
11	Sunday Apr 23	Hull FC	Castleford Tigers	KCOM Stadium	3pm
11	Saturday Apr 22 (Sky)	Warrington Wolves	Wakefield Trinity	Halliwell Jones Stadium	TBC
11	Friday Apr 21 (Sky)	Widnes Vikings	St Helens	Select Security Stadium	8pm
11	Sunday Apr 23	Wigan Warriors	Catalans Dragons	DW Stadium	3pm
12	Saturday Apr 29	Castleford Tigers	Wigan Warriors	The Mend-A-Hose Jungle	3pm
12	Friday Apr 28 (Sky)	Hull FC	Warrington Wolves	KCOM Stadium	8pm
12	Thursday Apr 27 (Sky)	Leeds Rhinos	Huddersfield Giants	Headingley Carnegie Stadium	8pm
12	Sunday Apr 30	Salford Red Devils	Widnes Vikings	AJ Bell Stadium	3pm
12	Friday Apr 28	St Helens	Leigh Centurions	Langtree Park	8pm
12	Sunday Apr 30	Wakefield Trinity	Catalans Dragons	Rapid Solicitors Stadium	3pm
13	Saturday May 6 (Sky)	Catalans Dragons	Leeds Rhinos	Stade Gilbert Brutus	6pm
13	Thursday May 4 (Sky)	Huddersfield Giants	Castleford Tigers	John Smiths Stadium	8pm
13	Saturday May 6	Leigh Centurions	Wakefield Trinity	Leigh Sports Village	6pm
13	Friday May 5 (Sky)	Warrington Wolves	St Helens	Halliwell Jones Stadium	8pm
13	Sunday May 7	Widnes Vikings	Hull FC	Select Security Stadium	3pm
13	Friday May 5	Wigan Warriors	Salford Red Devils	DW Stadium	8pm
14	Sunday May 21 (Sky)	Castleford Tigers	Leeds Rhinos	Sports Direct Arena	TBC
14	Sunday May 21 (Sky)	Catalans Dragons	Huddersfield Giants	Sports Direct Arena	TBC
14	Saturday May 20 (Sky)	Hull FC	St Helens	Sports Direct Arena	TBC
14	Sunday May 21 (Sky)	Leigh Centurions	Salford Red Devils	Sports Direct Arena	TBC
14	Saturday May 20 (Sky)	Widnes Vikings	Wakefield Trinity	Sports Direct Arena	TBC
14	Saturday May 20 (Sky)	Wigan Warriors	Warrington Wolves	Sports Direct Arena	TBC
15	Friday May 26	Castleford Tigers	Widnes Vikings	The Mend-A-Hose Jungle	8pm
15	Friday May 26	Hull FC	Leigh Centurions	KCOM Stadium	8pm
15	Friday May 26 (Sky)	Leeds Rhinos	Warrington Wolves	Headingley Carnegie Stadium	8pm
15	Friday May 26	Salford Red Devils	Catalans Dragons	AJ Bell Stadium	8pm
15	Thursday May 25 (Sky)	St Helens	Wigan Warriors	Langtree Park	8pm
15	Friday May 26	Wakefield Trinity	Huddersfield Giants	Rapid Solicitors Stadium	8pm
16	Monday May 29 (Sky)	Catalans Dragons	Hull FC	Stade Gilbert Brutus	TBC
16	Monday May 29	Huddersfield Giants	St Helens	John Smiths Stadium	TBC
16	Monday May 29 (Sky)	Leigh Centurions	Castleford Tigers	Leigh Sports Village	TBC
16	Monday May 29	Warrington Wolves	Salford Red Devils	Halliwell Jones Stadium	3pm
16	Monday May 29	Widnes Vikings	Leeds Rhinos	Select Security Stadium	TBC
16	Monday May 29	Wigan Warriors	Wakefield Trinity	DW Stadium	TBC
17	Sunday Jun 4	Castleford Tigers	St Helens	The Mend-A-Hose Jungle	3.30pm
17	Sunday Jun 4	Huddersfield Giants	Warrington Wolves	John Smiths Stadium	3pm
17	Friday Jun 2 (Sky)	Hull FC	Wigan Warriors	KCOM Stadium	8pm
17	Friday Jun 2	Leeds Rhinos	Leigh Centurions	Headingley Carnegie Stadium	8pm
17	Saturday Jun 3	Salford Red Devils	Wakefield Trinity	AJ Bell Stadium	TBC
17	Sunday Jun 4	Widnes Vikings	Catalans Dragons	Select Security Stadium	3pm

2017 BETFRED SUPER LEAGUE FIXTURES

RD	DATE	HOME TEAM	AWAY TEAM	VENUE	KO
18	Sunday Jun 11	Castleford Tigers	Warrington Wolves	The Mend-A-Hose Jungle	3.30pm
18	Saturday Jun 10 (Sky)	Catalans Dragons	Huddersfield Giants	Stade Gilbert Brutus	6pm
18	Thursday Jun 8 (Sky)	Leigh Centurions	Wigan Warriors	Leigh Sports Village	8pm
18	Sunday Jun 11	Salford Red Devils	Hull FC	AJ Bell Stadium	3pm
18	Friday Jun 9	St Helens	Widnes Vikings	Langtree Park	8pm
18	Sunday Jun 11	Wakefield Trinity	Leeds Rhinos	Rapid Solicitors Stadium	3pm
19	Friday Jun 23	Huddersfield Giants	Wigan Warriors	John Smiths Stadium	8pm
19	Friday Jun 23	Hull FC	Wakefield Trinity	KCOM Stadium	8pm
19	Friday Jun 23	Leeds Rhinos	Castleford Tigers	Headingley Carnegie Stadium	8pm
19	Friday Jun 23	St Helens	Salford Red Devils	Langtree Park	8pm
19	Saturday Jun 24	Warrington Wolves	Catalans Dragons	Halliwell Jones Stadium	3pm
19	Thursday Jun 22 (Sky)	Widnes Vikings	Leigh Centurions	Select Security Stadium	8pm
20	Saturday July 1	Castleford Tigers	Hull FC	The Mend-A-Hose Jungle	7pm
20	Saturday Jul 1 (Sky)	Catalans Dragons	Leigh Centurions	Stade Gilbert Brutus	6pm
20	Thursday Jun 29 (Sky)	Leeds Rhinos	St Helens	Headingley Carnegie Stadium	8pm
20	Sunday Jul 2	Salford Red Devils	Huddersfield Giants	AJ Bell Stadium	3pm
20	Saturday Jul 1	Wakefield Trinity	Warrington Wolves	Rapid Solicitors Stadium	6.30pm
20	Sunday Jul 2	Widnes Vikings	Wigan Warriors	Select Security Stadium	3pm
21	Saturday Jul 8 (Sky)	Catalans Dragons	Wigan Warriors	Stade Gilbert Brutus	6pm
21	Friday Jul 7	Huddersfield Giants	Widnes Vikings	John Smiths Stadium	8pm
21	Sunday Jul 9	Salford Red Devils	Leeds Rhinos	AJ Bell Stadium	3pm
21	Friday Jul 7	St Helens	Hull FC	Langtree Park	8pm
21	Thursday Jul 6 (Sky)	Wakefield Trinity	Castleford Tigers	Rapid Solicitors Stadium	8pm
21	Friday Jul 7	Warrington Wolves	Leigh Centurions	Halliwell Jones Stadium	8pm
22	Sunday Jul 16	Castleford Tigers	Salford Red Devils	The Mend-A-Hose Jungle	3.30pm
22	Friday Jul 14	Huddersfield Giants	Leigh Centurions	John Smiths Stadium	8pm
22	Friday Jul 14	Leeds Rhinos	Hull FC	Headingley Carnegie Stadium	8pm
22	Sunday Jul 16	St Helens	Catalans Dragons	Langtree Park	3pm
22	Friday Jul 14	Widnes Vikings	Wakefield Trinity	Select Security Stadium	8pm
22	Thursday Jul 13 (Sky)	Wigan Warriors	Warrington Wolves	DW Stadium	8pm
23	Saturday Jul 22 (Sky)	Catalans Dragons	Castleford Tigers	Stade Gilbert Brutus	6pm
23	Sunday Jul 23	Hull FC	Huddersfield Giants	KCOM Stadium	8pm
23	Sunday Jul 23	Leigh Centurions	Salford Red Devils	Leigh Sports Village	3pm
23	Sunday Jul 23	Wakefield Trinity	St Helens	Rapid Solicitors Stadium	3pm
23	Thursday Jul 20 (Sky)	Warrington Wolves	Widnes Vikings	Halliwell Jones Stadium	8pm
23	Friday Jul 21 (Sky)	Wigan Warriors	Leeds Rhinos	DW Stadium	8pm

All fixtures copyright of the RFL, and subject to change

2017 BETFRED SUPER LEAGUE - KEY DATES

FEBRUARY
Weekend of 9th-12th - Betfred Super League Round One
Weekend of 18th-19th - Dacia World Club Series

AUGUST
Weekend of 3rd-6th - Super 8s begin
26th - Ladbrokes Challenge Cup Final

APRIL
Weekend of 14th-17th - Easter Weekend

SEPTEMBER
30th - £1M Game and Betfred Super League semi-finals

MAY
Weekend of 5th-8th - England Mid-Season International
(Details TBC)
Weekend of 20th-21st - Dacia Magic Weekend

OCTOBER
7th - Betfred Super League Grand Final

6

www.missingpixel.co.uk

Family and lifestyle photography you'll be
proud to hang on your walls.....

Chairman MICHAEL NORRIS

IF 2015 was Leigh Centurions' year, it did leave us all disappointed after our dismal showing in the Qualifiers. It was only through the amazing generosity and foresight of our owner Derek Beaumont that we started the 2016 season in good fettle.

Derek made up the huge financial shortfall caused by finishing bottom of the 8s in one go and he continued to plough in a regular monthly investment to ensure we had our best possible chance of success.

The events of the winter are recounted in this yearbook. As a club we faced many challenges and as a Board we had to pull together and see out the bad times, confident that the good times were around the corner.

In retrospect the opening day defeat at Batley was a galvanising day on and off the field. We never looked back. Neil Jukes and Paul Anderson were key figures throughout the season and the way they handled many issues was an amazing achievement. Micky Higham led from the front as captain and the influence of other senior players was critical.

At the time it seemed like we were involved in some kind of soap opera but we stuck together, weathered the storm and the team developed a consistent and effective playing style as week by week they saw off the best of the Championship.

The Challenge Cup defeat in Toulouse was a shock, but also maybe a blessing as the team then entered a long unbeaten period that culminated in a third successive League Leaders' Shield. The doubters were still out as we entered the 8s but the preparation was spot-on and a return to Super League was achieved in thrilling and memorable style.

It was very humbling and fulfilling to be Chairman of Leigh Centurions in 2016. We had a motto- when someone leaves, replace them with someone better. A few people left and we wish them well in their future endeavours. In their place we recruited quality replacements, on and off the field, while the continued support of our valued sponsors and business partners was crucial.

The Leyther family grew in numbers and the fantastic following we enjoyed at home and away underpinned our push for honours. LSV remained a vibrant place on match day and we enjoyed several fantastic commercial days including a highly successful Golf Day and an end of season awards that would have done justice to a BBC Sports Awards night. As a community club, we delivered time and time again, interacting and involving our fans and keeping them informed.

As an organisation we geared up quickly and effectively for the new season and ended a momentous year in a good place as we look forward to the 2017 Betfred Super League campaign.

2016 was 'Our Time' and it was a special year to be a Leigh Centurions fan. We now face new challenges and I am confident we will not only meet them but smash them down. We are a special club and one that doesn't accept second best.

Let's enjoy the ride!

Yours in sport,
MICHAEL NORRIS
Chairman

Neil Jukes

HEAD COACH

Born: 23 May 1976
Heritage Number: 1084
Contracted to: November 2018
Sponsored by Ascot Services

Neil took over as Head Coach following Paul Rowley's resignation on the eve of the 2016 season. He steered the team to another successful season in the Championship before plotting a successful course through the Qualifiers to earn promotion to Super League.

A former Leigh player during the mid-1990s, Neil came up through the Academy ranks and made his first-team debut at loose forward against Swinton in January 1995. He made 32 appearances for the Club, but sadly his playing career was cut short by injury following a spell at Rochdale Hornets in 1998.

Neil then turned his attentions to coaching and built up a fine reputation in the amateur ranks with Ince Rose Bridge, also coaching Lancashire. He re-joined Leigh in 2009, and coached the Reserves team to Division One League success before becoming primarily involved with a wide range of first-team duties in his role of assistant coach.

Autograph

Paul Anderson

ASSISTANT COACH

Born: 2 April 1977 Heritage Number: 1160
Contracted to: November 2018
Sponsored by diddi dance Wigan and Leigh

An outstanding junior player, Leigh-born Paul was snapped up by St Helens as a youngster and represented Great Britain Academy on their tour of Australia in 1996. He made his Saints first-team bow against Wigan on Boxing Day 1995, and made 46 appearances for Saints before joining Sheffield Eagles.

He came to Leigh in July 1999, and made his debut against Rochdale in the second row before making one of the centre spots his own. He went on to score 50 tries in 103 appearances for Leigh, before finishing his career with short stints at Oldham and Rochdale Hornets. After building up a fine reputation as a coach in the amateur game, Paul joined the Centurions' staff and coached the Reserves team to Championship grand final success in 2014 and to a second successive League Leaders position in 2015.

Working closely alongside Neil Jukes, the pair jointly won the Special Award at the Club's 2016 annual awards dinner for their immense contributions towards achieving a place in Super League.

Paul Cooke ASSISTANT COACH

Born: 17 April 1981 Contracted to: November 2018
Sponsored by The Britannia

Paul joined Leigh midway through the 2016 season after finishing his commitments with Doncaster Knights RUFC where he had been skills and backs coach since 2013, working with director of rugby Clive Griffiths. Cooke was highly regarded in the union game as the Knights finished second in the Championship - just failing to earn a place in the Premiership after a play-off loss against Bristol.

A vastly experienced player and coach in Rugby League, Cooke played with distinction for Hull FC, Hull Kingston Rovers and Wakefield Trinity Wildcats, clocking up 280 Super League appearances in 12 seasons in the top flight. He is best remembered for scoring the match-winning try in Hull FC's dramatic 25-24 Challenge Cup Final victory over Leeds at Cardiff in 2005, and also played in Hull's 2006 Super League grand final

defeat at the hands of St Helens.
After leaving Wakefield, Cooke joined Doncaster as a player in 2012 and became head coach at the club after Tony Miller's departure at the end of 2013.

In his first full season as player-coach in 2014, he was chosen as Kingstone Press Championship Coach of the Year. He left Doncaster midway through the 2015 season and finished his distinguished playing career with a short stint at Featherstone Rovers. In September 2016 he unveiled his autobiography 'Judas', written in conjunction with Talk Sport broadcaster Adrian Durham.

Kieron Purtill ASSISTANT COACH

Born: 12 February 1977 Heritage Number: 1146
Contracted to: November 2018
Sponsored by Boomers & Swingers

Kieron joined Neil Jukes' coaching staff in time for the start of the current season after his release from Huddersfield Giants. A highly respected level 4 coach, Kieron has worked alongside some of the game's best coaches since his playing career at Leigh was cruelly ended by a recurring shoulder injury in 2002.

He worked for St Helens from 2002-2005, for Huddersfield Giants from 2006-2008 and then returned to Saints from 2009-2012 before returning to the Giants. After being appointed coach to Canada in 2010, he has since been a highly successful coach to England Knights.

After signing for Leigh from Wigan St Pats, Kieron followed his elder brother Dean in playing for the Centurions and earned Heritage Number 1146. He

made 85 appearances for the Club, scoring 18 tries and kicking one drop-goal, and was a member of the Leigh side that lost to Dewsbury Rams 13-12 in the Premiership Grand Final in 2000 - playing alongside fellow assistant coach Paul Anderson.

Kieron's cousin Craig Rodgers also played for Leigh while his wife Debbie's granddad was the brilliant scrumhalf Peter Riley, a star of the Leigh side in the immediate post war era. Peter Riley's nephew was of course the great John Woods, whose grandfather Herbert was a member of the 1906 Championship-winning side.

1. Mitch Brown

Born: 7 November 1987
Debut: 2016
Heritage Number: 1418
Height: 6ft 1in
Weight: 95kg
Contracted to: November 2018
Sponsored by EDP

The experienced NRL star was one of three crucial signings just ahead of the July transfer deadline, and his impressive displays in the Qualifiers were crucial in the run-in.

Born in Sutherland, New South Wales he is a former Gymea junior who represented the Australian Schoolboys in 2005, and made his NRL debut on the wing for Cronulla against Penrith in 2006.

He played for Cronulla until the end of 2009, before joining Wests Tigers and moved onto play for Canterbury Bulldogs early in the 2012 campaign. He was in the Canterbury side that lost to South Sydney in the 2014 NRL grand final.

Autograph

He returned to Cronulla to begin the 2015 season and, shortly before moving to England, missed best man duties at his brother's wedding to score a try against Penrith in the Sharks' 13th consecutive victory that enhanced their position at the top of the NRL ladder. Brown is credited with 39 tries in 132 NRL games.

PLAYING CAREER

Cronulla Sharks *(2006-2009, 2015-2016)*
44 games, 9 tries, 36 points

Wests Tigers *(2010-2011)*
40 games, 8 tries, 1 goal, 34 points

Canterbury Bulldogs *(2013-2014)*
48 games, 22 tries, 88 points

Leigh Centurions *(2016)*
7 games, 4 tries, 16 points

TOTALS
139 games, 43 tries, 1 goal, 174 points

2. Adam Higson

Born: 19 May 1987
Debut: 2008
Heritage Number: 1310
Height: 6ft 3in
Weight: 94kg
Contracted to: November 2018
Sponsored by Health Shack

Short-listed alongside Micky Higham for both the Coaches' and Players' Player of the Year awards in 2016 (both won by Dayne Weston), 'AJ' scored some outstanding tries in Leigh's promotion push and continued his rapid development.

A former Leigh Miners Rangers ARL product, he made his senior debut in 2008. But his career was interrupted by injuries, and he also spent one season playing for Swinton before making a successful return to the Centurions.

Adam enjoyed an outstanding 2014 campaign, scoring 17 tries in 26 games, including some spectacular efforts and made the right-wing spot his own.

He continued his consistent progress with another fine season in 2015 despite early injury setbacks, and after passing the 100-game landmark he was later rewarded with a contract extension.

Autograph

PLAYING CAREER
Leigh Centurions *(2008-2011, 2013-2016)*
140 games, 61 tries, 244 points
Swinton Lions *(2012)*
15 games, 10 tries, 40 points
TOTALS
155 games, 71 tries, 284 points

3. Ben Crooks

Born: 15 June 1993
Height: 6ft 2in
Weight: 90kg
Contracted to: Season-long loan
from Castleford Tigers,
to November 2017
Sponsored by 24/7 Technology

Ben joined the Centurions on a season-long loan in time for pre-season training, after scoring six tries in 28 games for the Tigers as they finished fifth in Super League in 2016.

The son of former Hull FC, Leeds and Castleford international Lee Crooks (and nephew of former Castleford international Steve 'Knocker' Norton), Ben comes from rich Rugby League stock. Like both his famous relatives, he tried his luck in the NRL - signing for Parramatta Eels in September 2014 - before returning to England.

After emerging through their academy ranks, he made his Super League debut for Hull FC in 2012. The following season he was chosen for the Super League Dream Team, scored 20 tries in 22 games and formed a prolific partnership with winger Tom Lineham.

Autograph

Leigh fans will recall Ben's role in their club's only league defeat of the 2014 season - on dual-registration from Hull FC he scored two tries as Doncaster defeated Leigh 24-16 at the Keepmoat Stadium. It was a result which helped earn then Doncaster player-coach Paul Cooke the Kingstone Press Championship Coach of the Year award.

PLAYING CAREER

Hull FC *(2012-2014)*
51 games, 31 tries, 30 goals, 184 points

Doncaster *(2014)*
3 games, 5 tries, 20 points

Castleford Tigers *(2016)*
28 games, 6 tries, 1 goal, 26 points

TOTALS
82 games, 42 tries, 31 goals, 230 points

Ben Crooks in action for Castleford against Leeds

PIC: Matthew Merrick

4. Willie Tonga

Born: 8 July 1983
Debut: 2016
Heritage Number: 1411
Height: 6ft 1in
Weight: 102kg
Contracted to: November 2017
Sponsored by Premier Sport

Injury restricted Willie to half a dozen appearances in his first year at the LSV, but he spent two months in intensive training in the USA prior to rejoining the squad in time for pre-season.

Signed following his release from Catalans Dragons, Willie continues the heritage of famous Australian players joining Leigh, sparked by the Club's first Australian signing Mick Bolewski over one hundred years ago.

Willie made his NRL debut with Parramatta Eels in 2002 after being scouted by former Australian Test greats Arthur Beetson and Noel Cleal at a country rugby festival, before joining Canterbury in 2004.

Autograph

PLAYING CAREER

Parramatta Eels *(2002-2003, 2012-2014)*
40 games, 8 tries, 32 points

Canterbury Bulldogs *(2004-2008)*
81 games, 37 tries, 148 points

North Queensland Cowboys *(2009-2011)*
60 games, 34 tries, 136 points

Catalans Dragons *(2015)*
19 games, 6 tries, 24 points

Leigh Centurions *(2016)*
6 games,1 try, 4 points

Australia *(2004-2011)*
12 games, 8 tries, 32 points

Queensland *(2004-2011)*
8 games, 3 tries, 12 points

TOTALS
226 games, 97 tries, 388 points

In his first year with the Bulldogs, he played a prominent role in their 16-13 Grand Final victory over Sydney Roosters in a side that also included former Centurions team-mate Reni Maitua.

Willie also made his Queensland and Australian Test debuts in his breakthrough year of 2004, going on to make eight appearances for the Maroons and 12 appearances for the Kangaroos. He also scored two tries in Australia's 44-4 Tri-Nations Final victory over Great Britain at Elland Road that year.

After joining North Queensland in 2009, Willie re-signed for Parramatta in 2012 before making the move to play with Catalans Dragons. He has scored 86 tries in 206 club appearances and 11 tries in 22 representative appearances - which also include games for the Prime Minister's XIII and the Indigenous All Stars. His younger brother Esi is also an established NRL player.

5. Matty Dawson

WINGER

Born: 2 October 1990
Debut: 2016
Heritage Number: 1416
Height: 5ft 11in
Weight: 95kg
Contracted to: November 2018
Sponsored by
Holiday Inn Express, Leigh

The former St Helens winger joined up at LSV just before the July transfer deadline, after the clubs agreed a five-figure transfer fee. He went on to play a massive role in the Qualifiers, scoring some crucial tries.

A former Castleford Tigers junior who was a regular at halfback in the Tigers' under-20s side in 2010, he joined Huddersfield Giants in October of that year - and went on to make his Super League debut on the wing against Warrington in 2012.

He made a further four appearances for the Giants in 2013, and also scored three tries in ten games for Doncaster on dual-registration before following former Giants coach Nathan Brown to St Helens.

Autograph

In three seasons at Saints, he scored 16 tries in 50 games and also enjoyed two productive dual-registration spells with Rochdale Hornets.

PLAYING CAREER

Huddersfield Giants *(2012-2013)*
5 games

Doncaster *(2013)*
10 games, 3 tries, 12 points

Rochdale Hornets *(2014-2015)*
6 games, 5 tries, 20 points

St Helens *(2014-2016)*
50 games, 16 tries, 64 points

Leigh Centurions *(2016)*
8 games, 9 tries, 36 points

TOTALS
79 games, 33 tries, 132 points

Martyn Ridyard

Born: 25 July 1986
Debut: 2009
Heritage Number: 1314
Height: 5ft 9in
Weight: 88kg
Contracted to: November 2018
Sponsored by
McLaughlin's Kitchens

Martyn topped the Club's goals and points charts for the fifth season in a row in 2016, a feat only previously achieved by Jimmy Ledgard in the 1950s.

During the season, he passed 200 appearances for the Club and ended the season with 1,793 points after moving above Neil Turley into third place in the Club's all-time points table. Only Jimmy Ledgard (1,043 goals and 2,194 points) and John Woods (997 goals and 2,492 points) have kicked more goals or scored more points for the Club than Ridyard.

Autograph

A Leigh-born former Leigh Miners star and BARLA Young Lions and GB Community Lions international, Martyn made his debut for the Centurions in 2009. Martyn enjoyed an outstanding 2014 campaign, and carried off the Kingstone Press Championship Player of the Year Award and the Tom Bergin Trophy as Man of the Match in the Grand Final victory over Featherstone Rovers.

In 2015 his halfback partnership with Ryan Brierley continued to earn critical acclaim, not least from former Great Britain star Garry Schofield, and he was instrumental in another successful season.

In 2016 Martyn struck up a highly successful partnership with Josh Drinkwater in the second half of the season, which proved crucial to the Centurions' promotion push.

PLAYING CAREER
Leigh Centurions *(2009-2016)*
217 games, 77 tries, 738 goals, 9 field goals, 1,793 points

7. Josh Drinkwater

HALFBACK

Born: 15 June 1992
Debut: 2016
Heritage Number: 1413
Height: 5ft 10in
Weight: 90kg
Contracted to: November 2019
Sponsored by
AGS Technical Solutions Ltd

Josh gave Leigh a major boost by agreeing a contract extension just before the crucial Qualifiers game against Huddersfield. After making a try-scoring debut in the victory at Swinton in May, he played a major part in the second half of the season, forming a fine halfback partnership with Martyn Ridyard and becoming a firm fans' favourite.

Sydney born and a former Manly junior, he made his NRL bow with St George Illawarra in 2013 and then joined Wests Tigers after a season in Super League with London Broncos. He was top points scorer for the Broncos in their relegation season of 2014.

Autograph

Prior to returning to England, he had been in impressive form in the New South Wales Cup and won the Man of the Match award in NSW Residents' victory over Queensland Residents. He joined Leigh initially on a contract until the end of the current season, after starting 2016 as a member of Wests Tigers' 30-man NRL squad.

PLAYING CAREER

St George Illawarra Dragons *(2013)*
5 games, 1 field goal, 1 point

London Broncos *(2014)*
25 games, 5 tries, 58 goals, 136 points

Wests Tigers *(2015)*
1 game

Leigh Centurions *(2016)*
15 games, 8 tries, 1 goal, 34 points

TOTALS
46 games, 13 tries, 59 goals, 1 field goal, 171 points

8. Gareth Hock

Born: 5 September 1983
Debut: 2015
Heritage Number: 1397
Height: 6ft 2in
Weight: 110kg
Contracted to: November 2018
Sponsored by Palatine Paints

A former Great Britain and England international forward, Gareth joined the Club in February 2015 following his release from Salford Red Devils.

Wigan born, he came through the Warriors' scholarship and academy ranks - and earned Great Britain Academy international honours in 2001.

Gareth made his first team debut in 2003 against Doncaster, earning Heritage Number 953 for the Warriors. He went on to score 11 tries in 32 appearances in his first season and soon established a reputation as one of the best forwards in the game.

Autograph

PLAYING CAREER

Wigan Warriors *(2003-2009, 2011-2012)*
191 games, 48 tries, 192 points

Widnes Vikings *(2013)*
18 games, 10 tries, 1 goal, 42 points

Salford Red Devils *(2014-2015)*
18 games, 6 tries, 24 points

Leigh Centurions *(2015-2016)*
40 games, 9 tries, 36 points

England 'A' *(2003)*
4 games, 2 tries, 8 points

Great Britain *(2006)*
4 games

England *(2008-2009, 2012)*
9 games, 2 tries, 8 points

TOTALS
284 games, 77 tries, 1 goal, 310 points

He appeared in two finals whilst with Wigan, but unfortunately ended up on the losing side on both occasions. He was a substitute in the 2003 Super League Grand Final reverse against Bradford at Old Trafford, and started in the second row in the Warriors' Challenge Cup final defeat to St Helens at Cardiff the following season.

He scored 48 tries in 191 games for Wigan before leaving to spend a season-long loan at Widnes in 2013.

In September 2013 he signed a four-year contract at Salford. With over 250 club games and 17 appearances on the international stage, he used all his experience to become a key member of the Centurions' pack.

In 2015 he launched his hard-hitting autobiography 'Hock: The Real Me', written in conjunction with Neil Barker, to critical acclaim.

9. Micky Higham

HOOKER

Born: 18 September 1980
Debut: 1999
Heritage Number: 1153
Height: 5ft 8in
Weight: 88kg
Contracted to: November 2018
Sponsored by 24/7 Technology

After capping an outstanding personal campaign by earning the prestigious Championship Player of the Year award and leading his hometown club back into Super League, Micky closed in on the major landmark of 500 career appearances.

When Micky rejoined Leigh from Warrington in 2015, the £50,000 transfer fee was a Club record for the summer era. He made his second debut in the Summer Bash game against Featherstone, nearly 15 years after his last Leigh appearance.

Autograph

PLAYING CAREER

Leigh Centurions *(1999-2000, 2015-2016)*
86 games, 36 tries, 144 points

St Helens *(2001-2005)*
116 games, 35 tries, 140 points

Wigan Warriors *(2006-2008)*
97 games, 17 tries, 68 points

Warrington Wolves *(2009-2015)*
175 games, 37 tries, 148 points

Super League Under-21s *(2001)*
1 game

England Under-21s *(2001)*
2 games, 1 try, 4 points

England 'A' *(2002-2003)*
4 games

Great Britain *(2004-2005)*
4 games

England *(2008-2009)*
4 games, 1 try, 4 points

TOTALS
489 games, 127 tries, 508 points

After initially signing from Leigh East, Micky came to the fore in the 2000 season - earning the Man of the Match Award as Paul Terzis's side suffered a 13-12 defeat at the hands of Dewsbury Rams in the Northern Ford Premiership Grand Final.

After that pivotal game, Micky then embarked on a fine career at the top level playing with distinction for St Helens, Wigan Warriors and Warrington Wolves.

Whilst with the Wolves, he featured in three victorious Challenge Cup Finals at Wembley, defeating Huddersfield 25-12 (2009), Leeds 30-6 (2010) and Leeds again (35-18, 2012).

Micky also joined the select group of Leigh-born players to represent Great Britain when he made his debut against New Zealand at Hull in the 2004 Tri-Nations, and made three further appearances in the 2005 Tri-Nations.

10. Dayne Weston

Born: 15 December 1986
Debut: 2016
Heritage Number: 1401
Height: 6ft 2in
Weight: 104kg
Contracted to: November 2019
Sponsored by
TRY Fitness Training

Dayne enjoyed a stand-out debut season in 2016, earning a notable hat-trick of awards as Coaches', Players' and LCTV Player of the Year.

He brought an imposing physical presence to the Centurions pack and was superbly consistent throughout the campaign, missing only one game.

Hailing from Goulburn in New South Wales, Dayne earned a scholarship with Illawarra Steelers and began his top-flight career with Cronulla in 2007. He subsequently played for North Queensland and Penrith, and in the Queensland Cup for Mackay Cutters and Burleigh Bears, before joining Melbourne Storm midway through 2013.

Autograph

Dayne readily agreed to become an ambassador for Leigh Community Trust, and devised an anti-bullying programme for local schools among his tireless work in the local community.

PLAYING CAREER

Cronulla Sharks *(2007)*
10 games

North Queensland Cowboys *(2008-2009)*
21 games, 2 tries, 8 points

Penrith Panthers *(2011-2012)*
33 games

Melbourne Storm *(2014-2015)*
16 games

Leigh Centurions *(2016)*
31 games, 6 tries, 24 points

TOTALS
111 games, 8 tries, 32 points

11. Cory Paterson — UTILITY

Born: 14 July 1987
Debut: 2016
Heritage Number: 1406
Height: 6ft 4in
Weight: 102kg
Contracted to: November 2018
Sponsored by Anytime Fitness

Joint Vice Captain in 2016 alongside his former Salford team-mate Harrison Hansen, Cory finished the campaign as top try-scorer (18) and became the first forward to top Leigh's scoring charts since Micky Higham in 2000.

Signed on a three-year contract, Cory is a vastly experienced utility player in both the NRL and Super League.

Born in Perth, Western Australia, Cory earned Australian Schoolboy honours and joined the Newcastle Knights, making his NRL debut in 2007. He later played for North Queensland Cowboys and Wests Tigers.

After a season with Hull KR in 2013, Cory came back to England to play for Salford Red Devils in the 2015 Super League campaign.

Autograph

PLAYING CAREER

Newcastle Knights *(2007-2011)*
77 games, 21 tries, 12 goals, 108 points

North Queensland Cowboys *(2011-2012)*
10 games, 4 tries, 16 points

Hull Kingston Rovers *(2013)*
17 games, 7 tries, 28 points

Wests Tigers *(2014)*
9 games, 1 try, 2 goals, 8 points

Salford Red Devils *(2015)*
21 games, 10 tries, 9 goals, 58 points

Leigh Centurions *(2016)*
21 games, 18 tries, 72 points

TOTALS
155 games, 61 tries, 23 goals, 290 points

12. Glenn Stewart

Born: 11 January 1984
Height: 5ft 10in
Weight: 99kg
Contracted to: November 2018
Sponsored by Lewis William

Arguably Leigh's major close season signing, Glenn was a regular in the Catalans pack in 2016 before agreeing a release one year into a three-year contract for family reasons.

Prior to moving to France, Stewart enjoyed a 13-year first-grade career in the NRL. He played 187 games for Manly Sea Eagles following his debut in 2003, and a further 19 for South Sydney in 2015.

Glenn has a wealth of representative experience - including five Australian caps and five appearances for New South Wales in State of Origin - and played in the 2008 World Cup Final.

Born in Wollongong, he played alongside his younger brother Brett, winning Premierships in 2008 and 2011 with grand final victories over Melbourne and New Zealand Warriors. In the latter grand final, he won the Clive Churchill Medal as the game's outstanding player.

Autograph

PLAYING CAREER
Manly Sea Eagles *(2003-2014)*   187 games, 27 tries, 108 points
South Sydney Rabbitohs *(2015)*   19 games
Catalans Dragons *(2016)*   30 games, 3 tries, 12 points
Australia *(2008-2009)*   5 games
New South Wales *(2009, 2011-2012)*   5 games
New South Wales, Country *(2008, 2010-2011)*   3 games
TOTALS   249 games, 30 tries, 120 points

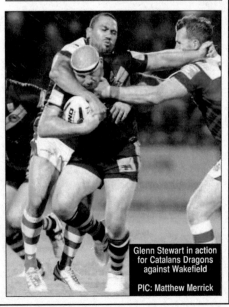

Glenn Stewart in action for Catalans Dragons against Wakefield

PIC: Matthew Merrick

13. Harrison Hansen

BACK ROW FORWARD

Born: 26 October 1985
Debut: 2016
Heritage Number: 1402
Height: 6ft 1in
Weight: 103kg
Contracted to: November 2017
(Club has further one year option)
Sponsored by JD's Diner

Joint Vice Captain in 2016, Harrison enjoyed a highly successful campaign and was consistently outstanding in the pack, justifying his decision to take a step down from Super League as he played a massive part in the Centurions' promotion push.

A vastly experienced forward who has achieved some of the game's highest honours, Harrison was born in Auckland, New Zealand. He was schooled in England, where his father Shane was a professional for both Salford and Swinton, earning a reputation as one of the game's best tacklers.

Harrison played for the famous Folly Lane club at junior level and came through the successful Wigan Warriors junior development scheme, making his first-team debut for the club in 2004.

Autograph

PLAYING CAREER

Wigan Warriors *(2004-2013)*
242 games, 43 tries, 172 points

Salford Red Devils *(2014-2015)*
52 games, 9 tries, 36 points

Leigh Centurions *(2016)*
29 games, 6 tries, 24 points

New Zealand *(2006)*
1 game

Samoa *(2007-2010)*
8 games, 3 tries, 12 points

The Exiles *(2013)*
1 game

TOTALS
333 games, 61 tries, 244 points

He went on to make 242 appearances for the Warriors, winning the Grand Final in 2010 against St Helens and the Challenge Cup in 2011 against Leeds. He then achieved the notable Super League and Challenge Cup double in the club's momentous 2013 campaign.

After earning England international honours at youth level, he represented New Zealand in 2006 and then went on to play for Samoa, featuring in the 2008 World Cup.

He was then chosen to captain Samoa in the 2013 World Cup, but had to subsequently withdraw from the squad due to injury.

Harrison turned down the opportunity of a testimonial at Wigan to join Salford, where he was one of the mainstays of their pack in a two-year stint.

14. Eloi Pelissier

HOOKER
Born: 18 June 1991
Height: 5ft 8in
Weight: 82kg
Contracted to: November 2018
Sponsored by
Polar Cooling Services Ltd

The French international hooker moved to Leigh from Catalans Dragons, and scored a try for France in their international against England in Avignon just before joining up with his new club.

PLAYING CAREER

Catalans Dragons
(2011-2016)
154 games, 27 tries,
1 field goal, 109 points

France *(2011-2014, 2016)*
14 games, 5 tries, 20 points

TOTALS
168 games, 32 tries,
1 field goal, 129 points

A product of the Dragons Academy and Perpignan born, he had trials with Wigan under-18s in 2008 and played for St-Esteve in the French Championship before making his Super League debut in 2011.

In each of the past five seasons he has been a regular in the Dragons' line-up, scoring 27 tries in 154 top flight appearances.

Autograph

16. Antoni Maria

FORWARD
Born: 21 March 1987
Height: 6ft 2in
Weight: 102kg
Contracted to: November 2018
Sponsored by
ACS Construction Group

Leigh confirmed the signing of the former Catalans Dragons international in the summer, and he linked up with his new club for pre-season training.

PLAYING CAREER

Toulouse Olympique
(2009-2011) 66 games,
12 tries, 48 points

Catalans Dragons
(2012-2016)
41 games, 1 try, 4 points

France *(2012-2015)*
9 games

TOTALS 116 games,
13 tries, 52 points

A regular in the French side, he represented his country in the 2013 World Cup.

After impressing with Saint-Gaudens in the French Elite Championship, Maria joined Toulouse Olympique for their previous stint in the RFL Championship. Between 2009 and 2011 he made 66 appearances, before his impressive performances earned him a contract with Catalans.

Autograph

15. Danny Tickle

Born: 10 March 1983
Debut: 2016
Heritage Number: 1416
Height: 6ft 1in
Weight: 105kg
Contracted to: November 2017
Sponsored by
LoveMyFurniture.co.uk

Leigh confirmed Danny's signing from Castleford just before the transfer deadline and he made his debut against Dewsbury at LSV, going on to play a key role in the successful Qualifiers series.

A product of the famous Golborne Parkside community club, Tickle's first professional club was Halifax, making his Super League debut as a teenager in 2000.

PLAYING CAREER

Halifax *(2000-2002)*
45 games, 10 tries, 100 goals, 2 field goals,
242 points

Wigan Warriors *(2002-2006)*
141 games, 34 tries, 217 goals, 2 field goals,
572 points

Hull FC *(2007-2013)*
177 games, 47 tries, 571 goals, 1 field goal,
1,331 points

Widnes Vikings *(2014-2015)*
45 games, 3 tries, 118 goals, 248 points

Castleford Tigers *(2016)*
11 games, 1 goal, 2 points

Leigh Centurions *(2016)*
7 games

England 'A' *(2002-2003)*
8 games, 4 tries, 37 goals, 90 points

England *(2009, 2012)*
2 games, 1 try, 4 points

TOTALS
436 games, 99 tries, 1,044 goals, 5 field goals,
2,489 points

Autograph

He moved on to Wigan in 2002 and then spent seven seasons with Hull FC, then two campaigns with Widnes Vikings. He joined Castleford in April 2016.

Few players can match Tickle's remarkable consistency and durability in topflight Rugby League, and he is also recognised as a top class goal-kicker and regular try-scorer.

He has made two appearances for England (in the game against Wales at Bridgend in 2009, Micky Higham was a team-mate) as part of over 400 senior appearances. He has scored 99 career tries and kicked over 1,000 goals.

Tickle won a European Championship winners medal with England 'A' in 2003, and while with Wigan was a runner-up in the 2003 Super League Grand Final and in the 2004 (with Wigan) and 2013 (with Hull FC) Challenge Cup finals.

17. Atelea Vea

FORWARD
Born: 27 November 1986
Height: 6ft 0in
Weight: 104kg
Contracted to: November 2018
Sponsored by O2 Leigh

Atelea has spent the past two seasons with St Helens, and after an injury curtailed 2015 campaign was a regular in the Saints pack in 2016.

Sydney born, he made his NRL bow with Cronulla and later played for Melbourne and St George-Illawarra before joining London Broncos.

A tough and direct powerhouse, 'Tils' looks sure to become a firm favourite with the Centurions' fans.

PLAYING CAREER

Cronulla Sharks *(2009)*
8 games

Melbourne Storm *(2011)*
11 games

St George Illawarra Dragons *(2012-2013)*
3 games

London Broncos *(2014)*
23 games, 2 tries, 8 points

St Helens *(2015-2016)*
40 games, 10 tries, 40 points

Tonga *(2009)*
2 games, 1 try, 4 points

TOTALS
87 games, 13 tries, 52 points

Autograph

19. Ryan Hampshire

UTILITY BACK
Born: 29 December 1994
Height: 5ft 9in
Weight: 85kg
Contracted to: November 2018
Sponsored by M Logan and Sons

Leigh confirmed the signing of utility back Ryan just before pre-season training.

Ryan spent 2016 on a season long loan at Castleford, scoring eight tries in 22 first-team appearances.

A product of Normanton Knights, he was spotted by Wigan at the age of 15. He played for Wigan's under-16s and under-18s in 2011, their under-18s and under-20s in 2012, and toured Australia with England Academy in 2012.

After making his Super League debut for Wigan at Widnes in June 2013, he went on to make 30 first-team appearances for the Warriors.

PLAYING CAREER

Wigan Warriors *(2013-2015)*
30 games, 9 tries, 24 goals, 84 points

Workington Town *(2015)*
1 game

Castleford Tigers *(2016)*
22 games, 8 tries, 32 points

TOTALS
53 games, 17 tries, 24 goals, 116 points

Autograph

18. Gregg McNally

Born: 2 January 1991
Debut: 2012
Heritage Number: 1350
Height: 5ft 10in
Weight: 84kg
Contracted to: November 2018
Sponsored by
CDA Business Solutions

Gregg battled back from a serious leg injury sustained in the warm up game at Warrington to regain his first-team place for the final two months of the 2016 season.

He emerged at hometown Whitehaven, and actually scored the last-ever try at Hilton Park in 2008. His performances earned him a contract at Huddersfield, but first-team chances were limited.

He has established himself as a top-class, try-scoring fullback and became only the second Leigh fullback (after Neil Turley) to top 20 tries in a season in 2014. He surpassed that total with 30 in 2015, and ended the year with a trio of Club Player of the Year awards, as voted for by the Head Coach, Leigh CPA and LISA respectively.

Autograph

PLAYING CAREER

Whitehaven *(2008-2010)*
36 games, 33 tries, 83 goals, 298 points

Oldham *(2010)*
12 games, 7 tries, 46 goals, 1 field goal, 121 points

Barrow Raiders *(2011)*
0 games, 3 tries, 5 goals, 22 points

Huddersfield Giants *(2011)*
1 game, 6 goals, 12 points

Leigh Centurions *(2012-2016)*
132 games, 88 tries, 20 goals, 392 points

Ireland *(2010-2012)*
6 games, 3 tries, 9 goals, 30 points

TOTALS
195 games, 134 tries, 169 goals, 1 field goal, 875 points

20. Ben Reynolds

Born: 15 January 1994
Debut: 2014
Heritage Number: 1398
Height: 6ft 0in
Weight: 94kg
Contracted to: November 2018
Sponsored by LISA

A talented goalkicking halfback or fullback, Ben joined Leigh Centurions on a free-transfer from Castleford Tigers on a full-time contract in time for the start of preseason training in November 2014.

He had come to the fore during that year, making two Super League appearances for Castleford and impressing on a dual-registration contract with Kingstone Press Championship One League Leaders York City Knights.

He was joint Championship One Young Player of the Year in 2014, alongside City Knights team-mate James Saltonstall, was one of the nominations for Championship One Player of the Year (won by York team-mate Jack Lee) and also selected in the Championship One All-Star team. He scored seven tries and kicked 70 goals in 16 appearances for York during that season.

Autograph

PLAYING CAREER

Castleford Tigers *(2013-2014)*
4 games

York City Knights *(2014)*
16 games, 7 tries, 70 goals, 168 points

Doncaster *(2015)*
3 games, 1 try, 1 goal, 6 points

Leigh Centurions *(2015-2016)*
26 games, 11 tries, 15 goals, 74 points

Dewsbury Rams *(2016)*
4 games, 1 try, 11 goals, 26 points

TOTALS
53 games, 20 tries, 97 goals, 274 points

A former Knottingley and Featherstone Lions ARL product, Reynolds graduated through the ranks of the Castleford Tigers Academy and had been training full-time with the Tigers' first-team squad since November 2012.

Though his first-team opportunities for Leigh were limited in 2015, he made eight appearances - scoring three tries and kicking six goals. He also spent a month loan at Doncaster early in the campaign.

Ben signed a three-year contract extension tying him to the Club until the end of 2018, and was involved in a season-long loan deal to Dewsbury Rams for the 2016 season to gain more first-team experience. He was later recalled by Head Coach Neil Jukes in March 2016 as an injury list mounted at the Club, and reappeared for the Centurions in their fine victory at Halifax, going on to play 18 games in the campaign.

21. Liam Hood

HOOKER

Born: 6 January 1992
Debut: 2016
Heritage Number: 1410
Height: 5ft 9in
Weight: 89kg
Contracted to: November 2017
Sponsored by
CTR Joinery Limited

Liam joined Leigh in March 2016 and he made his debut in the win at Halifax a few days later, quickly earning a regular place in the squad.

Bradford-born, he has played Super League for Leeds Rhinos and Salford Red Devils and has gained international experience with Scotland, featuring in the 2016 Four Nations series.

After signing professional forms from Stanningley he emerged through the ranks at Leeds, making his Super League debut in 2012. He was released by the Rhinos at the end of that season (after scoring three tries in five games) frustrated by the lack of first-team opportunities.

Autograph

PLAYING CAREER

Dewsbury Rams *(2012)*
12 games, 2 tries, 8 points

Leeds Rhinos *(2012)*
5 games, 3 tries, 12 points

Hunslet Hawks *(2013-2014)*
36 games, 18 tries, 72 points

Salford Red Devils *(2015)*
22 games, 1 try, 4 points

Swinton Lions *(2016)*
4 games

Leigh Centurions *(2016)*
19 games, 4 tries, 16 points

Scotland *(2012, 2015-2016)*
7 games, 1 try, 4 points

TOTALS
105 games, 29 tries, 116 points

Liam enjoyed a successful stint as a dual-registration player with Dewsbury Rams in 2012 and impressed with Hunslet Hawks in 2013 and 2014, starring in the Hawks' dramatic Championship One grand final success over Oldham.

He then got another opportunity of being a full-time player with Salford. Liam made 22 appearances for the Red Devils in 2015, and played against Leigh in the Challenge Cup tie between the two sides at LSV.

In 2016 he started the season with fellow Kingstone Press Championship club Swinton Lions, after cutting short an intended move to play in the Queensland competition. The Lions then agreed to release him when the opportunity of a full-time Centurions contract came along.

22. James Green

Born: 29 November 1990
Height: 6ft 7in
Weight: 112kg
Contracted to: November 2018
Sponsored by Balmer Wilcock

The giant forward joined the Club from Hull Kingston Rovers, where he made over 80 first-team appearances, and was a regular in the Robins' pack in each of the past four seasons.

With dual-registration experience at four clubs - Workington Town, Batley Bulldogs, Gateshead Thunder and Featherstone Rovers - earlier in his career, Beverley-born Green has already made over one hundred senior appearances since his Hull KR debut in 2012.

After graduating through the ranks of community club Skirlaugh, Green came to prominence in the successful Robins reserve side in 2011 and made his Super League debut against Bradford Bulls in August 2012.

In 2014, he won the Rovers Young Player of the Year award.

Autograph

PLAYING CAREER

Hull Kingston Rovers *(2012-2016)*
82 games, 3 tries, 12 points

Batley Bulldogs *(2012)*
9 games

Workington Town *(2012)*
3 games

Featherstone Rovers *(2013)*
3 games

Gateshead Thunder *(2013)*
5 games

TOTALS
102 games, 3 tries, 12 points

James Green in action for Hull KR against Castleford

PIC: Courtesy of Hull KR

23. Sam Hopkins

Born: 17 February 1990
Debut: 2011
Heritage Number: 1347
Height: 6ft 3in
Weight: 101kg
Contracted to: November 2017
Sponsored by Pam Ties

Sam capped a memorable 2016 campaign with a late call-up to the international stage, representing Wales in their crucial World Cup qualifying victory over Italy in Monza.

After leaving the Centurions to join Wigan Warriors at the end of the 2013 season, Sam was soon back at the LSV in 2014 and played 20 games on loan, impressing in Leigh's dominant pack.

The Centurions then extended that loan period to cover the whole of the 2015 season, before agreeing terms for a permanent move with the Warriors midway through the year.

After emerging through the ranks at Leigh East, Sam made rapid strides following his senior debut in 2011 and followed the lead of team-mate Chris Hill in signing for a Super League club.

He passed the landmark of 100 Leigh appearances late in the 2015 campaign, and also played one game for Workington Town on dual-registration from Wigan in 2014.

Autograph

PLAYING CAREER

Leigh Centurions *(2011-2016)*
135 games, 48 tries, 192 points

Workington Town *(2014)*
1 game, 1 try, 4 points

Wales *(2016)*
1 game

TOTALS
137 games, 49 tries, 196 points

Jamie Acton

Born: 4 April 1992
Debut: 2014
Heritage Number: 1389
Height: 6ft 0in
Weight: 106kg
Contracted to: November 2018
Sponsored by
Online Surface Coatings

London born Jamie first played Rugby League with Hemel Stags as a 16-year-old, having initially played rugby union.

He moved to Wigan Warriors and was a regular in their under-20s Academy side in 2011, and has also represented England and BARLA at under-18s level.

Jamie made his senior debut as a dual-registered player with South Wales Scorpions in 2012, and later that season played for Oldham.

In 2013 he was a regular in the Workington Town side, before joining Leigh in September 2013 and soon becoming a firm fans' favourite.

Autograph

PLAYING CAREER

South Wales Scorpions *(2012)*
3 games, 1 try, 4 points

Oldham *(2012)*
6 games

Workington Town *(2013)*
22 games, 2 tries, 8 points

Leigh Centurions *(2014-2016)*
57 games, 6 tries, 24 points

TOTALS
88 games, 9 tries, 36 points

25. Lee Smith

UTILITY BACK

Born: 8 August 1986
Debut: 2016
Heritage Number: 1404
Height: 5ft 11in
Weight: 97kg
Contracted to: November 2017
Sponsored by LISA

A vastly experienced and successful player at club and international level, Lee has spent most of his career at Leeds Rhinos.

Morley born, he was the Rhinos' Academy Player of the Year in 2003 and made his first-team debut against Wakefield in March 2005. He went to prove his versatility by playing for the Rhinos in three different positions in successive Super League Grand Final successes (all against St Helens).

He scored a try from the wing in the Rhinos' 33-6 victory in 2007 and scored a try from fullback a year later as Leeds defeated the Saints 24-16. His display at Old Trafford that evening won him the Harry Sunderland Trophy as man of the match.

In 2009, he scored two tries from centre in the Rhinos' 18-10 victory over the Saints at Old Trafford before embarking on what proved to be a short career in rugby union with London Wasps. Lee returned to Leeds in February 2010, and went on to make 156 appearances for the club.

Autograph

In the summer of 2012 he joined Wakefield Trinity Wildcats, but then returned to rugby union to play for Newcastle Falcons in February 2014. He briefly returned to Wakefield at the end of the 2015 season, when he crucially kicked a drop-goal in the Wildcats' 17-16 win at LSV in the Super 8s Qualifiers.

Lee made his England debut in their Federation Shield success in 2006, and also represented his country in the 2008 World Cup and 2009 Four Nations tournament.

After joining the Centurions and becoming Neil Jukes' first signing, Lee quickly scored the three tries he needed to join the elite band of players to score 100 tries in their senior Rugby League career and his experience, versatility and goal-kicking ability proved of immense value throughout the campaign.

PLAYING CAREER

Leeds Rhinos *(2005-2012)*
150 games, 60 tries, 94 goals, 1 field goal, 341 points

Wakefield Trinity Wildcats *(2012-2013, 2015)*
41 games, 23 tries, 79 goals, 3 field goals, 253 points

Leigh Centurions *(2016)*
23 games, 12 tries, 36 goals, 120 points

England *(2006, 2008-2009)*
8 games, 7 tries, 1 goal, 30 points

TOTALS
228 games, 110 tries, 150 goals, 4 field goals, 744 points

26. Lewis Foster

HALFBACK/HOOKER
Born: 21 December 1993
Debut: 2014
Heritage Number: 1391
Height: 5ft 9in
Weight: 80kg
Contracted to: November 2017
Sponsored by LISA

Formerly with St Helens, Lewis impressed playing for Paul Anderson's Reserves side in 2014 and made his senior debut against Doncaster in May of that year.

PLAYING CAREER
Leigh Centurions *(2014-2016)* 10 games, 1 try, 4 points
Oldham *(2016)* 7 games, 1 try, 4 points
TOTALS 17 games, 2 tries, 8 points

He was one of several Reserves team stand-outs to be offered full-time contracts and, viewed as an outstanding prospect for the future, his deal was then extended to the end of 2017.

He furthered his experience with a loan spell at Oldham during the 2016 campaign.

Autograph

27. David Thompson

WINGER
Born: 13 September 1995
Height: 6ft 1in
Weight: 103kg
Contracted to: November 2018
Sponsored by John Cisk & Sons

The Wigan born former England Academy three-quarter joined the Centurions from Warrington Wolves in time for pre-season training.

PLAYING CAREER
Hull Kingston Rovers *(2016)* 2 games

David previously spent time on loan at Hull Kingston Rovers, making two senior appearances late in the 2016 season.

After graduating through the Wigan Academy structure and representing the Warriors at under-19s level in 2015, Thompson featured regularly in Warrington Wolves' reserve side until the move to Humberside allowed him the opportunity to make his senior debut.

Autograph

28. James Clare

Born: 13 April 1991
Height: 6ft 2in
Weight: 88kg
Contracted to: November 2018
Sponsored by WL Piling

James came on board at LSV after Bradford Bulls' sad demise, as preparations for the start of the 2017 Super League campaign intensified.

The former Castleford Tigers and Bulls utility joined the Club on a two-year contract up until the end of November 2018, and linked up with his new teammates for the pre-season warm weather training camp at Club La Santa in Lanzarote.

Clare came up through the ranks of his hometown club Castleford after graduating from the well respected community club Lock Lane, and in 2010 was the Tigers' under-20s Player of the Year.

Autograph

He made his Super League debut for the Tigers against Huddersfield Giants in March 2012, and went on to score 24 tries in 38 games for the club before a mid-season move to Bradford in 2015. He scored 21 tries in 30 games for the Bulls, including three tries against Leigh during the 2016 campaign, two of them in the space of three minutes in the 32-32 draw at Odsal last February.

With additional dual-registration experience at Doncaster and York City Knights, his career tally of 55 tries has come in only 79 senior games.

PLAYING CAREER

Castleford Tigers *(2012-2015)*
38 games, 24 tries, 96 points

Doncaster *(2013)*
4 games, 1 try, 4 points

York City Knights *(2015)*
7 games, 9 tries, 36 points

Bradford Bulls *(2015-2016)*
30 games, 21 tries, 84 points

TOTALS
79 games, 55 tries, 220 points

Ste Maden

Nathan Pennington

Jonathan Skinner

Elizabeth Cunliffe

Paul Wood

Thomas Wood

Frank Taylor

Robert Stewart

Player Welfare Manager
Ste Maden

Head of Performance Analysis
Ste Mills
Sponsored by
AnalysisPro Ltd/Nacsport

Strength & Conditioning Coaches
Nathan Pennington
Paul Wood

Physiotherapists
Jonathan Skinner
Emma Fletcher
Elizabeth Cunliffe

Club Doctor
Dr John Morgan - Bucket &
Sponge Medical Services

Support staff
Robert Stewart (Masseur)
Cliff Sumner (Statistician)
Thomas Wood (Training assistant)
Sean Fairhurst (Kit)
Frank Taylor (Kit)

MIKE LATHAM looks back on a special year for everyone connected with Leigh Centurions

THE year began on a sad note as Life President Tommy Sale MBE passed away on Sunday morning, 3 January at the age of 97.

Tommy was the single most influential person in the history of Leigh Rugby League Club and his death occurred as the playing squad and staff were travelling to Lanzarote for pre-season, warm weather training. They were devastated to learn of the news when they landed. Leigh Centurions Players Association placed a book of condolence in reception at Leigh Sports Village and supporters began to lay floral tributes outside the stadium.

Born in Hindsford on 21 July 1918, Tommy's involvement with Leigh began when he worked on the scoreboard from an early age at the old Mather Lane ground. He later made his debut for the club in 1938 and returned after war service to not only become the club's first post war captain when the club reformed in 1946, playing at Charles Street but also act as groundsman and mastermind the building of the new ground at Kirkhall Lane in a remarkable community exercise, especially in the era of rationing and shortages.

Tommy, who also played briefly for Warrington and then for Widnes, captaining them in the 1950 Challenge Cup Final, later embarked on a coaching career with Wigan A, Leigh A and Liverpool City. He was also busy in his new career as a schoolteacher and was responsible for introducing the game of Rugby League to so many Leigh schoolchildren alongside his great pal Bert Causey and other dedicated schoolmasters and volunteers. He continued his links with Leigh by becoming a director of the Club and serving in many roles including secretary, assistant secretary, secretary of the Supporters' Club and he was also the long-serving timekeeper. Having missed very few Leigh games since the war

The late, great Tommy Sale MBE

Tommy was a regular attendee at Leigh Sports Village right until his death.

Club ambassador Alex Murphy OBE was one of many people to pay tribute to the man whose autobiography, brilliantly written by Andy Hampson, was fittingly entitled 'Mr Rugby Leigh' and stated how proud Tommy was to see Leigh on the up again under the leadership of club owner Derek Beaumont. Murphy said: "Leigh was Tommy's town and he did so much for so many people. He was a great teacher and he introduced so many to Rugby League. My own love for the Leigh club, the town and the fans is well known but Tommy's was absolutely incredible and his enthusiasm was remarkable. He was the ultimate ambassador. I could turn to him and know he was always there. His knowledge was vast.

"Derek is a strong, purposeful leader who is very much carrying on the good work and the standard set by Tommy all those years ago. Tommy will be greatly missed but the club is again strong and again ready to challenge. I have lost of great friend but believe me, the memory of Tommy Sale lives on forever in what is his town and his club."

39

Tom Armstrong returned to training after illness to join up with the squad in Lanzarote and Ryan Brierley was ahead of schedule in his recovery from ankle surgery. The week away went to plan and Head Coach Paul Rowley said: "We utilised our time really well and everyone worked and pushed really hard. Whilst we're certainly not coming back the finished article, we made some massive strides with the amount of new personnel we've got on board."

Rowley confirmed that Micky Higham would captain the side in 2016 with new signings Cory Paterson and Harrison acting as joint vice captains. Higham succeeded Oliver Wilkes in the role and was very honoured to take over as captain of his home town club.

Tommy Sale's funeral on Friday 15 January at Leigh Parish Church was one of the biggest ever held in the town. The church was packed to overflowing and many supporters stood outside to hear the service relayed on loudspeakers. Eulogies were delivered by the town's MP Andy Burnham, Lord Peter Smith and club director Mike Latham and a private gathering was later held at Leigh Sports Village. Mike Latham told the mourners: "Above all else Tommy Sale was a gentleman, he had time for everyone, was always cheerful and enthusiastic and he loved Leigh Rugby League Club with a burning passion. He'd seen the great days like Wembley 1971 when Alex Murphy led the team to Challenge Cup glory, especially fitting for Tommy who had been instrumental in Alex joining the club in the first place from St Helens. He'd seen them lift the Championship in 1982.

"But he also saw days and times when the Club was at a fearfully low ebb, struggling to survive. Leigh Rugby League Club will always survive as long as Tommy's legacy lives on through generations to come. He simply never, ever gave up. And he always wanted the Club to progress. Like everyone else he was sad to leave Hilton Park but he was excited about the possibilities that would open up at Leigh Sports Village. In the past two seasons he began to see those ambitions

come to fruition and he loved watching play from his wheelchair in the directors' box, and seeing the enthusiastic crowds. He would nod and have a word with many people over the course of a match day afternoon. Virtually everyone in Leigh knew Tommy Sale and he knew them."

Extensively covered on local television and radio, the funeral, though sad was an uplifting occasion, just as Tommy would have wanted it and two days later Wigan Warriors rolled into town for the first of the Warm Up games.

Tommy's face took centre stage on the club programme and a minute's applause took place in his honour before the Centurions gave an early indication of their intentions for the season, earning an exciting victory over their old rivals. In near-freezing temperatures after an overnight snowfall Leigh came back from 14-0 behind to post a 26-20 victory in the 'Battle of the Borough' in front of a 4,614 crowd. Jamie Acton twisted over by the side of the posts for what proved to be the winning try on the hour-mark as Centurions fans got a first look at Willie Tonga, Rangi Chase, Cory Paterson, Dayne Weston and Harrison Hansen in a Leigh jersey.

Though some critics described the Warriors side as 'inexperienced and youthful' no less than eight of the starting line-up and one of their bench players went on to feature in their grand final victory over Warrington nine months later. Harrison Hansen won the Arthur Thomas Memorial Trophy as man of the match; it was later revealed that due to a technicality on a one-match suspension carried over from the previous season that he was not eligible for the game, the RFL admitting an 'administrative error' while confirming there would be no repercussions for player or club.

Meanwhile Paul Rowley poured cold water on suggestions in Derek Beaumont's Leigh Observer column that the Centurions could better their recent record of losing just one league game in each of the previous two seasons. "I don't think you'll see a record like we've had for the next 20 years, never mind this

Leigh wore the new away strip for the first time as they visited the Halliwell Jones Stadium for their second and final Warm Up game against Warrington in the testimonial game for Simon Grix. Though the visitors took an early lead through an Adam Higson try Warrington showed their class, Ben Currie highly impressive in their 46-4 victory before a crowd of 4,963. The game was marred by serious injuries to Gregg McNally and Greg Worthington during the first half that severely hampered Rowley's plans ahead of the Championship opener at Batley. McNally was later ruled out for six months with a knee injury that required extensive surgery. New signing Willie Tonga also faced surgery on a knee problem. Meanwhile Gareth Hock extended his contract until the end of the 2018 season and Jake Emmitt penned a one-year extension.

On 28 January Leigh Centurions confirmed the resignation of Head Coach Paul Rowley who had decided to depart his role with immediate effect, releasing a personal statement via the TotalRL.com website after notifying the Board of Directors 15 minutes earlier in writing. He made the decision to stand down just over a week before the start of the season. Assistant coach Neil Jukes was immediately placed in charge of team affairs. "It's a challenge I'm excited by," Jukes said. "But on the other hand I'm hugely disappointed as I've been a work colleague of Paul's for seven years and within that time we've become very good friends, which we will remain. But this is sport and we have to move forward together again now as a club. The response of the captain and senior players in the squad has been very good and it's up to them, myself and the rest of the coaching staff to lead the group forward." The TotalRL.com website alleged that Ryan Brierley could leave the club as a free agent due to a clause in his contract concerning Rowley's departure.

Brian Bowman was appointed honorary life president, taking over from his long standing friend Tommy Sale MBE. "I am really honoured to accept this position," Mr

season," Rowley told League Express. "I think that would be disrespectful to our opposition."

The new Kukri away kit was unveiled alongside the home shirt at the Club's annual photo-call at LSV when all the playing and coaching staff had their photographs taken. CEO Allan Rowley said: "We are delighted to continue our relationship with Kukri and the away kit looks fantastic. As with the home shirt, the away shirt features our principal shirt sponsor AB Sundecks on the front and emblazoned with our other valued sponsors on the shirt and shorts. In addition the Lancashire Red Rose has been sublimated into the design."

The main sponsors for 2016 were as follows:

AB Sundecks
- main shirt sponsor front;
Evans Halshaw Vauxhall
- top rear of shirt;
Maxilead Metals
- bottom rear of shirt;
Fitfield - collar
(both sides and back);
Palatine Paints - Chest;
Bubbles and Dreams
- Shoulders;
Westco - Sleeve;
McLaughlin's Kitchens
- front of shorts;
Leigh Market
- rear of shorts.

Bowman said. "Tommy was a great friend of mine and we always got on very well. We had a great relationship and would speak two or three times a week about rugby almost right up to Tommy's passing." A regular Leigh supporter since the Club was reformed in 1946, Brian developed his own successful joinery business and became a Club Director in 1973, serving as Chairman from 1977 until 1983. That period coincided with some of the Club's greatest times notably in the 1981-82 season when Leigh lifted the Lancashire Cup and then became Champions of the Rugby League with a never-to-be-forgotten last day victory at Whitehaven. During his time as Chairman Brian was responsible for signing on two of the greatest players in the Club's history in Des Drummond and John Woods who both went on to achieve great things in the game. Brian also served on the Rugby League Council between 1977 and 1983 and was vice-chairman of the Disciplinary Committee for five years as well as being co-opted onto the Great Britain Selection Committee. He was also Lancashire RL President in 1982 and served on the County's selection committee.

Four days following Paul Rowley's departure Neil Jukes was confirmed as Head Coach. Owner Derek Beaumont said: "This is not a difficult appointment or one that needed much consideration, if any at all. As everybody knows I have a huge amount of respect for Rolls and value his opinion. In his letter to the Board he suggested that Neil should be promoted as his successor stating he was more than capable of coaching the team.

"The players themselves made contact with me, stating they believed Neil was the man for the job. Nothing is broken in terms of the Club's structures, schedules, facilities and styles of play so I was keen to ensure that wasn't disrupted. I have witnessed first-hand how involved Jukesy is with the team over the past two years and paid more attention to him by virtue of Rolls stating how good he was and how not many people realise how important Jukesy is to what we do.

"He also has a good background in business as a manager responsible for a large workforce so has good managerial skills and with that good discipline and procedures. I have always got on really well with him and he communicates well with me at ease so it is just a natural progression. He was involved in the creation of this team with Rolls many years ago and has the respect of those players as well as the respect of the senior players in the Club.

"We had a very easy conversation and have a good understanding of what is expected. It goes without saying that there is a lot of pressure associated with the position, more so this year with the investment in the squad and the clear intention to achieve Super League. Jukesy is more than happy to absorb that and he understands and accepts the challenge on a results-driven basis."

"I firmly believe he has the credentials and ability to achieve what we set out to achieve at the beginning and he knows that if we feel he needs support down the line we can look to add that if necessary."

Neil Jukes and Micky Higham were the main centres of attention for the press at the Championship launch at Worsley as they prepared for the start of the 2016 campaign with a visit to Batley Bulldogs.

Leigh's opening Championship fixture was a dramatic encounter at the Fox's Biscuits Stadium as John Kear's Batley came from 22-12 down to snatch victory with late tries by Chris Ulugia and Shaun Ainscough and a last minute 25-metre goal by Pat Walker after Rangi Chase failed to gather a high, hanging kick and

---

CHAMPIONSHIP ROUND 1

Sunday 7th February 2016

BATLEY BULLDOGS 24 LEIGH CENTURIONS 22

BULLDOGS: Dave Scott; Wayne Reittie; Shaun Squires; Chris Ulugia; Shaun Ainscough; Cain Southernwood; Dominic Brambani; Keegan Hirst; Luke Blake; Adam Gledhill; Sam Scott; Joe Chandler; Pat Walker. Subs (all used): Brad Day; James Davey; Tom Lillycrop; James Brown.
Tries: Brown (28), Ulugia (40, 68), Ainscough (77);
Goals: Walker 3, Brambani.
CENTURIONS: Rangi Chase; Adam Higson; Greg Worthington; Tom Armstrong; Liam Kay; Martyn Ridyard; Ryan Brierley; Fuifui Moimoi; Micky Higham; Dayne Weston; Harrison Hansen; Andrew Dixon; Jake Emmitt. Subs (all used): Reni Maitua; Tom Spencer; Lewis Foster; Sam Hopkins.
Tries: Dixon (19), Armstrong (33), Higham (49), Brierley (58);
Goals: Ridyard 3.
Half-time: 12-12; **Referee:** Gareth Hewer; **Attendance:** 1,678.

Jake Emmitt looks for a way past Batley's Cain Southernwood and Brad Day

then compounded his error by giving away a penalty for tripping. Chase, playing fullback, was one of four players on debut for the Centurions as Reni Maitua made his bow after missing the warm up games while his visa paperwork was completed.

Neil Jukes insisted that there was no panic in the Leigh ranks. "There certainly hasn't been any mention of the word 'crisis' here," he said. "I've been involved with teams before that have started strongly and finished poorly and maybe this year will be the opposite of that. We've got a long way to go but hopefully we can improve week on week and be a better side come the Qualifiers."

Reflecting on the Batley game in his programme column Club Captain Micky Higham wrote: " There was nothing we didn't expect. They were tough conditions, we didn't underestimate them and we prepared well. Batley played the conditions better than us, kicked better and in a game like that you have to take your chances and capitalise when you're on top. There are no excuses. At 22-12 up we should have closed out the game but we didn't and there a lot of lessons to be learned from that game."

Asked if playing at Mount Pleasant was a culture shock for some of the new players Higham replied: "No- I don't think

so- either way it's going to have to be something we deal with, week in and week out. No one has commented on it or complained. They all just get on with it. The Championship is a really tough competition in its own right. All the teams have strengthened and recruited well. There are no easy games and you have to be on top of your game to get through. It's as tough as it's ever been.

"We know what we have to do, the areas we have to address and we know that every week teams will be going all out to beat us as they see us as the Championship favourites. Everyone will raise their game and see us as a big scalp. That's not being big headed, just realistic, because that's the way it is. The way Batley celebrated was like they'd won the cup. Fair play to them, they had a right to celebrate but that has only sharpened our resolve and made us even more determined."

And reflecting on the coaching changes at the Club he added: "It was business as usual. Jukesy had a lot of input anyway as assistant and did a lot of the hands-on stuff. We let Jukesy down big time on Sunday. The preparation was spot-on and Batley didn't do anything we didn't expect or hadn't prepared for. It's up to the players to rectify that, starting now."

CHAMPIONSHIP ROUND 2

Sunday 14th February 2016

LEIGH CENTURIONS 48 OLDHAM 18

CENTURIONS: Lee Smith; Jonny Pownall; Adam Higson; Tom Armstrong; Liam Kay; Martyn Ridyard; Rangi Chase; Fuifui Moimoi; Lewis Foster; Dayne Weston; Harrison Hansen; Andrew Dixon; Gareth Hock. Subs (all used): Micky Higham; Sam Hopkins; Reni Maitua; Jake Emmitt.
Tries: Pownall (11), Smith (23), Higson (31, 36), Hopkins (45, 53, 58), Moimoi (60), Maitua (62); **Goals:** Ridyard 4, Smith 2.
OLDHAM: Richard Lepori; Adam Clay; Jack Holmes; Tom Ashton; Jamel Chisholm; Lewis Palfrey; Steve Roper; Phil Joy; Gareth Owen; Jack Spencer; Josh Crowley; Danny Langtree; Will Hope. Subs (all used): Sam Gee; Liam Thompson; Adam Files; Michael Ward.
Tries: Ashton (15), Clay (65), Palfrey (77); **Goals:** Palfrey 3.
Half-time: 20-6; **Referee:** Sam Ansell; **Attendance:** 3,371.

Leigh's first home game of the season saw them defeat Oldham 48-18 on Valentine's Day in front of 3,371 fans with a second half Sam Hopkins hat-trick, in the space of 13 minutes, the highlight. Hopkins had nearly been left out of the game after arriving late after his car ran out of fuel. Former international back Lee Smith, Neil Jukes' first signing since becoming head coach, made an impressive try-scoring debut and Reni Maitua scorched 70 metres for a glorious solo effort. Smith joined the Club as a free agent having spent the off season undergoing trials at Hull FC. His signing took the number of internationals in the Leigh Centurions playing squad to 13- an all-time Club record.

Fuifui Moimoi celebrates his try against Oldham in 'unique' style

After the Oldham game Leigh Centurions supporters were invited to a function at Leigh East when there was a disco and an opportunity to get photos and autographs with the players.

Haydock Park became the Main Match Sponsor for the next home game against London and in return staged a Leigh Centurions titled race as part of their Race Day on Wednesday 23 March when Centurions season ticket holders were able to gain free admission to the course. Leigh Centurions players joined race goers for an afternoon of thrills and spills at the superbly appointed racecourse that is just seven miles from LSV.

Operations Director Steve Openshaw summed up the feelings of the Board in his article From The Top in the next match day programme under the heading 'Unity - It's What Makes Us Strong.'

""Morning Steve, have you got a minute...what's happening down at the Club, I'm hearing all sorts of rumours and we're worried about it. It doesn't sound good."

"Those words weren't from a concerned fan on the market, a member of staff, or a sponsor in the Premier Club as may have ordinarily be expected.

"They were the first words out of Nigel Wood's mouth last Wednesday morning at a quarterly RFL meeting in Doncaster.

"Nigel Wood. Chief Executive of the RFL, the guy who's just appointed Wayne Bennett as England coach for the 2017 World Cup, asking me what's going wrong at Leigh Centurions. I'd not even taken my coat off.

"It was a question which deserved only one answer. "Nothing. Nothing is wrong. Far from it."

"Now normal respectful protocol is to keep discussions between the clubs and the hierarchy of the RFL private. In this instance its needs sharing. It needs sharing because it shows how detrimental rumours, tittle tattle, loose lips, half-truths, call it what you will has the potential to damage a Club, its community, and its reputation.

"Much has been written, primarily via social media, about the Club and its impending doom, a situation magnified immeasurably with an opening day defeat at Batley. Using those instances as a benchmark, one can only wonder the meltdown that must be happening at Headingley this week. Expect there isn't. There's an understanding that things happen, things change, things evolve, and that on the balance of probability Leeds Rhinos will be there or thereabouts come September.

"There will always be other clubs and fans wanting to see us fail. We accept that and it drives us. It's sport and it can be healthy. What's frustrating though is people closer to us doing the same. People with their own road show, legends of the tap room and banter pages, people who are have some perverse sense of achievement to see negativity, feeding it constantly. They know who they are. We know who they are.

"So let me counter that once and for all. Within the Club there is an even greater strength and unity from top to bottom, and we simply will not give in.

"If you believe the doubters, we've heard we are a Club in crisis. Laughable.

Ten minutes before last week's Oldham game I was called outside the stadium to greet a guest and noticed the queue for tickets. The queue, extended beyond the West Stand and around the corner to the South Stand. In all our time at LSV I have never seen a queue like it - apologies if you were in it but thanks for coming! I actually took a photo and showed it to Derek and Jukesy who stood in the tunnel just before kick-off, totally relaxed watching the lads make final pre-match preparations.

""Lads look at this" I said, showing them the photo just as Rangi Chase and Gareth Hock were returning to the changing room. "A Club in Crisis - there's 2,500 already inside and a hundred yard long queue for tickets outside."

"A club in crisis whose attendances have more than doubled in two years, record season ticket sales, a squad full of internationals, and a packed out Premier Club upstairs. If that is a Club in crisis then we are doing something right because that is the reality.

"As a Board we have but one goal. To get the Club to Super League and keep it there. As simple as that. No hidden agenda, no ulterior motive. Just a simple dream to share with the town. Whilst as a Board we may own the shares, they are not worth the paper they are written on, we are simply custodians of the Club. It's owned by the town, the fans, the community. It's over 100 years old, and in another 100 years someone else will hold the reins.

"We know there will be prickly moments and it's our job to deal with them. It's also our job to make tough choices and decisions. Some people won't like those decisions, that is life and we understand that, but each and every time it's done to achieve the dream. If we make a mistake we try to fix it. Our dream shared by thousands of loyal trusted dedicated fans who support the Club. They deserve that dream.

"The message from the Board is loud and clear. We are fans too, we've come from the terraces of Hilton Park, we want the same thing. And together, united, we can achieve it."

CHAMPIONSHIP ROUND 3

Sunday 21st February 2016

LEIGH CENTURIONS 24 LONDON BRONCOS 20

CENTURIONS: Lee Smith; Adam Higson; Greg Worthington; Richard Whiting; Jonny Pownall; Rangi Chase; Ryan Brierley; Fuifui Moimoi; Micky Higham; Dayne Weston; Harrison Hansen; Reni Maitua; Gareth Hock. Subs (all used): Lewis Foster; Sam Hopkins; Jamie Acton; Jake Emmitt.
Tries: Hopkins (38), Acton (67), Emmitt (70), Chase (72); **Goals:** Smith 4.
Sin bin: Weston (20); Emmitt (33).
BRONCOS: Alex Walker; Rhys Williams; Ben Hellewell; Wes Naiqama; Iliess Macani; Joe Keyes; Scott Leatherbarrow; Nick Slyney; James Cunningham; Mark Ioane; Alex Foster; Matt Garside; Jack Bussey. Subs (all used): Andy Ackers; Daniel Harrison; Jamie Thackray; Eddie Battye.
Tries: Foster (16), Cunningham (25), Williams (34), Hellewell (60);
Goals: Naiqama 2.
Half-time: 6-14; **Referee:** George Stokes; **Attendance:** 3,291.

London Broncos were next up and the visitors looked set to claim the spoils and inflict Leigh's first home defeat in the Championship since 2013 as the led 20-6 after an hour. But the Centurions came back strongly, Rangi Chase opening up the Broncos defence for Gareth Hock to send Jamie Acton over before Micky Higham created a try for Jake Emmitt. Just eight minutes remained when Chase scampered under the posts for the winning try and a hugely important victory. The experienced Richard Whiting came in for his debut after joining the club on an extended loan from Hull FC after the decision was taken to release French international centre Mathias Pala.

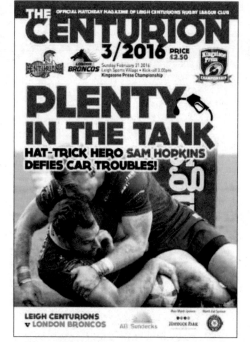

Gareth Hock on the charge against London Broncos

The trip to Odsal presented the Centurions with another stiff challenge but it was one they met head on, building a 32-6 advantage after 65 minutes to dampen what had been a highly charged atmosphere. Cory Paterson made a delayed debut after preseason surgery in a new halfback partnership with Ryan Brierley, whose two tries saw him overtake Neil Turley's tally for the Club and placed him in the top five try scorers in Leigh's history. Lee Smith's second try for the Club was his one hundredth career try.

CHAMPIONSHIP ROUND 4

Sunday 28th February 2016

BRADFORD BULLS 32 LEIGH CENTURIONS 32

BULLS: Richard Mathers; James Clare; Adrian Purtell; Kris Welham; Omari Caro; Lee Gaskell; Danny Addy; Adam Sidlow; Adam O'Brien; Rhys Lovegrove; Tom Olbison; Kurt Haggerty; Jay Pitts. Subs (all used): Dale Ferguson; Matty Blythe; Mitch Clark; Jonathan Walker.
Tries: Welham (28), Clare (65, 67), Purtell (71), Addy (75), Caro (78);
Goals: Addy 4.
CENTURIONS: Lee Smith; Jonny Pownall; Greg Worthington; Richard Whiting; Adam Higson; Cory Paterson; Ryan Brierley; Fuifui Moimoi; Micky Higham; Dayne Weston; Harrison Hansen; Gareth Hock; Jamie Acton. Subs (all used): Lewis Foster; Sam Hopkins; Reni Maitua; Jake Emmitt.
Tries: Pownall (3), Brierley (8, 55), Smith (43), Maitua (45); **Goals:** Smith 6.
Sin bin: Higson (39).
Half-time: 6-14; **Referee:** Richard Silverwood; **Attendance:** 6,563.

But then in an amazing finale Bradford Bulls mounted the unlikeliest of comebacks, scoring an incredible five tries with Danny Addy's touchline conversion to Omari Caro's last minute try sealing a 32-32 draw just as the hooter sounded.

"It just goes to show that it's never over until it's over," Neil Jukes said. "We just dropped off, we couldn't kick the ball and then they scored three times without us touching the ball and we just couldn't stop the flow. I think we would have taken a point before the game as we've got our injuries and haven't been firing on all cylinders at the start. We're not the finished article but we've shown what we can do."

Leigh served notice on Dewsbury Rams of their intention to recall Ben Reynolds from his seasonal loan as the injury crisis among the backs deepened. Reynolds had impressed during his time with the Rams. "We will try and thicken up the squad for the short term," Neil Jukes explained. "Hopefully we'll have some decent numbers again in a few weeks' time."

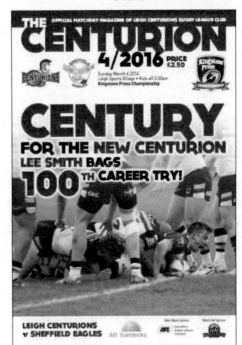

An unconvincing home win over Sheffield Eagles saw Leigh creep into the top four in the Championship as the season moved into March. Eze Harper was drafted in for his debut when Lee Smith pulled out in the warm-up and Super League loan signings Richard Owen and Lewis Charnock were other newcomers. With off-field speculation casting a shadow over the Club, it was a gutsy performance especially as the Eagles had fought back from trailing 26-10 at one stage to draw level at 28-

Jonny Pownall crashes past Bradford duo Tom Olbison and Omari Caro to score the opening try at Odsal

---

CHAMPIONSHIP ROUND 5

Sunday 6th March 2016

LEIGH CENTURIONS 36 SHEFFIELD EAGLES 28

CENTURIONS: Jonny Pownall; Eze Harper; Adam Higson; Richard Whiting; Richard Owen; Martyn Ridyard; Lewis Charnock; Fuifui Moimoi; Micky Higham; Dayne Weston; Harrison Hansen; Gareth Hock; Cory Paterson. Subs: Lewis Foster (not used); Tom Spencer; Reni Maitua; Jake Emmitt.
Tries: Weston (7), Higson (10), Higham (28), Charnock (39), Maitua (44), Paterson (78); **Goals:** Ridyard 6.
Sin bin: Hock (58).
EAGLES: Quentin Laulu-Togagae; Rob Worrincy; Menzie Yere; George Tyson; Ben Blackmore; Cory Aston; Dave Hewitt; Scott Wheeldon; Keal Carlile; Adam Neal; Michael Knowles; Duane Straugheir; Matt James. Subs (all used): Matty Fozard; Mitchell Stringer; Elliot Minchella; Mark Mexico.
Tries: Worrincy (17, 71), Laulu-Togagae (31, 75), Yere (50);
Goals: Knowles 4.
Sin bin: Stringer (58).
Half-time: 22-10; **Referee:** Chris Kendall; **Attendance:** 3,282.

Reni Maitua touches down against Sheffield

apiece with five minutes remaining. But Martyn Ridyard kept his cool to nail a late penalty before Cory Paterson's late try sealed a nervy victory after the Eagles, one of four full-time teams in the Championship, had impressed with their fluent second half attacking display. Leigh played in their away strip for this game as the Eagles' away strip had yet to arrive from the manufacturer.

Ridyard moved into third place above Neil Turley in the Club's all-time points-scoring chart with the third of his six goals and was later presented with a framed certificate by Turley to mark the achievement. The former amateur international had now scored 1,527pts in 195 games for his hometown club since his debut in 2009 and only John Woods (2,492pts) and Jimmy Ledgard (2,194pts) were ahead of him in Club records.

Three days prior to the game Ryan Brierley had been pictured watching Salford's game with Warrington alongside several current and former colleagues as news emerged on Sky Sports that he had formally handed in his notice to the club, citing a clause in his contract. The following night the Centurions issued a detailed statement from the Board suspending Brierley and stating they may seek a legal redress. The statement was as follows: "It is extremely concerning to

again see confidential and sensitive information surrounding Leigh Centurions appearing in the public domain, particularly when it continually centres on Ryan Brierley. It can be confirmed that Ryan Brierley emailed the Board of Directors on Monday evening, 29th February 2016 purporting to give four weeks' notice to terminate his contract with the Club.

"The Board responded to Ryan Brierley as we have previously done by outlining our position that we do not believe the alleged clause to be enforceable and confirming that he is contracted to the Club until 30th November 2016. As the matter is being dealt with by the Club's legal advisors the Club will not be commenting further on this. However, we can confirm that the Club will explore all legal avenues to protect its interests which, if necessary, will include taking legal action against Ryan Brierley and any associated third party."

The statement continued: "On Tuesday 1st March 2016 (Leigh Centurions Head Coach) Neil Jukes informed Club Owner Derek Beaumont that he had spoken to Ryan Brierley to ascertain his reasons for purporting to invoke the alleged clause, given he had continually stated privately and in public that he was committed to Leigh Centurions until the end of 2016 and wanted to achieve Super League with the Club.

"Derek was informed by Neil that Ryan Brierley stated another Championship Club (named by Ryan Brierley as Bradford Bulls) had made him a lucrative offer until the end of the season and that he would then be a free agent. However, should his contract be increased by £15,000 then he would consider staying. Derek informed Neil that the Board would consider the Club's position for a few days and that Derek would speak to Ryan Brierley at the appropriate time. The Board was therefore saddened and disappointed to see the information detailed on Sky Sports along with pictures of Ryan Brierley at the game prior to Derek having the opportunity to discuss this with him."

The statement added: "Given the serious number of recent breaches of confidential information surrounding Ryan Brierley the Club has taken the decision to suspend him with immediate effect in order that we can fully investigate how these matters came into the public domain. During this time Ryan Brierley will not attend the Club and will not be available for selection."

The statement concluded: "The Club has faced some difficult times recently with continuous injuries on the field and various issues off it. However, we are all confident that Neil and the team are pulling together and will fight hard through this adversity. We will be a very strong group once we come out the other side. The Board of Directors would like to take this opportunity to thank our loyal fans for their continued support which is greatly appreciated."

Brierley's detailed reply was again exclusively revealed on the TotalRL.com website.

Brierley, sidelined with a dead-leg anyway, was one of ten senior players unavailable for the Sheffield game. Neil Jukes said: "My focus more than ever is to have a squad that stays strong. That can only be achieved by having strong, committed people at the club. I feel we are still well on the way to achieving that."

Chief Executive Allan Rowley announced his retirement ahead of his 65th birthday later in the year and stepped down from the board of directors, later being awarded life membership of the club. Mr Rowley said: "We have experienced many highs and some lows during my time at Leigh but I am grateful to the Club for my time here, where I have made many friends throughout the game which has left me with many memories. I am now looking forward to watching the team reach our Super League target and I wish Derek and Neil and the team all the very best and will be shouting as loud as anyone albeit from the lofty heights of a life member's seat."

Director Steve Openshaw filled in as CEO until the Centurions made the significant appointment of sports lawyer Matthew Chantler, 30, in the role a few days later. Mr Chantler also joined the board of directors. A practicing solicitor specialising in sports law and a lifelong Leigh Centurions fan who lives locally, Mr Chantler had been acting as the Club's legal advisor. He said: "I am absolutely delighted to accept the position of Chief Executive with my hometown Club. Although this was a significant decision for me, stepping away from a successful career in law, I feel that it is a fantastic opportunity that was simply too good to turn down.

"Personally, I have accepted the position with the aim of being the Chief Executive of a Super League club and I am extremely confident that this is an achievable goal. Derek Beaumont often talks of his strong belief that he will lead the team out at Wembley and my grandmother often talks of her wish to watch Leigh at Wembley again; I certainly hope that I am in the stand with her, as Chief Executive of the Club, watching such an occasion!

"I have heard comments that the Leigh team is of Super League quality. I want to ensure that this also applies off the field and that the Club is run as effectively and as professionally as possible. Solid foundations have been laid by my predecessor Allan Rowley and I am confident in my ability to build on them with the complete backing of the Board of

Directors and Derek who has invested, and continues to invest, considerable amounts into the Club.

"The Leigh Sports Village is of Super League quality and I am confident Neil Jukes and the team will also demonstrate that they are too by achieving promotion. I will take up the position, at the very least, until the end of 2018. As custodian of the Club during my tenure, I can guarantee the Leigh public that I will give my all, not just for the Club but also the town. I strongly believe that the Club can be a flagship for the town, community and can inspire the younger generation of Leigh. I will work tirelessly to build on the links with our community partners, clubs and schools, will ensure that the Leigh Community Trust is backed by the Club with both time and investment, and that the Club engages with local businesses as I passionately believe that the support of these parties are integral to the success of the Club.

"I strongly request that everyone fully supports the Club by any means that they can, should that be attending a home game or simply by sharing the club's social media posts to help us raise the profile of our great Club. I also implore our business community to continue to back the Club and to add to not just the success of the club but the town which will also be of benefit to them.

"Support the Club, the town and BeLeighve!"

Leigh's trip to the Shay Stadium was another severe test for their injury-hit side and memories were still strong of their dismal performance against Halifax in the Qualifiers at the end of the previous season. After trailing 6-0 at the interval Leigh turned the tide with second half tries by Reni Maitua, Lee Smith, Gareth Hock and Micky Higham to earn a hard fought 26-18 win sealed by Martyn Ridyard's last minute penalty goal and move up to third, level on points with Batley and one point behind leaders London Broncos. Former Leeds and Salford hooker Liam Hood, signed from Swinton Lions was the latest player on debut as Bob Beswick continued to struggle with an injury picked up in pre season.

The long running Ryan Brierley saga was finally completed when he signed a four-and-a-half year contract with Huddersfield Giants after they agreed terms for an undisclosed transfer fee from Leigh. Brierley scored 133 tries in 125 Leigh games. Leigh Centurions Owner Derek Beaumont said: "He has been an outstanding ambassador in the community over the years. He was always happy to go above and beyond the call of duty for the benefit of those in the community and he should be remembered and commended for that.

"There has always been a lot of media attention around Ryan and over a number of years I worked closely with him to protect him from that. I was disappointed with his article in the magazine (Rugby League World) particularly referring to me as 'the owner.' I understand his

Reni Maitua takes on Halifax duo Ben Heaton and Ben Johnston

CHAMPIONSHIP ROUND 6

Sunday 13th March 2016

HALIFAX 18 LEIGH CENTURIONS 26

HALIFAX: Miles Greenwood; Tom Saxton; Ben Heaton; Steve Tyrer; James Saltonstall; Gareth Moore; Ben Johnston; Richard Moore; Ryan Maneely; Mitch Cahalane; Adam Tangata; Dane Manning; Adam Robinson. Subs (all used): Luke Ambler; Connor Robinson; Gavin Bennion; Andy Bracek. **Tries:** Saxton (20), Tangata (52), C Robinson (77); **Goals:** Tyrer 3. **Sin bin:** Manning (78).
CENTURIONS: Lee Smith; Jonny Pownall; Richard Whiting; Adam Higson; Liam Kay; Martyn Ridyard; Ben Reynolds; Fuifui Moimoi; Micky Higham; Dayne Weston; Harrison Hansen; Gareth Hock; Cory Paterson. Subs (all used): Liam Hood; Sam Hopkins; Reni Maitua; Jake Emmitt. **Tries:** Maitua (46), Smith (60), Hock (63), Higham (72); **Goals:** Ridyard 5. **Sin bin:** Hock (78).
Half-time: 6-0; **Referee:** Richard Silverwood; **Attendance:** 2,706.

Cory Paterson hands off Graeme Mattinson on the way to his fourth try against Workington

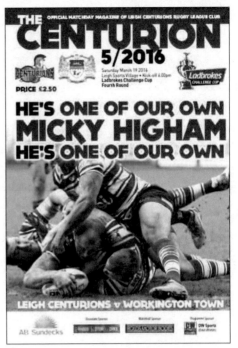

relationship with Paul (Rowley) and him wanting to support him, but I felt I deserved better than that.

"However, I am bigger than that and I wish Ryan well at Huddersfield and genuinely hope he makes a fist of Super League."

Taking a break from Championship action ahead of the Easter programme, Leigh began their Ladbrokes Challenge Cup campaign with a 68-14 victory over an injury depleted Workington Town at LSV. Cory Paterson scored four of Leigh's twelve tries with Martyn Ridyard kicking ten goals. The Australian became only the sixth forward in Leigh history to score four tries in a game for the Club. Andrew Dixon and Tom Armstrong returned after injury and Willie Tonga was included in the

squad for the first time. Rangi Chase was also ready soon to return to training, leaving just Bob Beswick, Greg Worthington and Gregg McNally on the injury list. "Last week we had 25 players running at training - it felt like a different club," Neil Jukes said. "We have been running drills like eight against seven, but this week we could put a full 13 out against 12 defenders."

Neil Jukes, his assistant Paul Anderson and conditioners Paul Wood and Nathan Pennington were all handed extended and improved contracts until the end of November 2018. "All the support staff have been working non-stop in recent weeks and that has played a big part," Jukes added. "It is a huge honour to be head coach at Leigh Centurions and I am really privileged to be holding this position at this great club. The potential is here for us to go on and achieve great things. If you turn up each day and work hard with a smile on your face, you have a chance to succeed in whatever job you are doing.

"That's something we all do at this club and we are a really happy, committed and determined group with a real family feel."

CHALLENGE CUP ROUND 4

Saturday 19th March 2016

LEIGH CENTURIONS 68 WORKINGTON TOWN 14

CENTURIONS: Lee Smith; Jonny Pownall; Adam Higson; Tom Armstrong; Liam Kay; Martyn Ridyard; Ben Reynolds; Jamie Acton; Liam Hood; Dayne Weston; Andrew Dixon; Gareth Hock; Cory Paterson. Subs (all used): Lewis Foster; Tom Spencer; Sam Hopkins; Harrison Hansen. **Tries:** Paterson (3, 10, 21, 68), Reynolds (6), Hood (12), Pownall (16), Smith (45), Hansen (54, 63), Acton (70), Hopkins (79); **Goals:** Ridyard 10. **TOWN:** Jack Murphy; Chris Murphy; Declan Hulme; Jason Mossop; Theerapol Ritson; Carl Forber; Jarrod Sammut; Kris Coward; Graeme Mattinson; Oliver Gordon; Brett Phillips; Perry Whiteley; Marc Shackley. Subs (all used): Liam McAvoy; Ryan Verlinden; Jamie Doran; Callum Phillips. **Tries:** Sammut (25), Ritson (36), Whiteley (59); **Goal:** Forber. **Half-time:** 32-10; **Referee:** Chris Kendall; **Attendance:** 2,049.

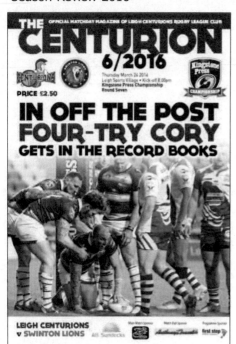

Reni Maitua tries to shake off ex-Centurion Stuart Littler, during the home clash with Swinton

Leigh began the Easter matches with the Maundy Thursday derby against Swinton Lions at LSV and moved to the top of the Championship on points difference with a 42-12 victory. From that day on the Centurions were never to lose pole position in the Championship. Despite having four players ruled out by illness Leigh had the key players in Martyn Ridyard and Micky Higham and Tom Armstrong's individual 67th minute try, Leigh's seventh of the evening, put

them 42-0 up before the Lions staged a late rally to post two tries through winger Liam Marshall. Willie Tonga made his delayed Centurions debut, earning Heritage Number 1411, the twelfth debutant already of the campaign.

Leigh met a determined Workington Town side on the trip to Derwent Park on Easter Monday but completed their holiday matches with a 40-24 victory. Four second half tries, including a brace by Reni Maitua calmed the nerves of the travelling fans after their side had laboured to a 16-14 lead at the interval. Andrew Dixon was ruled out for up to ten weeks after sustaining a medial ligament during the game.

Eze Harper closed down by Workington's Brett Phillips and Jamie Doran

CHAMPIONSHIP ROUND 7

Thursday 24th March 2016

LEIGH CENTURIONS 42 SWINTON LIONS 12

CENTURIONS: Lee Smith; Richard Owen; Tom Armstrong; Willie Tonga; Adam Higson; Martyn Ridyard; Ben Reynolds; Fuifui Moimoi; Micky Higham; Dayne Weston; Reni Maitua; Andrew Dixon; Harrison Hansen. Subs (all used): Lewis Charnock; Richard Whiting; Sam Hopkins; Jake Emmitt.
Tries: Smith (7), Owen (11), Weston (21), Hopkins (33), Higham (49), Hansen (61), Armstrong (66); **Goals:** Ridyard 7.
Sin bin: Reynolds (46).
LIONS: Kieran Hyde; Shaun Robinson; Stuart Littler; Macauley Hallett; Liam Marshall; Ben White; Chris Atkin; Rob Lever; Anthony Nicholson; Jordan Hand; Connor Dwyer; Rhodri Lloyd; Andy Thornley. Subs (all used): Ben Austin; Corbyn Kilday; Josh Barlow; Matty Beharrell.
Tries: Marshall (72, 77); **Goals:** Atkin 2.
Sin bin: Littler (46).
Half-time: 24-0; **Referee:** Chris Campbell; **Attendance:** 3,230.

CHAMPIONSHIP ROUND 8

Monday 28th March 2016

WORKINGTON TOWN 24 LEIGH CENTURIONS 40

TOWN: Jack Murphy; Chris Murphy; Perry Whiteley; Jason Mossop; Theerapol Ritson; Carl Forber; Jarrod Sammut; Kris Coward; Jamie Doran; Marc Shackley; Brett Phillips; Jarrad Stack; Liam McAvoy. Subs: Oliver Gordon; Ryan Verlinden (not used); Tom Walker (not used); Brett Carter (not used).
Tries: C Murphy (9), Ritson (15), Sammut (32), B Phillips (55), Mossop (78); **Goals:** Sammut 2.
CENTURIONS: Lee Smith; Adam Higson; Richard Whiting; Tom Armstrong; Eze Harper; Martyn Ridyard; Ben Reynolds; Fuifui Moimoi; Liam Hood; Dayne Weston; Reni Maitua; Andrew Dixon; Jake Emmitt. Subs (all used): Micky Higham; Sam Hopkins; Jamie Acton; Harrison Hansen.
Tries: Emmitt (19), Hansen (25), Armstrong (38), Maitua (60, 69), Hopkins (64), Moimoi (74); **Goals:** Ridyard 5, Reynolds.
Half-time: 14-16; **Referee:** Gareth Hewer; **Attendance:** 787.

Ben Reynolds celebrates his try at Dewsbury with Dayne Weston

Another tough away game in Yorkshire provided the next challenge for Neil Jukes' side but they again produced a strong second half showing to win 40-18 at Dewsbury Rams after leading 12-8 at half-time. Four tries in an inspired ten-minute spell turned a tight and tetchy game Leigh's way with Ben Reynolds, Liam Kay, Cory Paterson and Richard Whiting all crossing. Leigh were now two points clear of second placed Batley with London and Bradford, both with a game in hand, also in the top four and Halifax and Featherstone Rovers fifth and sixth respectively.

In a concerning incident Harrison Hansen was carried off the field after being injured in the tackle. Later, CEO Matthew Chantler reflected: "The injury to Harrison was very concerning at the time but 'H' received expert medical care straight away and as ever we are extremely thankful to the club's medical staff, and that of Dewsbury in giving our players the best possible care. Harrison was quickly well on the way to a full recovery and that was great news for many concerned people last Sunday evening."

Asked if Leigh's style of play had changed since last season Club Captain Micky Higham said: "There's no doubt it has and I'd like to get back to the old style in patches if we could as it is very hard to defend against. But last season was based around the core of a team that had played together for a few seasons and now we have different players in the pivotal positions so it will take time to develop that innate understanding you get from playing together regularly."

Martyn Ridyard reached the milestone of 200 Leigh games and became only the third player in the summer era to achieve the feat, following in the footsteps of Ste Maden and John Duffy. Maden was on hand to present him with a framed certificate to mark the achievement when Whitehaven visited LSV ahead of another break for Challenge Cup action.

CHAMPIONSHIP ROUND 9

Sunday 3rd April 2016

DEWSBURY RAMS 18 LEIGH CENTURIONS 40

RAMS: Josh Guzdek; Dale Morton; Jason Crookes; Etuate Uaisele; Dalton Grant; James Glover; Paul Sykes; Toby Adamson; Dom Speakman; Jonathan Walker; Scott Hale; Shane Grady; Joel Farrell. Subs (all used): Jack Teanby; Luke Adamson; Nathan Conroy; Kyle Trout.
Tries: L Adamson (26), Morton (77), Teanby (79); **Goals:** Sykes 3.
Sin bin: Crookes (74).
CENTURIONS: Lee Smith; Adam Higson; Tom Armstrong; Richard Whiting; Liam Kay; Martyn Ridyard; Ben Reynolds; Sam Hopkins; Micky Higham; Dayne Weston; Reni Maitua; Gareth Hock; Cory Paterson. Subs (all used): Liam Hood; Jake Emmitt; Jamie Acton; Harrison Hansen.
Tries: Hopkins (10, 14), Higson (44), Reynolds (60), Kay (65), Paterson (67), Whiting (69); **Goals:** Ridyard 6.
Sin bin: Hock (55); Acton (74).
Half-time: 8-12; **Referee:** Sam Ansell; **Attendance:** 1,691.

Leigh gave their most fluent attacking display of the season so far, running in eleven tries to record a 60-6 victory over 'Haven in front of just over 3,000 fans. Cory Paterson led the way with a first-half hat-trick and Greg Worthington made a successful return from injury. Prior to the game there was one minute's applause in respect of Isaac Haggerty, who had passed away following a courageous battle with a rare form of leukaemia.

Isaac was the son of former Widnes, Salford and Harlequins player Gareth Haggerty, and the nephew of former Leigh Centurions player Kurt Haggerty who was now at Bradford Bulls. Meanwhile Leigh revealed their special Team Isaac Summer Bash strip in support of the charity set up in his memory. In a gesture of great generosity, Leigh Centurions' main club sponsor AB Sundecks donated their space on the front of the Summer Bash Special Limited Edition shirt to the Team Isaac charity. This is a fund close to Leigh Centurions Owner Derek Beaumont's heart and despite the sad passing of young Isaac there is still an opportunity to raise funds in his memory, to assist the Alder Hay Children's Hospital's in house Loukaemia research programme. The research is undertaken specifically by the three consultants that looked after Isaac tirelessly throughout his short life. In addition to the exposure of the Team Isaac logo, Leigh Centurions would also donate the profit made from the shirt sales to the fighting fund, and the cheque presentation was made at the final home game of the season.

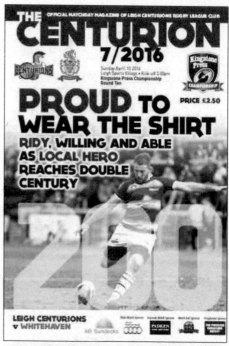

Liam Hood heads for the line against Whitehaven

CHAMPIONSHIP ROUND 10

Sunday 10th April 2016

LEIGH CENTURIONS 60 WHITEHAVEN 6

CENTURIONS: Lee Smith; Adam Higson; Greg Worthington; Tom Armstrong; Liam Kay; Martyn Ridyard; Ben Reynolds; Tom Spencer; Micky Higham; Dayne Weston; Reni Maitua; Gareth Hock; Cory Paterson. Subs (all used): Liam Hood; Jamie Hopkins; Richard Whiting; Jamie Acton.
Tries: Paterson (14, 20, 24), Armstrong (29), Acton (33), Reynolds (38), Maitua (45), Kay (50, 52), Weston (67), Hood (73); **Goals:** Ridyard 8.
WHITEHAVEN: Louis Jouffret; Ed Chamberlain; Chris Taylor; Jessie Joe Parker; Craig Calvert; Dion Aiye; Grant Gore; Glenn Riley; Liam Carberry; Ted Chapelhow; Dave Allen; Scott McAvoy; Ben Davies. Subs (all used): Steve Fox; James Newton; Ryan Duffy; John-Paul Brocklebank.
Try: Riley (61); **Goal:** Jouffret.
Half-time: 36-0; **Referee:** Chris Kendall; **Attendance:** 3,089.

Every club has their unsung heroes and one of them was a special guest of the Club at the Whitehaven game together with his wife. Derek Taylor, 79, is perhaps the Superleigh Lottery's longest serving agent, starting in March 1960. He spoke to Andrew Parkinson about his involvement that goes back an incredible 56 years. "I remember one game I was stood on the terrace at Kirkhall Lane," recalled Derek. "It was March 1960, and an announcement was made that volunteers were needed to sell draw tickets. So I went round to the back of the stand and got £1'sworth, tickets were one shilling each. So I went away, and sold them to friends family and the like.

"When I brought the money back I was given one shilling and sixpence back. 'What's that?' I asked? 'That's your commission' the gentleman said, which surprised me as I didn't know I'd be getting commission. From there I went from strength to strength, and back in the '70s and '80s when I worked at David Browns, I was bringing in £40 a week. I used to sell Bingo tickets and all sorts for Leigh. You name it, I sold it. Things have tapered off a bit since I retired, but I still bring a few pounds in every week. There was a snippet once in the Journal about a 'Super Agent' who sold four top prizes of £50 in one week. If anybody out there remembers that, then that was me.

"I always make sure I pay in for 100percent of my members, too. If they haven't paid I put it in out of my own pocket. I've perhaps lost a couple of hundred quid down the years doing that,

but it all goes to help the club. Once they got to owing about six pounds or so that was the limit and I'd cancel them off. I've been supporting Leigh since I was eight or nine years old. We played at Charles Street then, and Tommy Sale was on the wing. Then when we moved to Kirkhall Lane I can remember slipping out of school to help paint the outer fences green. The fences were made out of old air raid shelters.

"I've been following Leigh ever since, and former Chairman Brian Bowman (Hon Life President) sometimes used to take me to the away games. I suppose I've kept collecting all these years because I love Leigh Rugby Club, and it all helps the club."

Meanwhile a new corporate partnership initiative was unveiled by the Club, aimed at rewarding and benefiting loyal season ticket holders for their continued support. Several businesses began offering discount offers and packages to season ticket holders on product of their season ticket and the initiative gathered momentum throughout the year. The Club also broke more new ground by producing an exclusive business directory. Many local businesses and high profile companies were supportive of an exciting and innovative corporate venture instantly benefited many people within the local community and beyond. The directory offered a wide range of top class professional services spanning airport travel to car valets.

Leigh had been handed a trip to the South of France for the next round of the Ladbrokes Challenge Cup against Kingstone Press League One newcomers Toulouse Olympique. Around one hundred Leigh fans followed their favourites on the 1,800 mile round trip for the Saturday afternoon kick-off at the Stade Ernest Argeles, those remaining at home relying on Dave Parkinson's excellent commentary on MixLR and Twitter updates from Club Chairman Mike Norris with the normal Twitter expert, the widely followed Mark Taylor missing a Leigh game, a rare occurrence indeed.

CHALLENGE CUP ROUND 5

Saturday 16th April 2016

TOULOUSE OLYMPIQUE 10 LEIGH CENTURIONS 8

OLYMPIQUE: Mark Kheirallah; Kuni Minga; Bastien Ader; Gregory White; Tony Maurel; Johnathon Ford; Arthur Gonzales-Trique; Bastien Canet; Kane Bentley; Clement Boyer; Sebastien Planas; Rhys Curran; Andrew Bentley. Subs (all used): Mourad Kriouache; Samy Masselot; Maxime Puech; Anthony Marion.
Try: Canet (5); **Goals:** Kheirallah 3.
CENTURIONS: Jonny Pownall; Adam Higson; Greg Worthington; Tom Armstrong; Liam Kay; Martyn Ridyard; Ben Reynolds; Jake Emmitt; Micky Higham; Dayne Weston; Richard Whiting; Reni Maitua; Cory Paterson. Subs (all used): Lewis Foster; Tom Spencer; Jamie Acton; Sam Hopkins.
Try: Hopkins (44); **Goals:** Ridyard 2.
Half-time: 8-0; **Referee:** Chris Kendall; **Attendance:** 2,133.

Jake Emmitt tackled by Toulouse's Rhys Curran

Despite meticulous preparation for the journey Leigh lacked any attacking fluency in a stop-start cup-tie that was littered with handling errors and went down to a 10-8 defeat. The visitors trailed 8-0 at the break but pulled back to level with a Sam Hopkins try and two Martyn Ridyard goals only for Mark Kheirallah to seal victory for the home side with a penalty as the storm clouds rolled in and the closing stages were played out in torrential rain.

Reflecting on the game Neil Jukes said: "It was good for the group to spend some time together. Our preparation was good and where we stayed was great but ultimately the performance wasn't good enough. We defended well but attacked poorly and that certainly put a dampener on the weekend.

"While last year it was great to get as far as we did in the Challenge Cup it gave us a backlog of fixtures that did us no favours. It's possibly a blessing in disguise. Certainly that is one less excuse we can use as a club in the Middle 8s this year."

Meanwhile in an exclusive interview with the Sydney Telegraph Fuifui Moimoi revealed that he feared for his life after spending two weeks in intensive care with a serious infection. Moimoi had lost around 15kg over the course of two weeks in hospital but was happily now back on the road to recovery.

A testing trip to the Big Fellas Stadium awaited Leigh on their return from France as April was coming to a close. It was another game from which the Centurions earned two points from a hard fought and tight game. They led 22-8 at the break including a try for Jamie Acton, who had recently extended his contract until the end of 2018 and another for Rangi Chase, making his first appearance for two months. But ultimately the Centurions were grateful for Liam Kay's 64th minute try from Martyn Ridyard's clever kick and a Ridyard penalty after Jon Sharp's side had the better of the second half and drew level at 24-24 on the hour-mark. After holding out in a tense finish and surviving a few alarms Leigh now led London by one point at the top of the highly competitive Championship with the Bulls, despite having a game in hand five points behind while fourth-placed Batley had now dropped nine points in their first eleven games. Bradford coach James Lowe had resigned his post during the previous week for personal reasons.

Leigh Centurions were saddened to hear of the passing of their former player Wally Tallis, who had died in his native

Dayne Weston drives forward at Featherstone

Harrison Hansen barges through the Batley defence to score

Queensland aged 75. A gentle giant of a man, he signed for Leigh in late 1964 from the Townsville Past Brothers team. His son Gorden went on to become one of Australia's finest ever forwards and once called in at Hilton Park during an Australian tour to be presented with a Leigh club tie in honour of his father when he was said to be very moved by the way his father was remembered at the club.

Batley's visit to LSV on the first day of May gave the Centurions an opportunity to avenge that opening day defeat and put

further daylight between them and John Kear's side. It was a dramatic game as again Leigh found a way to win despite a stirring comeback from their opponents. Leigh lost Rangi Chase to a back injury midway through the first half and Chase was destined never to play again for the Club. Later in the month he was released from his contract by mutual consent and after some time away from the game he re-joined his old club Castleford.

Leigh looked set for victory as they built a 25-12 lead just before the hour-mark, including a brace for Harrison Hansen who was proving to be an outstanding acquisition. But just as they had back in February John Kear's side showed their Bulldog spirit, inspired by halfback Dominic Brambani, turned the game on its head to score three tries inside ten minutes and take a five-point lead. Neil Jukes' side recovered their composure just in time, Lee Smith following up his own kick to notch an opportunist converted try with less than two minutes on the clock. There was just time for Sam Hopkins to seal an important win with a last gasp score.

CHAMPIONSHIP ROUND 12

Sunday 1st May 2016

LEIGH CENTURIONS 37 BATLEY BULLDOGS 30

CENTURIONS: Lee Smith; Adam Higson; Richard Whiting; Tom Armstrong; Liam Kay; Martyn Ridyard; Rangi Chase; Jake Emmitt; Micky Higham; Dayne Weston; Reni Maitua; Gareth Hock; Harrison Hansen. Subs (all used): Jamie Acton; Tom Spencer; Sam Hopkins; Liam Hood. **Tries:** Kay (19), Hansen (35, 43), Hood (56), Smith (78), Hopkins (79); **Goals:** Ridyard 6; **Field goal:** Ridyard (40).
BULLDOGS: Dave Scott; Alex Brown; Greg Minikin; Callum Casey; Shaun Ainscough; Cain Southernwood; Dominic Brambani; Keegan Hirst; James Davey; Sean Hesketh; Joe Chandler; Alex Bretherton; Luke Blake. Subs (all used): Tom Lillycrop; Alistair Leak; James Harrison; Dave Petersen. **Tries:** Ainscough (28), Leak (50), Bretherton (65), Brambani (69), Harrison (74); **Goals:** Brambani 5.
Half-time: 13-6; **Referee:** Chris Campbell; **Attendance:** 3,389.

The Leigh Head Coach, meanwhile, held a long and productive talk with match officials' representative Steve Presley over the number of penalties his side had been conceding. "We've got a few technical bits to fix-up and we're working hard on it," said Jukes. "Overall, I want us to be proud of our discipline but be aggressive. We don't want to become a soft team." Elsewhere Toronto Wolfpack director of rugby Brian Noble targeted a place in Super League for the newly-launched Canadian side who, it was revealed, would begin life in League One in 2018. Former Leigh Head Coach Paul Rowley was appointed coach and several former and current Leigh players were linked in the media with moves to the new club. One of the first to join up was assistant coach Simon Finnigan who left Leigh to link up again with his former boss.

After a fortnight's break caused by their cup exit Leigh travelled for the first time to Stalybridge Celtic's Bower Fold, Oldham's new home ground with Hull FC forward Brad Fash having bolstered their ranks following a loan move. This was the start of a four-match away run for the Centurions while LSV underwent annual renovations to its immaculate playing surface. "We're top of the league without playing great, but we are working hard" Neil Jukes said. "If we keep working hard on and off the field it should stand us in good stead for the tougher games that lie ahead."

Leigh scored ten tries against Oldham with Reni Maitua notching a brace and the other eight being shared by eight different

Try time for Reni Maitua at Oldham

players before the home side, just as they had at LSV, staged a late revival to score two late tries. The Centurions had now opened up a three-point lead at the top over London, who lost at Featherstone, and were eight points clear of fifth-placed Batley as the battle to qualify for the top four intensified. While Neil Jukes' side was now churning out wins week after week their challengers were dropping points consistently. One of the fancied sides in pre season had been Sheffield Eagles, especially after they went full-time after their success in the Middle 8s in 2015 but after suffering a shock home defeat by Whitehaven they had now lost eight of their 13 games while Halifax were only one place higher.

Two days after the Oldham game Leigh Centurions staged a highly successful annual Golf Day at Houghwood on which was a complete sell out. Massive sponsorship and healthy corporate support was provided and every single four-ball team (24 in total) was allocated at one of the North West's premier parkland courses as directors, players and coaches joined the sponsors at a hugely successful event.

CHAMPIONSHIP ROUND 13

Sunday 15th May 2016

OLDHAM 14 LEIGH CENTURIONS 56

OLDHAM: Jared Simpson; Adam Clay; Liam Johnson; Danny Grimshaw; Jamel Chisholm; Steve Roper; Gareth Owen; Phil Joy; Kruise Leeming; Michael Ward; Gary Middlehurst; Liam Thompson; Will Hope. Subs (all used): Joe Burke; Sam Gee; Kenny Hughes; Danny Langtree.
Tries: Grimshaw (14), Johnson (74), Langtree (77); **Goal:** Roper.
CENTURIONS: Lee Smith; Adam Higson; Greg Worthington; Tom Armstrong; Liam Kay; Martyn Ridyard; Ben Reynolds; Jamie Acton; Micky Higham; Dayne Weston; Richard Whiting; Reni Maitua; Gareth Hock. Subs (all used): Harrison Hansen; Liam Hood; Jake Emmitt; Brad Fash.
Tries: Maitua (18, 47), Smith (24), Ridyard (34), Kay (37), Hood (40), Armstrong (50), Reynolds (54), Acton (66), Weston (69); **Goals:** Ridyard 8.
Half-time: 6-26; **Referee:** Scott Mikalauskas; **Attendance:** 1,489.

The tournament was presented by Mr Jason Huyton of Palatine Paints. Westco were the event's associate sponsor and Bents Garden and Home, Maxilead Metals, TTR Construction, Tim Philbin (Design Business Interiors), Chilli Dip Golf, CS Civils and Preston Audi also kindly provided additional sponsorships.

Another away trip and another new ground for Leigh fans to tick off as they made the short journey to Heywood Road in Sale, Swinton Lions' new home. While Leigh's 48-6 victory appeared convincing, it came at a cost with Gareth Hock sent-off and two players sin-binned while Swinton incurred two red and two yellow cards. Despite both sending in letters of apology for their conduct, Hock and Jamie Acton both later incurred lengthy bans arising from the game. Leigh held a 26-6 lead at the break and added four tries amid the second half mayhem.

As Leigh prepared for the Summer Bash game at Blackpool, Josh Drinkwater jetted in from Australia to join the squad and made a try-scoring debut off the bench against the Lions. The 23-year-old former London Broncos halfback had impressed playing in the NSW Cup for Wests Tigers' feeder club and was spotted by assistant coach Paul Anderson during his regular reviews of the Australian game.

Club Captain Micky Higham also signed an extended contract at the Club until the end of November 2018. The next year (2017) was a playing contract and

Jonny Pownall steps inside Swinton's Shaun Robinson

the second year (2018) had an option at the Club's discretion, either as a playing contract or as a role on the coaching or conditioning staff.

Another significant recruit was that of Paul Cooke to join the coaching staff after his commitments at Doncaster Knights RU club finished following their two-leg play-off defeat against Bristol saw their hopes of a place in the Premiership ended. Cooke had built a growing reputation in the union game working under head of rugby Clive Griffiths at the Knights having previously been Championship Coach of the Year with Doncaster in 2014, when they were the only side to defeat Leigh in the Championship. Best remembered as a player for scoring the match-winning converted try in Hull FC's dramatic 25-24 Challenge Cup Final victory over Leeds at Cardiff in 2005 Cooke, 35, played with distinction for Hull FC, Hull Kingston Rovers and Wakefield Trinity Wildcats, clocking up 280 Super League appearances in 12 seasons in the top flight.

CHAMPIONSHIP ROUND 14

Sunday 22nd May 2016

SWINTON LIONS 6 LEIGH CENTURIONS 48

LIONS: Kieran Hyde; Shaun Robinson; Stuart Littler; Rhodri Lloyd; Mike Butt; Ben White; Chris Atkin; Ben Austin; Anthony Nicholson; Andy Bracek; Andy Thornley; Connor Dwyer; Josh Barlow. Subs (all used): Daniel Fleming; Matty Beharrell; Stephen Nash; Zach Johnson.
Try: Nicholson (14); **Goal:** Atkin.
Dismissals: Johnson (45); Barlow (45).
Sin bin: Butt (45); Fleming (77).
CENTURIONS: Lee Smith; Adam Higson; Tom Armstrong; Willie Tonga; Jonny Pownall; Martyn Ridyard; Ben Reynolds; Jake Emmitt; Micky Higham; Dayne Weston; Richard Whiting; Reni Maitua; Gareth Hock. Subs (all used): Josh Drinkwater; Brad Fash; Sam Hopkins; Jamie Acton.
Tries: Armstrong (7), Smith (24, 40), Pownall (27), Whiting (34), Ridyard (55), Weston (60), Reynolds (66), Drinkwater (78);
Goals: Ridyard 5, Reynolds.
Dismissal: Hock (45).
Sin bin: Higson (45); Emmitt (77).
Half-time: 6-26; **Referee:** Andrew Sweet; **Attendance:** 1,413.

Micky Higham celebrates his winning try against Bradford at The Summer Bash with Gareth Hock and Sam Hopkins

Leigh also announced that Kieron Purtill would join the Centurions coaching staff later in the year once he had obtained his release from Huddersfield Giants. The former Leigh player and captain had been placed on gardening leave from his role as assistant coach by the Giants following the departure of head coach Paul Anderson. A highly regarded level 4 coach Purtill had worked alongside some of the game's most highly regarded coaches since his playing career at Leigh was cruelly ended by a recurring shoulder injury in 2002.

Welcoming the appointments Neil Jukes said: "It was important for me and the whole structure of the club to get back to four coaches and with the appointments we have made we are stretching ourselves from grass roots to first grade.

"I have never doubted Paul's coaching ability or knowledge of the game. In his heyday he was a very smart player and his head worked two seconds faster than the opposition. I'm looking forward to him bringing those 'smarts' to our team.

"And once I knew Kieron was available it was a no-brainer. We are constantly trying to raise the bar off the field just as much as on it and Kieron will no doubt help us achieve that."

Meanwhile Tom Spencer moved to Oldham on a month's loan after struggling to get sufficient game time.

The May Bank Holiday weekend saw Leigh make a return trip to Bloomfield Road for the eagerly awaited Summer Bash game against Bradford Bulls. Games between the two sides in the past two years had been memorable for different reasons and this was to be no exception. Scheduled as the fourth and final game on the Saturday evening the match was a thriller, with Leigh edging home 24-20 thanks to Micky Higham's dramatic winning try two minutes from time after he fastened onto Drinkwater's deft kick to win the race for the touchdown in the in-goal area, sending the Centurions fans in the 9,521 crowd into raptures.

CHAMPIONSHIP ROUND 15 - SUMMER BASH

Saturday 28th May 2016

BRADFORD BULLS 20 LEIGH CENTURIONS 24

BULLS: James Clare; Omari Caro; Matty Blythe; Kris Welham; Danny Williams; Oscar Thomas; Richard Mathers; Adam Sidlow; Danny Addy; Mitch Clark; Tom Olbison; Dale Ferguson; Jay Pitts. Subs (all used): Adam O'Brien; Steve Crossley; Alex Mellor; Kurt Haggerty.
Tries: Williams (6), Clark (10), O'Brien (53), Addy (75); **Goals:** Addy 2.
CENTURIONS: Lee Smith; Adam Higson; Greg Worthington; Tom Armstrong; Liam Kay; Ben Reynolds; Josh Drinkwater; Harrison Hansen; Micky Higham; Dayne Weston; Reni Maitua; Richard Whiting; Gareth Hock. Subs (all used): Liam Hood; Sam Hopkins; Jake Emmitt; Jamie Acton.
Tries: Kay (16), Drinkwater (38), Higson (43), Higham (78);
Goals: Reynolds 4.
Half-time: 10-10; **Referee:** Sam Ansell; **Attendance:** 9,521
(at Bloomfield Road, Blackpool).

It was a fitting climax to what had been a great advertisement for the Championship with Bradford seemingly having clinched victory in a see-saw game when Danny Addy scrambled over with seven minutes remaining. The Sky Sports cameras were on hand to capture the drama and the Leigh Centurions players, in their specially designed Team Isaac playing strip danced jigs of delight on the Bloomfield Road pitch as they celebrated a significant victory.

A scorching hot early June Saturday saw Leigh make another trip to the West Cumbrian coast for the return game against Whitehaven. Temperatures had barely fallen in time for the early evening kick-off and the game became as much a battle against the elements on a rock hard pitch against a fired-up home side. Leigh won comfortably enough in the end but 'Haven came out of the game with plenty of credit, holding the visitors to 12-12 at the break. Leigh's new 32-year-old Australian signing Travis Burns, who had joined the club on loan from St Helens for the rest of the season proved the difference on debut, scoring two second half tries to cap an influential display. Warrington prop Ben Evans also joined the club on a one month's loan deal while Lewis Foster and Jonny Pownall went to Oldham on a similar arrangement and Eze Harper joined several of his former Leigh team-mates at Barrow for a month.

With 16 rounds played Leigh still held a three-point lead over London with Batley eight points adrift in third and Bradford

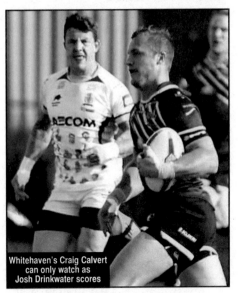

Whitehaven's Craig Calvert can only watch as Josh Drinkwater scores

were now in sixth position and in danger of missing out on the Qualifiers after suffering a shock 16-14 home defeat against Dewsbury.

The Club mourned the passing of former Great Britain forward Alan Rathbone at the age of 57. Rathbone, a former amateur boxer and GB Schoolboys and BARLA Under-19s forward, began his professional career with Leigh after signing from the Colts side, making his debut at Castleford in September 1976, retrospectively earning Heritage Number 860. Kevin Ashcroft was the Leigh coach at the time and took him under his wing. Rathbone, who grew up in the Bewsey area of Warrington, soon earned a reputation as a hard man and encountered disciplinary issues from the off, but Ashcroft saw the potential in him.

"Alan was one hard lad," Ashcroft recalled. "He was wayward but he never gave me an ounce of trouble and he was a top rate professional. The problem was he didn't know how to channel his football ability against his aggression. You've got to have both to be successful in Rugby League but it's a case of getting the balance right. Opposing teams used to know this and wind him up and all too often he took the bait. Alan was frightened of nothing and nobody. If King Kong was

CHAMPIONSHIP ROUND 16

Saturday 4th June 2016

WHITEHAVEN 12 LEIGH CENTURIONS 36

WHITEHAVEN: Louis Jouffret; Ryan Ince; Ed Chamberlain; Connor Holliday; Craig Calvert; Dion Aiye; Grant Gore; Anthony Walker; Thomas Coyle; Ryan Duffy; Ugo Perez; Steve Fox; John-Paul Brocklebank. Subs (all used): Jessie Joe Parker; Ben Davies; Liam Carberry; Ted Chapelhow.
Tries: Brocklebank (17), Jouffret (39); **Goals:** Jouffret 2.
Sin bin: Calvert (68).
CENTURIONS: Lee Smith; Adam Higson; Greg Worthington; Tom Armstrong; Liam Kay; Ben Reynolds; Josh Drinkwater; Fuifui Moimoi; Liam Hood; Dayne Weston; Reni Maitua; Cory Paterson; Harrison Hansen. Subs (all used): Brad Fash; Sam Hopkins; Travis Burns; Richard Whiting.
Tries: Drinkwater (5), Higson (10), Burns (48, 66), Paterson (68), Worthington (79); **Goals:** Reynolds 3, Burns 3.
Sin bin: Weston (38).
Half-time: 12-12; **Referee:** Jon Roberts; **Attendance:** 782.

stood in front of him he wouldn't back down. If an elephant charged at him he wouldn't move.

"There was one famous story that Brian Bowman, then Leigh Chairman offered him a turkey for Christmas if he didn't get sent off. That was in September. Alan got sent off the next match. Brian came into the dressing room and said: 'Alan, you've missed out on your turkey.' Alan replied: 'Mr Chairman, you can shove that turkey up you a***.' Brian still laughs about that now."

Rathbone was transferred to Rochdale Hornets but came back to Leigh in September 1979 and earned Great Britain Under 24s honours a few months later, playing against the French at Hilton Park alongside Leigh team mates Malcolm Swann, Des Drummond and John Woods. The second-rower or loose-forward, who had the nicknames 'Action' and 'Rambo', was transferred to Bradford Northern in June 1981 for £17,000 and went on to make five appearances for Great Britain, making his debut against the great 1982 Kangaroos. He later moved to Warrington in June 1985 and to Leeds in 1987. Ironically his debut for Leeds was against Leigh at Headingley and Rathbone incurred a severe jaw injury in the first half and never played again.

"It was no surprise to me when Alan played for Great Britain as he always had that potential," Ashcroft says. "He played every game like it was his last and like many players of his generation the injuries took their toll. When I last saw him he was suffering terribly with arthritis in his knees,

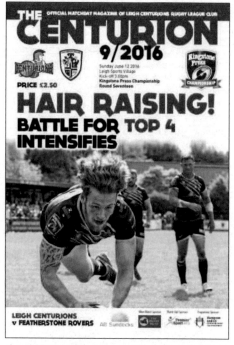

shoulders and hands and it was so sad to see a lad who had been so active being so incapacitated. He was a great lad was Alan and will be remembered fondly by many people."

Leigh's return to LSV after a six-week absence saw them take on fourth-placed Featherstone Rovers in another vital game. They were without Gareth Hock, Jamie Acton and Micky Higham, suspended for a combined total of 13 matches in the fall-out from the stormy game against Swinton and Jon Sharp's Rovers side again provided a stern challenge.

In a game in which defences were well on top Leigh just edged the game 16-12 despite Rovers' resilience with tries by Liam Kay and Greg Worthington giving them a 10-6 lead before Tom Armstrong ended a tense stalemate with a clinching try following a deft Adam Higson kick four minutes from time. Rovers showed their fighting qualities with a second try just before the hooter but had just fallen short again despite causing the Centurions plenty of problems.

CHAMPIONSHIP ROUND 17

Sunday 12th June 2016

LEIGH CENTURIONS 16 FEATHERSTONE ROVERS 12

CENTURIONS: Lee Smith; Adam Higson; Tom Armstrong; Greg Worthington; Liam Kay; Travis Burns; Josh Drinkwater; Fuifui Moimoi; Liam Hood; Dayne Weston; Reni Maitua; Cory Paterson; Harrison Hansen. Subs (all used): Sam Hopkins; Ben Reynolds; Brad Fash; Ben Evans.
Tries: Kay (23), Worthington (53), Armstrong (76);
Goals: Burns, Drinkwater.
ROVERS: Danny Craven; Kyran Johnson; Ian Hardman; Jamie Cording; Jamie Foster; Kyle Briggs; Anthony Thackeray; Darrell Griffin; Andy Ellis; Jordan Baldwinson; Tim Spears; John Davies; Bradley Knowles-Tagg. Subs (all used): Colton Roche; Jack Ormondroyd; Andrew Bostock; Robbie Ward.
Tries: Ellis (28), Knowles-Tagg (78); **Goals:** Foster 2.
Half-time: 6-4; **Referee:** Sam Ansell; **Attendance:** 3,503.

Debutant Ben Evans tackled by Featherstone's Colton Roche

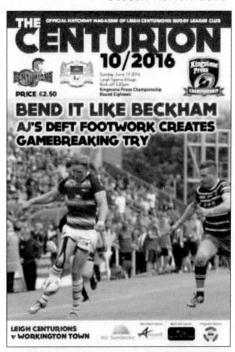

The North Stand watches on as Cory Paterson makes a break against Workington

Workington Town made their second visit of the season to LSV the following Sunday and again conceded over 50 points as Leigh ran in nine tries. Ben Reynolds and Josh Drinkwater led the way with two tries apiece and Lee Smith kicked nine goals from as many attempts to set up the Centurions for their top-of-the table game at London. Town battled bravely and won plenty of admirers for their non-stop efforts despite losing three players to injury during the game.

Anthony's Travel became the first company to take advantage of Leigh Centurions' new Community Match Day Sponsorship initiative pioneered by the Club in association with Leigh Community Trust.

Leigh Community Trust is a registered charity and aims to be an integral part of the Leigh Community by creating high quality, vibrant and innovative community programmes that enhance the lives of everyone in the area. The Trust has over 30 years' experience of working with children and young adults and has a positive reputation for delivering sports, health, education and inclusion projects.

CHAMPIONSHIP ROUND 18

Sunday 19th June 2016

LEIGH CENTURIONS 54 WORKINGTON TOWN 12

CENTURIONS: Lee Smith; Adam Higson; Tom Armstrong; Greg Worthington; Liam Kay; Josh Drinkwater; Travis Burns; Fuifui Moimoi; Ben Reynolds; Dayne Weston; Reni Maitua; Cory Paterson; Ben Evans. Subs (all used): Martyn Ridyard; Harrison Hansen; Brad Fash; Tom Spencer. **Tries:** Reynolds (14, 75), Worthington (18), Drinkwater (20, 56), Kay (35), Spencer (61), Higson (70), Paterson (77); **Goals:** Smith 9.
TOWN: Jack Murphy; Theerapol Ritson; Declan Hulme; Perry Whiteley; Jason Mossop; Jamie Doran; Jarrod Sammut; Oliver Gordon; Callum Phillips; Marc Shackley; Brett Phillips; Matty Gee; Liam McAvoy. Subs (all used): Graeme Mattinson; Karl Olstrum; Alex Szostak; Ryan Verlinden. **Tries:** Mossop (45), Whiteley (52); **Goals:** Sammut 2.
Half-time: 24-0; **Referee:** Scott Mikalauskas; **Attendance:** 3,002.

The idea behind this new initiative is to reach out to disadvantaged groups of the local community, and give them the opportunity to experience the thrills and spills that live Rugby League has to offer.

Meanwhile Fred Longworth, St Mary's Catholic High School, Atherton Community High School and Bedford High School had all joined the Centurions High School Partnership, which is run in conjunction with Leigh Community Trust. Each school was designated its own designated Player Ambassadors, who will take three coaching sessions per year and will be present at the school's presentation evening. The school will also benefit from the Centurions Respect Assembly, which has been formulated to combat all kinds of bullying.

Jake Emmitt was released from his contract after revealing his wish to travel and play in Australia. Neil Jukes revealed he would not seek an immediate replacement for the popular forward, who made a total of 89 appearances for the Centurions as Gareth Hock and Micky Higham had served their three match bans and Sam Hopkins was available again after finger surgery. He said: "Jake has had a long held desire to get over to Australia and travel and discussions have been going on quite a while. Throughout the process Jake has remained really professional and it has all been amicable. I'd like to wish him all the best for the future as the rest of the players and staff will do." Emmitt's Australian adventure did not last long for he later joined Swinton for the rest of the season before teaming up with Toronto.

Towards the end of June Leigh Centurions launched a new website created by the Club's IT manager Andrew Parkinson.

Another former Leigh player was mourned after the passing of halfback Graham Smith at the age of 71 on 30 June. After signing for his hometown club on his 16th birthday Graham made his debut as a 17-year-old against Wakefield Trinity on 20 April 1962, retrospectively earning Heritage Number 707. He went on to play 61 games for Leigh, scoring six

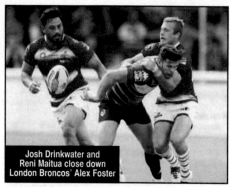

Josh Drinkwater and Reni Maitua close down London Broncos' Alex Foster

tries and kicking 14 goals, making his last appearance in October 1966.

London Broncos had moved to the Ealing Trailfinders Stadium from their previous home at The Hive and to prepare for the 3G pitch they would encounter at the new venue Neil Jukes' side trained on the artificial surface at Leigh East in readiness. All the preparation paid off as the Centurions gave arguably their most complete all-round team performance of the year to date to record an impressive 38-12 victory that extended their lead at the top to five points and opened up an 11pt lead over fifth-placed Bradford.

Leigh set the standards in a near flawless first-half performance that saw them open up a 28-0 lead with Cory Paterson and Greg Worthington each scoring two tries. Worthington was now putting behind him an injury ravaged first half of the season and was in the middle of a purple run of form that saw him score tries in six consecutive games.

CHAMPIONSHIP ROUND 19

Sunday 26th June 2016

LONDON BRONCOS 12 LEIGH CENTURIONS 38

BRONCOS: Elliot Kear; Rhys Williams; Ben Hellewell; Alex Foster; Iliess Macani; Api Pewhairangi; Scott Leatherbarrow; Nick Slyney; James Cunningham; Mark Ioane; Daniel Harrison; Matt Garside; Mark Offerdahl. Subs (all used): Jack Bussey; Jon Magrin; Eddie Battye; Jamie Thackray. **Tries:** Ioane (43), Pewhairangi (65); **Goals:** Pewhairangi 2. **Sin bin:** Ioane (22). **On report:** Bussey (40). **CENTURIONS:** Lee Smith; Adam Higson; Greg Worthington; Tom Armstrong; Liam Kay; Josh Drinkwater; Travis Burns; Fuifui Moimoi; Micky Higham; Dayne Weston; Reni Maitua; Cory Paterson; Gareth Hock. Subs (all used): Liam Hood; Harrison Hansen; Sam Hopkins; Ben Evans. **Tries:** Drinkwater (3), Paterson (10, 25), Worthington (35, 72), Kay (39), Higson (58); **Goals:** Smith 5. **Sin bin:** Hood (61). **Half-time:** 0-28; **Referee:** Joe Cobb; **Attendance:** 1,234.

Lee Smith gets ready to meet Bradford's Kieren Moss head on

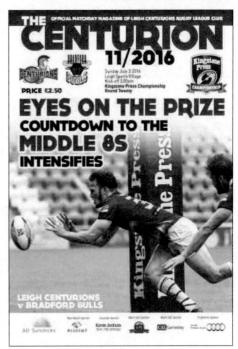

Bradford Bulls were next up at LSV in a match that was by now looking far more important for their season's objectives than Leigh's. It was another titanic struggle watched by a crowd of over 5,000 with the Centurions again just edging home. The game followed a similar path to the Summer Bash encounter as the Bulls fought back from trailing 14-4 to lead 20-16 with early second half tries by Alex Mellor and James Clare. Just two minutes remained when Reni Maitua fastened onto Josh Drinkwater's defence-splitting pass to cross and Lee Smith showed nerves of steel to land the match-winning

conversion. "I'm delighted," said Leigh Head Coach Neil Jukes. "Credit to Bradford, we knew they would bring their A game and they did."

After the game the Centurions staged a Family Fun Day at Leigh Miners, when all the Leigh Centurions players and coaching staff were in attendance and the host club provided food, music and a bouncy castle. It was a great opportunity for fans to mingle with the players, collect autographs and take photographs while children played on the pitch.

With three games remaining in the regular Championship season Leigh played hosts to Halifax knowing that victory would confirm a third successive League Leaders Shield. The visitors were fighting desperately to repeat last season's top-four finish but on the day they were no match for the Centurions who scored ten tries to record a resounding 58-18 victory. Cory Paterson and the fit again Andrew Dixon each scored two tries while Martyn Ridyard kicked nine goals. After a spell out with injury and being out of favour Ridyard had been linked with a move away from the Club but his display highlighted his

---

CHAMPIONSHIP ROUND 20

Sunday 3rd July 2016

LEIGH CENTURIONS 22 BRADFORD BULLS 20

CENTURIONS: Lee Smith; Adam Higson; Tom Armstrong; Greg Worthington; Liam Kay; Josh Drinkwater; Travis Burns; Fuifui Moimoi; Micky Higham; Dayne Weston; Reni Maitua; Cory Paterson; Gareth Hock. Subs (all used): Martyn Ridyard; Harrison Hansen; Sam Hopkins; Brad Fash. **Tries:** Smith (3), Hock (15), Worthington (27), Maitua (78); **Goals:** Smith 3. **BULLS:** Kieren Moss; James Clare; Matty Blythe; Kris Welham; Omari Caro; Danny Addy; Oscar Thomas; Ben Kavanagh; Stuart Howarth; Adam Sidlow; Joe Philbin; Kurt Haggerty; Tom Olbison. Subs (all used): Adam O'Brien; Jay Pitts; Epalahame Lauaki; Alex Mellor. **Tries:** Caro (19), Moss (34), Clare (51), Mellor (56); **Goals:** Addy 2. **Half-time:** 16-10; **Referee:** Chris Campbell; **Attendance:** 5,111.

Fuifui Moimoi sends Halifax's Brandon Moore flying

Eze Harper gets to grips with Sheffield's Cory Aston

growing partnership with Josh Drinkwater and his desire to remain at LSV.

The Halifax game also promoted the Club's newest Community venture in collaboration with Leigh Community Trust - LCT Forces. The Centurions invited both serving and ex-forces soldiers to the game to take part in the launch and the front of the stadium was full of organisations and charities that represented the armed forces including the local cadet forces paintball range, an army assault course, WW2 Pegasus artillery gun and vehicle and much more.

Inside the stadium the local cadets and standard bearers lined the pitch and Afghanistan veteran Andy Reid brought out the match ball. The match day marked the hard work of the Trust over the last two years to move into providing services for the local ex-forces community. At present the Borough has 22,000 ex-forces families.

CHAMPIONSHIP ROUND 21

Sunday 10th July 2016

LEIGH CENTURIONS 58 HALIFAX 18

CENTURIONS: Ben Reynolds; Adam Higson; Greg Worthington; Lee Smith; Liam Kay; Martyn Ridyard; Josh Drinkwater; Sam Hopkins; Liam Hood; Tom Spencer; Andrew Dixon; Cory Paterson; Harrison Hansen. Subs (all used): Fuifui Moimoi; Dayne Weston; Gareth Hock; Micky Higham. **Tries:** Paterson (4, 47), Smith (18), Higson (20), Worthington (25), Drinkwater (30), Dixon (38, 64), Moimoi (75), Kay (77); **Goals:** Ridyard 9.
HALIFAX: Ben Johnston; James Saltonstall; Ben Heaton; Steve Tyrer; Will Sharp; Gareth Moore; Scott Murrell; Mitch Cahalane; Connor Robinson; Adam Tangata; Simon Grix; Matt Sarsfield; Jacob Fairbank. Subs (all used): Luke Ambler; Gavin Bennion; Ed Barber; Brandon Moore. **Tries:** Johnston (14, 49), Sharp (56); **Goals:** Tyrer 3.
Half-time: 34-6; **Referee:** Robert Hicks; **Attendance:** 4,052.

CHAMPIONSHIP ROUND 22

Friday 15th July 2016

SHEFFIELD EAGLES 30 LEIGH CENTURIONS 34

EAGLES: Quentin Laulu-Togagae; Garry Lo; Menzie Yere; Nathan Chappell; Ben Blackmore; Stan Robin; Cory Aston; Steve Thorpe; Keal Carlile; Scott Wheeldon; Matt James; Duane Straugheir; Thibaut Margalet. Subs (all used): Matty Fozard; Adam Neal; Mark Mexico; Michael Knowles. **Tries:** Yere (4, 66), Straugheir (17), Wheeldon (21), Chappell (52); **Goals:** Aston 5.
CENTURIONS: Gregg McNally; Eze Harper; Lee Smith; Tom Armstrong; Liam Kay; Martyn Ridyard; Travis Burns; Tom Spencer; Liam Hood; Sam Hopkins; Andrew Dixon; Reni Maitua; Harrison Hansen. Subs (all used): Ben Reynolds; Gareth Hock; Brad Fash; Fuifui Moimoi. **Tries:** McNally (13), Armstrong (31), Ridyard (35), Dixon (56), Harper (64), Hock (79); **Goals:** Ridyard 5.
Half-time: 16-18; **Referee:** Callum Straw; **Attendance:** 774.

Leigh's final away game of the regular season again saw them break new ground with Sheffield Eagles' new home at the Sheffield Hallam University Sports Park the destination on a hot and sunny Friday evening. It was far from one of the Centurions' best display and they were indebted to a late Gareth Hock try to keep their long unbeaten run going with a 34-30 success. Cory Aston's penalty had given the Eagles the lead at 30-28 only for Hock to surge through from Martyn Ridyard's pass with the last play of the game. On the plus side Gregg McNally made a long-awaited return from serious injury and marked the occasion with an early try while Eze Harper also scored a maiden try on his third and final Leigh appearance. It was also the last game in Leigh's colours for Toronto bound winger Liam Kay.

With the deadline for new signings ahead of the Qualifiers looming Leigh strengthened their squad with a trio of acquisitions, bringing in Cronulla back Mitch Brown, St Helens winger Matty Dawson and Castleford forward Danny Tickle. All were to play significant roles during the remainder of the season. There was also great speculation over a short term move for Australian superstar Jarryd Hayne who was without a club after missing out on selection for the Fiji RU Olympic Sevens team and having left NFL franchise San Francisco 49ers. Club owner Derek Beaumont later revealed that Leigh came desperately close to securing Hayne's services in what would have been one of the most audacious signings in history.

UP, UP AND AWAY...

LIAM AND THE TRIPLE SHIELD WINNING CENTURIONS ARE FLYING HIGH!

There was a celebratory atmosphere around LSV the Centurions marked the end of another successful Kingstone Press Championship campaign against Dewsbury Rams. League leaders three years in a row, the Centurions had lost only three league games, one a season during that time, all away from home and the Rams were never going to spoil the party.

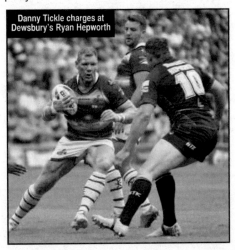

Danny Tickle charges at Dewsbury's Ryan Hepworth

CHAMPIONSHIP ROUND 23

Sunday 24th July 2016

LEIGH CENTURIONS 58 DEWSBURY RAMS 0

CENTURIONS: Gregg McNally; Adam Higson; Willie Tonga; Greg Worthington; Matty Dawson; Martyn Ridyard; Josh Drinkwater; Fuifui Moimoi; Micky Higham; Dayne Weston; Reni Maitua; Cory Paterson; Harrison Hansen. Subs (all used): Ben Reynolds; Jamie Acton; Andrew Dixon; Danny Tickle.
Tries: McNally (3, 15, 18), Maitua (12), Worthington (32), Higson (45, 55, 58), Reynolds (65), Higham (68); **Goals:** Ridyard 9.
RAMS: Josh Guzdek; Dale Morton; Paul Sykes; Jason Crookes; Etuate Uaisele; Dom Speakman; Bobbie Goulding; Mitchell Stringer; Tom Hemingway; Matt Groat; Kyle Trout; Lucas Walshaw; Luke Adamson. Subs (all used): Tony Tonks; Joel Farrell; Nathan Conroy; Ryan Hepworth.
Half-time: 28-0; **Referee:** Tom Grant; **Attendance:** 3,498.

Three tries from Gregg McNally inside the opening quarter set up Leigh for another high-scoring victory as they passed the 50-point mark for the sixth time during the season. Adam Higson notched a second half hat-trick in his side's 58-0 victory in front of 3,498 fans.

Martyn Ridyard completed one hundred goals for the fifth season in succession with the fifth of his nine goals and became only the second player in Club history to achieve the feat of kicking over one hundred goals in five successive seasons. After taking over the goal-kicking duties from Mick Nanyn, Ridyard kicked 133 goals in 2012, 123 goals in 2013, 167 goals in 2014 and 159 goals in 2015. The only player to have also achieved this feat for the Club is the late, great Jimmy Ledgard.

The former GB international fullback favoured the traditional toe-ended kicking style and had the old leather balls to contend with. Ledgard, who cost Leigh a RL record fee of £2,650 from Dewsbury in 1948, repaid that investment many times over. He kicked 125 goals in 1951-52, 116 goals in 1952-53, 104 goals in 1953-54, 165 goals in 1954-55 and 148 goals in 1955-56.

Leigh had won the Championship by a margin of nine points ahead of second placed London Broncos and were the highest points-scorers and had the second meanest defence. That particular accolade fell to Featherstone Rovers who, on a dramatic final day defeated Bradford Bulls 20-0 to clinch the fourth Qualifiers spot alongside Leigh, London and Batley. In a demonstration of just how competitive the Championship as a competition was, three of the sides that made the top four in 2015 Halifax, Bradford and Sheffield missed out repeating that feat in 2016, making the Centurions' achievement all the more praiseworthy.

Reflecting on a third League Leaders Shield Club Captain Micky Higham said: "It's a remarkable effort and I don't think some people realise just how special it is. I don't think the league leaders get the recognition they deserve with all the attention switching to the 8s. Of course,

that will be our main focus now but at least for one day we can reflect on a great effort, particularly after all the disruption we suffered in pre season and early in the season.

"Leigh Centurions have lost three league games in three years, at Doncaster in 2014, London last year and Batley this year and we have remained unbeaten at home throughout that period. That is a really special achievement, particularly when you consider that the Championship gets tougher every year and there are some very good teams and players in there. Look at Sheffield - they went full-time and are at the wrong end of the table, yet they have a really talented side. That shows how hard the Championship is and you only have to look at some of the other games being played on the last day of the regular season to realise how desperate teams are to make the top four."

Looking back to that black day at Batley in February Higham was asked if he had any doubts. "No, I didn't," he replied. "I knew we had a really talented squad and that it might take a while to gel, and in that Batley game, though we didn't play well, we still led late in the game and only lost to a penalty. I knew we would come together as a team and the way we quickly recovered from that disappointing start spoke volumes for the character and talent in the side and also the great work of the coaching staff and the back room team. There was no panic, just a steely determination to learn the lesson from that defeat and that is something we did pretty quickly. Since then we have come a long way as a club and a team and ticked a lot of boxes."

Neil Jukes insisted his club were better prepared for the challenge ahead than they had been in 2015 when they won only one of seven games in the Qualifiers and finished bottom of the pile. The celebrations that followed the Dewsbury game, with the players parading the Championship Shield in front of the fans also came after another busy week in which Martyn Ridyard penned a new two-year deal and Leigh confirmed the signing of Catalans forward Antoni Maria on a two-year contract.

"I think we're better prepared, I really do," Jukes said. "As a squad we're better prepared but at the same time the challenge will be a lot harder. We'll give it our best shot and treat every game like we want to win it."

By now Leigh knew the challenge that faced them in the Qualifiers with home games against Super League sides Salford and Huddersfield and Championship rivals London and Batley. They would face away trips to Hull KR, last season's treble winners Leeds Rhinos and Featherstone Rovers.

"Hull KR are a better side than last year and Leeds have certainly picked up in recent weeks," Jukes said. "Salford are by rights a mid-table team- they are not in the Qualifiers because of performance, but because of their points deduction. And Huddersfield on their day can beat any team in Super League."

The Ladbrokes Challenge Cup Semi-Finals gave Leigh a weekend off before the arrival of London Broncos marked the start of the Qualifiers campaign. After being given a few days off following the Dewsbury game the players returned to find their team room and gym completely transformed as Club Owner Derek Beaumont and Head Coach Neil Jukes had worked tirelessly to bring in new furniture, laptops to analyse performance and motivational signs with the strap-line "#Superleague20172018" highlighting the club's ambition to achieve top-flight status

within the next two years.

Club captain Micky Higham was upbeat as he looked ahead to the Qualifiers. "We've got the best chance we've had for a long time now," he said. "It would be a dream come true for me to captain these boys into Super League.

"It's the same with the other players. They've not come here to sit back and relax, they've come here to add competition for places and take the club to another level. They're desperate to do that and everything's there for us now. It's just down to us to perform for the next seven weeks."

The Centurions duly opened their Qualifiers campaign with a victory against the Broncos but were left hanging on desperately at the end as the visitors mounted an amazing late revival. When Matty Dawson went over for his second try of the game with 12 minutes remaining Leigh held a seemingly impregnable 34-8 advantage, having built on their narrow 14-8 half-time lead with further tries by Reni Maitua and Mitch Brown (his second) while Martyn Ridyard kicked seven from seven.

SUPER 8s (THE QUALIFIERS) ROUND 1

Saturday 6th August 2016

LEIGH CENTURIONS 34 LONDON BRONCOS 30

CENTURIONS: Gregg McNally; Adam Higson; Mitch Brown; Greg Worthington; Matty Dawson; Martyn Ridyard; Josh Drinkwater; Fuifui Moimoi; Micky Higham; Dayne Weston; Reni Maitua; Cory Paterson; Gareth Hock. Subs (all used): Harrison Hansen; Jamie Acton; Ben Reynolds; Danny Tickle. **Tries:** Dawson (22, 68), Brown (37, 62), Maitua (47); **Goals:** Ridyard 7. **Dismissal:** Worthington (72). **Sin bin:** Paterson (32).
BRONCOS: Alex Walker; Rhys Williams; Ben Hellewell; Elliot Kear; Iliess Macani; Api Pewhairangi; Jamie Soward; Nick Slyney; Andy Ackers; Mark Ioane; Daniel Harrison; Matt Garside; Jack Bussey. Subs (all used): James Cunningham; Eddie Battye; Jamie Thackray; Jon Magrin. **Tries:** Hellewell (25), Pewhairangi (72, 75), Ackers (77), Harrison (79); **Goals:** Soward 2, Pewhairangi 3. **Dismissal:** Soward (72). **Half-time:** 14-8; **Referee:** Ben Thaler; **Attendance:** 4,041.

Cory Paterson closes in on London Broncos' Rhys Williams

But in an amazing finish the Broncos ran in four tries and clawed their way back to within four points before time ran out. The match had exploded when Greg Worthington and Broncos' halfback Jamie Soward were both sent-off for fighting in the build-up to the Api Pewhairangi try that sparked the Broncos' ultimately unavailing revival.

"I thought we looked nervous before the game and we were a little bit like they were at their place," Neil Jukes later reflected. "We were like rabbits caught in the headlights; they wrestled us and we couldn't get on the front foot.

"In the first half we were off, loose defensively and our completion rate was really poor. They kicked early and we gave them scraps. We addressed everything at half-time and did it from 40 minutes to probably the 69th minute. We were perfect, absolutely perfect and then that last 11 minutes was just a schnozzle wasn't it?"

The celebrations begin after victory against Salford

Leigh's home game against Salford Red Devils, televised live on Sky Sports on Saturday afternoon now assumed extra importance. Salford had defeated Huddersfield in round one of the Qualifiers but Leigh moved up several gears from their display against London to record a thrilling 32-26 victory. Adam Higson emerged as a key player, scoring a crucial try and saving at least three in defence while Leigh's former Salford contingent of Gareth Hock, Cory Paterson, Liam Hood, Harrison Hansen and Reni Maitua all played crucial roles. Captain Micky Higham was another Leigh stand-out, but arguably Dayne Weston towered above

them all as he produced his best display in an already hugely impressive debut season.

The Centurions led 20-10 at half-time and extended their lead to 32-16 when Matty Dawson went over from Willie Tonga's fantastic inside pass. Salford had no less than four second half tries ruled out by the video referee but still clawed their way back to within six points at the end of a simply outstanding game. The only downside in the aftermath to the game from a Leigh point of view was Jamie Acton picking up another ban, this time for four games for contrary behaviour.

"We spoke all week about attacking the game," Neil Jukes revealed afterwards. "It was the first time this season we've faced Super League opposition when it meant something. We just spoke about attacking it, running out of subs if we needed to, just attack it and not hang about waiting to see what they were going to throw at us. I think we did that, especially in the first half.

"One thing we learnt from last year is that win, lose or draw we have to dust ourselves down and go again. Our motto is 'No Regrets' and we are looking forward, but the job is nowhere near done."

SUPER 8s (THE QUALIFIERS) ROUND 2

Saturday 13th August 2016

LEIGH CENTURIONS 32 SALFORD RED DEVILS 26

CENTURIONS: Gregg McNally; Adam Higson; Mitch Brown; Willie Tonga; Matty Dawson; Martyn Ridyard; Josh Drinkwater; Sam Hopkins; Micky Higham; Dayne Weston; Reni Maitua; Cory Paterson; Gareth Hock. Subs (all used): Jamie Acton; Liam Hood; Danny Tickle; Harrison Hansen.
Tries: Maitua (7), Paterson (12), McNally (22), Higson (74), Dawson (76);
Goals: Ridyard 6.
RED DEVILS: Gareth O'Brien; Niall Evalds; Junior Sa'u; Josh Griffin; Mason Caton-Brown; Robert Lui; Michael Dobson; Craig Kopczak; Logan Tomkins; George Griffin; Ben Murdoch-Masila; Feleti Mateo; Mark Flanagan. Subs (all used): Weller Hauraki; Luke Burgess; Olsi Krasniqi; Sean Kenny.
Tries: Caton-Brown (15, 79), Evalds (31), Lui (55), Murdoch-Masila (77);
Goals: O'Brien 3.
Half-time: 20-10; **Referee:** Chris Campbell; **Attendance:** 4,547.

Gregg McNally collared by Featherstone's Steve Snitch

Round three of the Qualifiers saw Leigh back at the Big Fellas Stadium against a Featherstone Rovers side that had given them two really hard games in the Championship. They knew this was a crucial game in their Super League quest as all the hard work would be undone if they failed to come out without a win.

There was a tangible sense of relief as the Centurions achieved their objective, Martyn Ridyard's late penalty followed by Gareth Hock's converted try sealing a 30-18 victory against a Rovers side that again gave them an almighty fright. Early tries by Reni Maitua and Mitch Brown had looked to put Leigh in command but Rovers dominated the rest of the first half and trailed by only four points at the

interval. Second half tries by Matty Dawson and Micky Higham again seemingly put the visitors in control but Rovers fought back to within four points in a tense and highly charged last quarter.

"To have six points from six gives us a really good chance," Neil Jukes reflected later. "We are in and around the Million Pound Game ballpark with what we've got; we're two points above Hull KR as it stands."

The break for the Challenge Cup Final allowed Leigh's players to take a breather and focus on the final month of the campaign. But the Club was represented at Wembley Stadium by 12-year-old season ticket holder Molly Bullough. It was the culmination of a journey that began when Molly was nominated to represent Leigh Centurions as part of a Fans Choir on BBC's Songs of Praise programme. The 32 choir members joined Aled Jones to sing the traditional Challenge Cup curtain raiser Abide With Me.

Molly reflected: "Walking out and singing Abide with Me on the actual Wembley turf in front of 76,235 fans was the best experience any rugby fan could ask for. What made it even better was that we stayed on the pitch as the players walked out! I would recommend entering

---

SUPER 8s (THE QUALIFIERS) ROUND 3

Sunday 21st August 2016

FEATHERSTONE ROVERS 18 LEIGH CENTURIONS 30

ROVERS: Danny Craven; James Duckworth; Ian Hardman; Misi Taulapapa; Luke Briscoe; Kyle Briggs; Anthony Thackeray; Darrell Griffin; Andy Ellis; Jordan Baldwinson; Bradley Knowles-Tagg; Josh Walters; Tim Spears. Subs (all used): Sam Day; Steve Snitch; Luke Cooper; Jack Ormondroyd.
Tries: Walters (13), Briscoe (68), Ormondroyd (70); **Goals:** Briggs 3.
CENTURIONS: Gregg McNally; Adam Higson; Mitch Brown; Tom Armstrong; Matty Dawson; Martyn Ridyard; Josh Drinkwater; Fuifui Moimoi; Micky Higham; Dayne Weston; Reni Maitua; Cory Paterson; Gareth Hock. Subs (all used): Liam Hood; Danny Tickle; Harrison Hansen; Sam Hopkins.
Tries: Maitua (4), Brown (7), Dawson (54), Higham (60), Hock (79); **Goals:** Ridyard 5.
Half-time: 8-12; **Referee:** Jack Smith; **Attendance:** 3,644.

the competition to anyone and I would like to thank the Songs of Praise team, and all the Leigh Centurions fans who sent good luck messages before the big day."

There was also time to fit in a glittering, sell-out awards evening at LSV when popular Australian prop Dayne Weston carried off the twin accolades as Players' Player and Coaches' Player of the Year ahead of fellow nominees Micky Higham and Adam Higson.

Derek Beaumont handed out a joint Special Award to Neil Jukes and Paul Anderson for their huge contributions to the season and Neil Barker won the Clubman of the Year Award for his efforts on the club's flourishing commercial department after switching careers following 32 years in journalism. Martyn Ridyard's try at Swinton, following a thrilling length-of-the-field move involving several players won Try of the Year and there was an emotional video presentation to the retiring Reni Maitua featuring some of the world's greatest players.

A host of the sport's greatest names including Jonathan Thurston, Sonny Bill Williams, Jarryd Hayne, Braith Anasta, Willie Mason, Steve Price, Nathan Myles and Frank Pritchard paid video tributes along with Reni's family. Reni's great friend and teammate Willie Tonga also presented him with a signed photographic compilation by Club Photographer Paul McCarthy.

Later, in an interview with Dave Parkinson on LCTV Maitua said: "I've thoroughly enjoyed coming here and have no regrets whatsoever. I never thought I'd end up on this side of the world and what a way to finish my career at a club like this. It's been an absolute pleasure. The club has welcomed myself and my partner Holly with open arms."

He went on to thank all the Leigh fans that have supported and sent him messages throughout the year: "Everyone has been fantastic and I look forward to saying goodbye to everyone over the next few weeks."

But Weston deservedly dominated the evening with Derek Beaumont also revealing that he had agreed a new three-year contract, tying him to the Club until the end of the 2019 season. Weston, who had been a model professional on and off the field in his first season in England was typically modest as he received his awards, thanking his team mates, coaches and all the Club's supporters for making him and his family feel so welcome despite being 12,000 miles from home.

Guests enjoyed a Champagne reception, a three course meal and fabulous entertainment from table magician Jason Rey, comedian Pete Emmett and singer Martin Gregory-Lambert in addition to the awards presentations. The Awards Dinner main sponsor was 24/7 Technology Limited. The Associate Sponsors were CAL Sameday, O2 Leigh and Palatine Paints and the Award Sponsors were Bradshawgate Cafe, Collins and Darwell, Kukri, Leigh Cables, Preston Audi and The Boars Head.

Reflecting on the occasion, Club Captain Micky Higham said: "Dayne's been great in his first season over here and thoroughly deserved his awards. He's really taken to life in Leigh and as Jukesy said it's not just the 80 minutes you see at the weekend it's the way that he goes about his business around the club, pushing up the standards in training and preparation along with a lot of other players. Off the field he's done some great work in the community and earned a lot of respect for the way he always has time for everyone.

"I thought it was a great evening and showed that on and off the pitch we are striving to get better and put on a show. The presentation was a bit like watching the BBC Sports Personality of the Year awards and the tributes to Reni (Maitua) at the end were really emotional. It was fantastic to see so many great players from Australia, almost like a Who's Who of the game, paying tribute to Reni but also wishing Leigh Centurions well. Maybe Fui's signing was the catalyst to all that, as his signing created world-wide interest in the club and showed that under Derek's leadership we really meant business.

Andrew Dixon races
past Ben Cockayne in
the rain at Hull KR

"Fui has since been followed by some great players and I look around our changing room and have to pinch myself sometimes that so many internationals, NRL players and established Super League players are all playing for Leigh. And the best thing is, we are all as one, the team spirit on and off the field is fantastic and we are all striving for the same thing. Off the field the club has developed its commercial arm and made great strides and that's a tribute to all the hard work and foresight of a lot of people."

Neil Jukes was keen to keep his

players' focus purely on the next game, an intriguing match-up at Hull KR rather than the bigger prize ahead. "There's enough experience in the room to know that, while we've given ourselves a good opportunity, we haven't achieved anything yet," he said.

"Hull KR away is a tough trip and then we've got Huddersfield at home and on their day they're still a very good side. We've still got Batley, who have been really good twice against us before finishing off at Leeds. Nobody is getting carried away here. we're just taking it one game at a time. Last week's win at Featherstone was big for us. We put a lot of focus on that game. Now we've got another big one at Hull KR."

The KCOM Lightstream Stadium, or New Craven Park in old money can be an intimidating place for visitors and Leigh have had precious few wins at Hull KR in the past 40 years. Memories of older supporters drifted back to Leigh's dramatic Challenge Cup win at the old Craven Park in a tie televised on BBC in 1982 and a 24-0 victory in the same competition at the new ground in the mid 1990s.

SUPER 8s (THE QUALIFIERS) ROUND 4

Saturday 3rd September 2016

HULL KINGSTON ROVERS 18 LEIGH CENTURIONS 25

ROVERS: Ben Cockayne; Ken Sio; Thomas Minns; Iain Thornley; Josh Mantellato; Matthew Marsh; Maurice Blair; Dane Tilse; Shaun Lunt; Mitchell Allgood; James Greenwood; Chris Clarkson; Adam Walker. Subs (all used): Kevin Larroyer; James Donaldson; George Lawler; Rob Mulhern.
Tries: Sio (6), Mantellato (11), Marsh (65); **Goals:** Mantellato 3.
CENTURIONS: Gregg McNally; Adam Higson; Mitch Brown; Greg Worthington; Matty Dawson; Martyn Ridyard; Josh Drinkwater; Gareth Hock; Micky Higham; Dayne Weston; Reni Maitua; Cory Paterson; Danny Tickle. Subs (all used): Harrison Hansen; Sam Hopkins; Andrew Dixon; Liam Hood.
Tries: Hopkins (25), Dixon (46), Dawson (49), Drinkwater (52);
Goals: Ridyard 4; **Field goal:** Ridyard (78).
Half-time: 12-6; **Referee:** Robert Hicks; **Attendance:** 7,363.

But hopes of a repeat looked a distant dream as Rovers dominated the early stages and built a 12-0 lead before Sam Hopkins somehow grounded the ball over the home line in a massed tackle to bring Leigh back into the game. Trailing 12-6 at the break Leigh came to life, scoring three glorious tries within 12 minutes of the resumption as the fit-again Andrew Dixon, Matty Dawson and Josh Drinkwater all crossed.

Rovers got back to within four points before Martyn Ridyard's nerveless penalty gave Leigh a six-point lead with ten minutes remaining. Ridyard then sent the travelling Leigh fans into seventh heaven as he kept his cool to pot the match-clinching drop-goal two minutes from time and secure a priceless 25-18 win.

Neil Jukes continued to keep his feet on the floor. "I'm delighted. It's a big win, but it's nowhere near job done," he said. "Mathematically even ten points doesn't get you there, so we've got to keep working hard. Make no mistake, to come to a place like Hull KR and do that on the back of the poor start we had is an incredible effort."

Josh Drinkwater gave the club a massive boost ahead of one of their biggest games in the summer era by penning a three-year deal. "Josh re-signing now shows a lot of confidence in what we are doing," said Jukes. "He has shown great commitment to the club and he is pivotal to what we are wanting to build here. He has had genuine offers from Super League clubs, but the fact that he wants to carry on with us shows faith in the staff and the players and shows that he has bought into our vision." After all the injury concerns early in the season Jukes went into the game with only the suspended Jamie Acton unavailable from the 27-man squad.

Meanwhile Jason Huyton accepted a unanimous invitation to join the Board of Directors of the Club. He took up his duties with immediate effect as Commercial Director to join Owner Derek Beaumont, Chairman Michael Norris, CEO Matthew Chantler, Operations Director Steve Openshaw and Media &

Communications Director Mike Latham on the six-man Board.

The managing director of Palatine Paints, prominent sponsors of the Club in recent years Mr Huyton, 39, brought a wealth of commercial experience to the role and his company, Palatine Paints were Main Match Sponsors for the Super 8s Qualifiers Round 5 game against Huddersfield Giants when Jason's daughter Amy was be one of the Match Day Mascots.

Leigh Centurions Owner Derek Beaumont said: "When I suggested inviting Jason onto the Board with the opportunity to purchase shares to the other directors they were unanimous in their support. I have always stated I want to build this Club for the future and adding quality, proven business people in particular that have a passion for the Club and the town will only enable this to happen. Jason will take control of the commercial department and I have no doubt he will continue to drive the great work that is already being done there."

Jason Huyton said: "I am a true Leyther in every sense of the term, originating around the Wigan Road area of Leigh. I am very proud of my roots as they have developed me into the person I am today. I still live in Leigh, around a mile from LSV, with my wife Adele, daughter Amy and my youngest brother Jordan who came to live with me in February when our mum passed away.

"Leigh Centurions has a place in my heart from standing on the terracing at Hilton Park to now cheering on from the North Stand. In the last few seasons, especially with the guidance and persistence of Adele and Amy the Centurions have taken a prominent part in our family lives.

"I have worked at my company Palatine Paints (est. 1946) which is situated on Smallbrook Lane in Leigh for 22 years. When I bought the company we had three staff, but with 50 years of experience between us. Now the company has 12 staff and has seen a remarkable growth of business in such a short time. This has enabled me to offer support to

Leigh Centurions with sponsorship whilst at the same time raising the profile of my company and building a great relationship with the Club, leading to being a shirt sponsor this season.

"The corporate section of the Club is second to none and the warmth and professionalism shown to me and my family has been overwhelming and it's here where I started to see just how passionate are the people running the Club. Most notably Derek Beaumont, who has been the biggest influence on me with his enthusiasm, desire and single mindedness (which I love) and it is difficult not to buy into this belief. When I was asked by Derek to join the Board I was filled with huge pride. I see it as an honour to be joining such an already formidable Board to which I hope to offer the skill sets that I possess to help the Club achieve all its ambitions, both on and of the pitch.

"I see my role as Commercial Director as a great area to be operating in as I already have a great relationship with both Amanda Lee and Neil Barker. I am convinced that with our friendly approach, together we can continue to push the Club forward with existing and new businesses and I will be looking to speak to all existing sponsors in the coming months as well as introducing new business to the Club. I would like to personally thank the sponsors for supporting the Club's drive to Super League as this along with the support of our great vociferous fans is an integral part of the Club's future.

"I would like to finish by thanking Adele for supporting me through everything and to Derek and the Board for giving me such a privileged opportunity. These great individuals and a wonderful Club deserve the success heading our way."

Saturday 10 September 2016 will remain a date firmly etched on the minds of Leigh Centurions supporters. It was the day the club finally clinched their place back in Super League after a simply sensational game against Huddersfield Giants played out before nearly 6,000 fans at LSV and an equally enthralled audience on Sky Sports. The final score-line of 48-40 sounds amazing in itself, but the drama

behind it was something else.

Leigh's first half performance was quite stunning and Huddersfield's players looked shell shocked as they made their way up the tunnel at half-time, trailing by 42-10. Leigh scored seven tries with some scintillating attacking play, all converted by Martyn Ridyard. It was the stuff of which dreams are made.

Matty Dawson, such a crucial late season acquisition, scored a sparkling first-half hat-trick and Ridyard bagged two tries- one a length-of-the-field interception

SUPER 8s (THE QUALIFIERS) ROUND 5

Saturday 10th September 2016

LEIGH CENTURIONS 48 HUDDERSFIELD GIANTS 40

CENTURIONS: Gregg McNally; Adam Higson; Mitch Brown; Greg Worthington; Matty Dawson; Martyn Ridyard; Josh Drinkwater; Gareth Hock; Micky Higham; Dayne Weston; Reni Maitua; Cory Paterson; Danny Tickle. Subs (all used): Harrison Hansen; Sam Hopkins; Andrew Dixon; Liam Hood. **Tries:** Worthington (1); Dawson (7, 12, 32), Ridyard (27, 39), Paterson (35), Brown (48); **Goals:** Ridyard 8.
GIANTS: Jake Connor; Jermaine McGillvary; Leroy Cudjoe; Joe Wardle; Aaron Murphy; Danny Brough; Jamie Ellis; Sebastine Ikahihifo; Ryan Hinchcliffe; Craig Huby; Michael Lawrence; Ukuma Ta'ai; Oliver Roberts. Subs (all used): Sam Rapira; Josh Johnson; Kruise Leeming; Nathan Mason. **Tries:** Lawrence (17), Murphy (24), Connor (53), Cudjoe (63, 65), Ellis (70, 76); **Goals:** Brough 6.
Half-time: 42-10; **Referee:** Robert Hicks; **Attendance:** 5,934.

Greg Worthington mobbed after scoring the opening try against Huddersfield

with Greg Worthington and Cory Paterson also going over in a spellbinding 40 minutes. It got even better when Mitch Brown extended the lead to 48-10 with an eighth Leigh try early in the second half.

But the Giants then mounted an incredible comeback, Jake Connor's try followed by a Leroy Cudjoe brace, then by a brace from ex-Leigh favourite Jamie Ellis. 48-10 became 48-40 and never have Leigh players or fans been more relieved to hear the final hooter.

"I felt they would come back at us," Neil Jukes said. "What we have always done is hung in there, whether that be a one-point win or a two-point win. As a group from the game against Dewsbury they've just got closer and closer. It's not been the prettiest at times, but the gutsiest without a shadow of a doubt. And now they can dream.

"What we've got to do is stay strong as a team and never forget this group of players or backroom staff, the board, Derek (Beaumont). We've got to make sure that we are continually working hard in what we are doing.

Gareth Hock looks to get a pass away under pressure from Huddersfield's Craig Huby

"To put 42 points on Huddersfield by half-time was electric, absolutely electric. We were on the money and defensively very good and we did enough in that first half to win the game. We've achieved our goal."

Club captain Micky Higham said: "Hometown club, hometown boy. It's a special moment. It's been building for a long time. It's been a great Championship team for years and now we've stepped up and finally made our mark. The hard work has paid off but we know now there's a lot more hard work next year.

"It was surreal and it's not really sunk it yet. It was a bit weird as after the game there was no winners' board or a trophy awarded. But it was job done and to do it with a couple of games to go really hit home. It's a remarkable achievement in what was a far stronger competition than the Qualifiers last year."

Former Great Britain coach Malcolm Reilly, one of the game's greatest players and a 1970 Ashes winner was a club guest at the game and thoroughly enjoyed the occasion and was hugely impressed with Leigh's display. Reilly was one of many high profile sports stars to be guests in Premier Club during the season, the list including fellow Rugby League stars Bill Ashurst, Andy Gregory, Bev Risman, Alex Murphy OBE, Reg Bowden, Steve Nash, Kevin Ashcroft, Darren Abram, Neil Turley and John Woods, footballers Joe Corrigan, Francis Lee, Fred Eyre, David Lee and Tony Kelly, cricketers Gary Pratt and Steve Mullaney and rugby union star Fran Cotton, accompanied by his brother Dave, a former Leigh player.

Higham capped a momentous personal season by winning the prestigious Kingstone Press Championship Player of the Year award at the annual dinner in Leeds. He beat fellow nominees Dominic Brambani (Batley) and Featherstone's Misi Taulapapa to the award. In the Coach of the Year Neil Jukes was pipped by Batley coach John Kear, in his final year in the role ahead of a move to Wakefield Trinity as football director. Leigh Centurions were named Championship Club of the Year, a fitting accolade to a season of hard work

and achievement on and off the field.

Micky Higham said: "I'm a team player and have always regarded individual awards as secondary to the team effort but I must admit it was a nice accolade and it was a lovely evening in Leeds. I was blown away to be honest with the award and as I said on the night I picked it up on behalf of the squad of 27 players who have all contributed hugely. It was a real team effort this year and you can't achieve anything without the efforts of your team-mates and the coaching and support staff who have all been brilliant.

"It was strange at the awards dinner as I met up with Anthony Murray who is now the coach at North Wales Crusaders. Anthony is a great lad and he was the first choice hooker when I was coming through the ranks. But he was absolutely brilliant with me. He's a good person and though I eventually took his place he never held it against me and always encouraged me. I have nothing but admiration for him and we had a good chat as we always do. He always had time to spend with younger players and he's taken that into his coaching and has done a great job in that role and I'm sure he will have a great coaching career. I had five years with Keiron Cunningham at Saints and he was just the same as Anthony in the way he helped me. After losing in the 2000 Premiership grand final with Leigh I always felt I had unfinished business and 16 years on I put that one to bed."

The final home game of the season was a time for celebration and in an amazing act of generosity owner Derek

---

SUPER 8s (THE QUALIFIERS) ROUND 6

Saturday 17th September 2016

LEIGH CENTURIONS 42 BATLEY BULLDOGS 24

CENTURIONS: Lee Smith; Adam Higson; Mitch Brown; Willie Tonga; Matty Dawson; Ben Reynolds; Travis Burns; Fuifui Moimoi; Liam Hood; Dayne Weston; Cory Paterson; Andrew Dixon; Brad Fash. Subs (all used): Harrison Hansen; Tom Spencer; Lewis Foster; Sam Hopkins. **Tries:** Moimoi (17), Higson (21), Paterson (31), Foster (35), Burns (46), Tonga (63), Weston (75); **Goals:** Smith 7.
BULLDOGS: Dave Scott; Wayne Reittie; Sam Smeaton; Chris Ulugia; Shaun Ainscough; Pat Walker; Dominic Brambani; Keegan Hirst; Alistair Leak; Alex Rowe; Brad Day; Alex Bretherton; Luke Blake. Subs (all used): James Davey; Adam Gledhill; Joe Chandler; Tom Lillycrop. **Tries:** D Scott (8), Leak (27), Hirst (70), Reittie (79); **Goals:** Walker 4. **On report:** Bretherton (60).
Half-time: 24-12; **Referee:** Chris Kendall; **Attendance:** 10,556.

Adam Higson beats Batley's Shaun Ainscough to score in the corner in front of a packed LSV

Beaumont threw open the turnstiles and made it free admission for all, in order to celebrate the club's promotion to Super League, and to re-introduce the club to a larger audience.

The Centurions wore the special Team Isaac Summer Bash shirt for this fixture, and the proceeds from the profits of shirt sales of this special edition garment were presented to Gareth Haggerty at half-time (on behalf of Team Isaac). The Centurions concluded the day with a lap of honour around the stadium, to thank the fans for their support.

A crowd of 10,556, easily the highest for a Leigh game at the LSV and their biggest home crowd for nearly 30 years packed out the stadium and Mr Beaumont added to the party mood by flying in by helicopter and landing on the adjoining Leigh Harriers ground just before kick-off after a business trip down south. The pre match events were extensively covered by ITV Granada for their tea-time news programme.

Club legend John Woods, in the month in which he celebrated his 60th birthday saw a statue in his honour unveiled outside the stadium and was guest of honour as he accepted the invitation to become a Life Member. John followed in the footsteps of his grandfather Herbert (#164), a member of Leigh's Championship-winning team in 1906, when then player-coach Kevin Ashcroft handed him his Leigh debut in 1976, retrospectively earning Heritage #858. John's uncle Peter Riley (#449) was a brilliant scrum-half in the Leigh team of the immediate post war side.

In two spells at Leigh John Woods scored 152 tries and kicked 997 goals (including 13 drop-goals) in 349 appearances, amassing 2,492 points. He is the highest points-scorer in Leigh's history and only the great Mick Martyn scored more tries; only the late, great Jimmy Ledgard kicked more goals.

John was a star of the Leigh championship-winning season in 1981-82 and represented Great Britain, earning the Player of the Tour award from the RL International Supporters Association in 1979. He also played with distinction for Bradford Northern, Warrington and Rochdale Hornets and when his professional career was over was player-coach at Leigh Miners. In his professional career he scored 236 tries and kicked 1,591 goals (including 22 drop-goals) for 3,985 points in 553 games.

Only four players in the history of the game- Neil Fox, Jim Sullivan, Kevin Sinfield and Gus Risman have scored more points in a career.

Mike Latham wrote: "Statistics do not do justice to John Woods for he cared little for them. He was a natural rugby player, capable of playing with equal success in any back position. His brilliant tackling technique was often overstated. He would glide through a gap, create openings, tackle the hardest and most redoubtable of forwards and kick goals from all over the park like he was shelling peas.

"Above all he loved playing for Leigh and when his career was over his cap size

The John Woods statue, outside Leigh Sports Village

was the same as when he started. To Leigh supporters who had the honour of seeing him play he was simply a living legend, the greatest player who ever donned the Cherry and White."

Leigh Centurions Owner Derek Beaumont said: "I am delighted that John has accepted our invitation to become a Honorary Life Member of the Club. It is a massive year for John, celebrating his 60th birthday and is an appropriate time to bestow such an honour on him to coincide with his statue which will be positioned at the ground.

"John was many a person's hero in his playing days and was certainly mine. I never managed to get his tie-ups as he was always mobbed first so I used to pick a different player that I had more chance of success. John is a fantastic person, very quiet and unassuming for someone who is a legend in his own town having achieved what he did. Our history is vital to our future and John is a very big part of that."

Before the game Micky Higham, on behalf of the club presented Batley coach John Kear with an inscribed glass ornament to mark the final away game of his illustrious coaching career.

In the match day programme Centurions Chairman Mike Norris wrote: " I have been a fan of Leigh Rugby League Club since I was playing with my pals on the old training pitch one Saturday afternoon and wandered into the ground where the A team were playing, probably around 1973. There were no ball boys at the game and so I found myself running around the terracing retrieving the ball after each kick which was really exciting for my nine-year-old self and from then on I was hooked!

"There have been some incredible highs, the Championship winning game at Whitehaven being the greatest, but also some painful lows - unfortunately more of the latter than the former. From my first season ticket aged 11 through sponsoring the odd game with Café Inns and then Honeycombe Leisure I arrived at a point in April 2013 when my beloved club was once again in crisis and I was asked if I would be able to help out. Not living in Leigh I didn't know the other people who I was meeting, one Friday afternoon, at the suggestion of my old mate Neil Wilcock but sat around a pub table we decided we would do what we could to save our club.

"Two of the guys at that meeting were Ste Openshaw and Derek Beaumont - big men with big hearts. As we approached our Championship victory in 2014 Derek suggested that he would be prepared to support the club to go full-time for the following season and Ste and I, together with Mike Latham who by now we had persuaded to return to his first love, agreed to support him wholeheartedly.

"2015 was a fantastic year for the club (who can forget the Fuifui Moimoi welcome night?) as we romped through the regular season and had a great run in the Challenge Cup only to see things falter badly in the Qualifiers. I still have a mocking text from the Chairman of one of our competitors after we came bottom of the 8 - I have resisted the temptation to reciprocate this season as it would be like kicking a puppy...

"After our defeat to Widnes in the final game of 2015 our RFL funding had fallen significantly whilst our peers had seen theirs increase and I was unsure how we would move forward. I needn't have worried as Derek phoned BBC Radio Manchester on the way home from the match and told them that we were going again in 2016 - bigger and better in all ways!

"What followed were a few months which would have been crossed out of a soap opera as too farfetched!

"Big names arrived - Chase, Hansen, Paterson, Tonga. Big names left - Chase, Brierley and the head coach. Neil Jukes was trusted to move the club forward and the first match of the season saw the aforementioned defeat to Batley.

"Derek's reaction was to give Neil a long term contract and to put total faith in him to get us into the top 6 in the Qualifiers - always our only target for the year. What a good call that was. As we approached the business end of the season more quality - Josh, Danny, Mitch, Matty - was added to the squad and we entered the play-offs quietly confident.

"And the rest, as they say, is history!

"We stand here today as a Super League club and will share an incredible day with our friends from Batley. I hope that the town of Leigh has responded to the offer of free entry and the ground is packed to cheer the lads on today. I will be raising a glass today in celebration of what has been achieved in three-and-a-half years on the back of Derek's investment and unrivalled drive, and I hope you all come back to see us in our adventure in 2017 - who knows what may happen!!!"

Meanwhile Micky Higham looked ahead briefly to 2017: "We have gone up so many levels from last year when I re-joined the club and have made massive strides so we are capable of climbing a few more rungs. It's all about looking to improve the things that all combine to make a difference, like professionalism, discipline and punctuality and getting to training half an hour before rather than ten minutes before so you can prepare properly, get strapped or watch some videos of games.

"So there are lots of things we need to improve upon to help up that intensity week in, week out. No disrespect to the teams in the Championship but there are occasions we could have put 70pts on teams. Now we are in Super League we'll be playing the likes of Wigan, Hull, Warrington and so on week in, week out and as was the case last week, if you switch off for 15 minutes you can get 30pts put on you.

"We have undoubted quality in the team and I'm sure with the quality of player we can attract that we will be ready and prepared come the start of next season. There's a massive rumour mill in Super League and lots of people have been speculating about the players Derek and Jukesy want to bring in. Above all, we'll want to avoid the bottom four and get in the top eight like teams like Wakefield and Widnes have done this year."

With promotion assured Neil Jukes gave the remaining squad members a first game in the 8s, the popular Tom Spencer playing his 99th and final game for the club ahead of a move to London Broncos alongside Lewis Foster, Travis Burns, Ben Reynolds, Brad Fash and Lee Smith. Reflecting on his time at the Club in an interview with Dave Parkinson on LCTV Tom Spencer said: "There were some good victories and good trophies we've won. Back in 2013 there was the Northern Rail Final, and also the League Leaders over the last few years and the Championship Grand Final. There have been lots of great moments along the way, good times with good people."

Tom also paid tribute to Leigh Community Trust, where he is an Ambassador. "When I first came onboard permanently with Leigh, the club wasn't full time. I have to thank LCT, Hannah and Heather for giving me an enjoyable job. It was very rewarding. I managed to reach out through various programmes, myself, Liam Kay and Ryan Brierley to the local community and we did a lot of work with less fortunate kids. We also did a lot of work with kids interested in rugby and provided a nice link between the club and the community."

Paying tribute to Spencer and other departing players in his programme notes Club Captain Micky Higham wrote: " There are some really good people and really good players who will be playing their last Leigh game at LSV. To pick out Andrew Dixon, he's been admirable and I'm disappointed he's leaving- he's very professional and his standards are very good. Same applies to Greg Worthington who has been one of our form players lately and will leave a big void to fill. Tom Spencer is a good lad and loves this club to the bones. He always has a smile on his face and will be a big loss. He's a big character. He's a nice lad with his best years still ahead.

"Then there is Reni who it's been an absolute pleasure to play alongside. The lads who haven't played week in, week out have been a massive influence. They are all professional and have kept up standards in training. Look at Lee Smith for instance- he's played at the top level of the game and is chomping at the bit to play and yet his standards on the training field have never faltered. And to top it all off, today we unveil the John Woods statue. The greatest player to ever play for Leigh in the opinion of many people, who would have been fantastic in the Super League era. To unveil his statue on a day that we have already secured a place back in Super League and just days after his 60th birthday is a fairytale. But then it's been that kind of season."

The game was never a classic but once Fuifui Moimoi got Leigh's scoring underway they never looked in serious trouble of losing against a Batley side that again competed well. Lewis Foster and Willie Tonga notched their first Leigh tries. Leigh's 42-24 victory saw them to their sixth win out of six in the Qualifiers and they went into their final game at second placed Leeds Rhinos looking to top the table and also earn the specially commissioned Bev Risman Trophy, in honour of the 1960s Leigh and Leeds favourite and dual international. It also preserved Leigh's unbeaten home record.

"It was good to get the result," Neil Jukes said. "It was always going to be a big occasion and the added pressure of over 10,000 people in here, so it was important we gave our own players a send-off, but also for some of the new guys and neutrals that came, we wanted it to be a spectacle.

"We were probably a little bit rusty on occasions and we said that. We made seven changes but it was all about making sure we came through with a good attitude and lots of energy and being physical. I'm really pleased and would have taken the score-line before the game, that's for sure."

After the game Dayne Weston was awarded the Tommy Sale Memorial Trophy as the LCTV Player of the Year, with Reni Maitua and Greg Worthington the other nominees. Dave Parkinson said: "All three earned their nominations on merit through the year. Reni for becoming one of the most popular players to ever pull on the jersey and scoring some crucial tries, Greg for his unwavering professionalism and dedication, not to mention brilliant form when he worked his way back into the team and Dayne for his consistency, leadership, great sporting nature and charity work for Ben's Wish."

Dave added: "It was a tough decision, but ultimately Dayne just edged it and I asked the LCTV team to present the award which is in honour of the great Tommy Sale MBE who passed away in January. Every week during our coverage we have mentioned the great man when nominating our Man of the Match. It was the least we could do to remind people of everything Tommy stood for and the legacy he left behind. I was delighted when Tommy's daughter Jean and the rest of the family donated this stunning trophy.

"All at Leigh Centurions TV would like to congratulate Dayne on winning the award and extending his time with the club. We also want to express our thanks to the Sale family for their generosity in purchasing and donating the trophy."

As plans for life in Super League continued apace, the Club confirmed that Ste Maden would take up a full-time position as the Club's Player Welfare Officer on an initial two-year contract starting in late October. The highly popular former player who made 210 appearances for the Club and also played for St Helens, Warrington Wolves and Whitehaven, had previously been carrying out the role on a part-time, voluntary basis.

Leigh Centurions Owner Derek Beaumont said: ,"I am delighted to welcome Ste on board in a full-time capacity. He's a cracking lad and a personal friend and has a great family and values. It is great to build the Club around people who have contributed so much. He is a distinguished former player who understands the game and the Club. He is passionate about the game and as a players' man he understands the issues and potential pitfalls that players face, not only while they are playing but in planning for their futures for when the day comes that their career is over.

"Ste is well versed in forming a career outside of rugby as it is something he has done successfully himself and which he has kindly diverted from in order to take up this role. His role is very important and varied but one of the main objectives will be to assist our players to plan their futures outside of rugby. It is a great reward for Ste who has been performing the role successfully on a voluntary basis in what have proved at times to be very difficult and challenging circumstances.

"As part of getting into Super League it is important to grow the business incrementally and Ste's appointment is another statement of our intent to be a competitive Super League side."

Ste Maden said: "I feel like I've been through it all at Leigh, from days of despair to the success we have enjoyed this season and I'd like to give Derek massive thanks for bringing me back to care for the players on and off the field. I'd also especially like to thank Jukesy for his support and faith in me. It's a massive role and a very important one and covers many different aspects. I was fortunate enough to be a full-time player for about four years out of my career, the rest part-

Leigh's Travis Burns dragged down by Leeds' Jamie Jones-Buchanan at Headingley, during the Centurions' final game of the 2016 season

time, and I understand how players can feel in limbo when their contract ends.

"The RFL has been very proactive in the area of player welfare and lots of players now have a plan and know what they are going to do when their playing career is

---

SUPER 8s (THE QUALIFIERS) ROUND 7

Thursday 22nd September 2016

LEEDS RHINOS 37 LEIGH CENTURIONS 12

RHINOS: Ashton Golding; Tom Briscoe; Kallum Watkins; Jimmy Keinhorst; Ryan Hall; Liam Sutcliffe; Joel Moon; Brad Singleton; James Segeyaro; Jamie Jones-Buchanan; Brett Ferres; Stevie Ward; Adam Cuthbertson. Subs (all used): Sam Hallas; Ash Handley; Cameron Smith; Josh Jordan-Roberts. **Tries:** Ferres (13), Keinhorst (25, 29), Segeyaro (34), Golding (49), Moon (54), T Briscoe (67); **Goals:** Watkins 4; **Field goal:** Moon (79). **Sin bin:** Jones-Buchanan (4).
CENTURIONS: Lee Smith; Mitch Brown; Greg Worthington; Willie Tonga; Matty Dawson; Martyn Ridyard; Josh Drinkwater; Fuifui Moimoi; Micky Higham; Dayne Weston; Andrew Dixon; Reni Maitua; Gareth Hock. Subs (all used): Danny Tickle; Harrison Hansen; Sam Hopkins; Travis Burns. **Tries:** Hopkins (36), Dawson (57); **Goals:** Ridyard 2. **Sin bin:** Smith (73).
Half time: 18-6; **Referee:** Gareth Hewer; **Attendance:** 14,747.

---

over. I am comfortable being around players and in that environment and I can't wait to get started. As Derek says, building an infrastructure on and off the field is vital as the Club progresses and looks to establish itself in Super League and it will be an honour to be part of that process."

The Sky Sports cameras covered Leigh for the fourth time in the Qualifiers as their season ended at Headingley Carnegie on the penultimate Thursday in September. Viewers in the pre match build-up were treated to a superb mini documentary by Angela Powers that featured, among other things, Derek Beaumont, Neil Jukes, Micky Higham and Martyn Ridyard being unveiled on the famous Wall of Fame outside the Centurion pub alongside club greats such as Alex Murphy, John Woods, Kevin Ashcroft, Tony Cottrell and Neil Turley.

After the drama and emotion of the previous few weeks Leigh never really got going and they went down to a 37-12 defeat against the Rhinos before a noisy 14,747 crowd - the highest for a Leeds-Leigh game since the early 1960s. Leigh's season ended as it began, with a defeat in Yorkshire in a game refereed coincidentally by Cup Final referee Gareth Hewer. In between they lost only one game, at Toulouse in the Challenge Cup-a remarkable achievement. Reni Maitua was given a guard of honour by his team-mates as he left the playing field for the final time in his illustrious career and it was the last game in England for Travis Burns and the last in a Leigh shirt, too, for Fuifui Moimoi, Greg Worthington and Andrew Dixon. Worthington, outstanding in the second half of the season was helped off with medial ligament damage after a dangerous tackle.

Neil Jukes was pragmatic in his final summary of the season. "If you play as poorly as we did with the ball, how we finished our sets and our ill-discipline on last plays against any team, you'll get done," he said. "We didn't do ourselves justice and went into our shell a little bit. Automatic promotion is an incredible feeling; this group of players won't be together again and they've left a legacy.

"It shows how far we've come as a club and a group of players that we're disappointed to have lost at Leeds. People tipped us to go well because of the money we've spent, but to play four Super League clubs and be able to get points off three of them is remarkable.

"I'm not sure it will ever be done again. I'm really proud, certainly over the last nine-week period when the players have put everything into it."

Derek Beaumont had promised his players that they would watch the Million Pound Game in the sunshine if they achieved their goal of automatic promotion. He was as good of his word and a 27-strong party of directors, staff and players jetted off to Portugal as Salford and Hull KR played out a nerve-wracking encounter to decide who would join Leigh, Leeds and Huddersfield in Super League for 2017. The events surrounding the game, particularly the dramatic ending as Salford drew level with two late tries, then clinched the spoils with Gareth O'Brien's long range drop-goal in extra-time were a remarkable ending to a season which saw Leigh Centurions re-join the elite and Hull KR relegated to the Championship.

Nothing ever stands still in Rugby League and plans were already underway for 2017 as soon as the final champagne corks were cracked open in the Headingley dressing room. Australian great Glenn Stewart joined up after cutting short a stint at Catalans for family reasons and was quickly followed by his team-mate Eloi Pelissier, the French international hooker. Saints Tongan forward Atelea Vea, Hull KR forward James Green and Warrington winger Dave Thompson were other acquisitions and they were followed by Wigan Warriors utility back Ryan Hampshire and Castleford Tigers centre Ben Crooks on a season long loan.

In no time at all the players were reporting back for pre-season training and the plans for the 2017 Super League campaign were underway.

Leigh Centurions' preparations for Super League continued apace as Betfred was confirmed as the new competition sponsor.

For some Leigh players there was international duty to look forward to and hooker Liam Hood distinguished himself with three outstanding performances for Scotland in the Four Nations tournament, capped by a stunning 18-18 draw against New Zealand at Workington in their final game. Hood, whose mother was born in Greenock, told LCTV's Drew Derbyshire: "I love coming to play for Scotland at the end of the year. It is a great camp, there is always a top bunch of lads and I always have a good time.

"You have to go out with the physical approach against all three teams in the Four Nations. The game against Australia was by far the quickest game I have ever played in. You realise in the Four Nations that you need to nail every detail and every one per-center because they are the difference at the end of the day."

Hood revealed he was honoured to play against world superstars in the autumn tournament and thinks it can only better his abilities. "Cameron Smith is probably the best nine in the world so it is always great to come up against people like him and have a dig against them. I tried to get his shirt after the game but Broughy (Danny Brough) had already asked him at Anfield (at the tournament launch)!"

By virtue of his Welsh grandfather Sam Hopkins was called up at the last minute for Wales' vital game against Italy in Treviso when a hard-fought 20-14 win secured John Kear's side a place in the 2017 World Cup. Meanwhile Eloi Pelissier capped an impressive performance with an early try in France's 40-6 defeat against England at Avignon when Mathias Pala featured on the wing.

The 2017 fixtures were revealed with Leigh Centurions set to begin their campaign with a trip to The Mend-A-Hose Jungle to take on Castleford Tigers on Friday 10th February (8pm) in a game covered live by Sky Sports.

Leeds Rhinos are the first visitors to Leigh Sports Village the following Friday in a game brought forward from Round 11. This game is again covered live on Sky Sports on Friday 17th February (8pm). The big games follow thick and fast with St Helens next in town the following Friday evening (8pm).

The first of the eagerly awaited Battle of the Borough games takes place when the Centurions travel to the DW Stadium to face defending champions Wigan Warriors on Friday 3rd March (8pm).

Leigh Centurions Owner Derek Beaumont said: "No doubt everybody will be excited reading through the fixtures as the reality of the Leigh Centurions competing in Super League firmly hits home.

"I am sure there will be plenty of holiday requests handed in tomorrow for the Catalan trip and I expect some on my desk in the morning also. For many it will be the highlight of the season in terms of the away games and it's a great time to go from a supporters' point of view with great weather expected at the height of summer.

"It is interesting that we have nine appearances on Sky Sports and this is fantastic for our deserved sponsors who will get great exposure."

Mr Beaumont added: "It is an extremely tough start with an away trip to Castleford followed by three of this year's top four within the next six rounds but we have to play them all at some point in the season and the boys will be keen to get up to speed hitting the ground running after a big pre-season.

"It was extremely difficult to try and achieve a blend of fixtures that had achievable turnarounds that weren't detrimental to the squad. I really am looking forward to this season with great optimism and anticipation. Everyone has worked hard to achieve this and I would urge everyone to enjoy it. The atmosphere is going to be electric throughout the whole stadium wherever you are sat so If you are unable to get in the North Stand please still ensure you get down for what promises to be the most exciting season of rugby ever experienced at the LSV."

Leigh Centurions and Salford Red Devils entered an innovative and reciprocal ticket incentive scheme for their respective season ticket holders for the 2017 season. Under the terms of the scheme Leigh Centurions season ticket holders can buy tickets for Salford's home games in the 2017 Betfred Super League at half price with the same applying to Salford Red Devils' season ticket holders for Leigh home games.

Tickets may also only be bought at the respective club's ticket office less than two hours before kick-off on the day of the game and the season ticket must be presented for inspection at the ticket office and then on entry at the turnstile alongside the match ticket. The only provisos are that the half-price scheme does not apply for games between Leigh and Salford.

LSV staged another international game as Italy thrashed Russia 76-0 to claim the fourteenth and final place in the 2017 World Cup. Terry Campese's fine individual performance and his 24-point haul was the highlight of Italy's 14-try rout of a depleted Russia side. Russia had only 16 men to call on after injuries ruled out three of their squad from the week before against Ireland and there was not time to obtain visas for replacements.

On Sunday 6 November, Leigh Centurions were extremely saddened to learn of the passing of Tommy Martyn Senior at the age of 70. Tommy was part of the Martyn dynasty that produced three of the most charismatic and talented players of the post war years, all of whom served the Leigh club with distinction. Tommy's elder brother Mick was a one club man who created the record of scoring the most tries ever by a Leigh player- 189 in 329 games between 1954 and 1967 and played for Great Britain.

So Tommy had tough boots to step into when he too pursued a career in the professional game after playing in Leigh Miners' first-ever team. He started off, like many Leigh born players did in the late 1960s at Batley - a legacy of Terry Gorman, a Leigh born halfback having a coaching spell at Mount Pleasant and recruiting many of his home town players to bolster the Gallant Youths' ranks.

Tommy made 60 appearances for Batley, scoring 14 tries before he joined Leigh for the first time in October 1971, just after the club's Wembley triumph. It was a period of transition for the club and though Tommy soon became a regular, playing 97 times over the course of the next three years it was hard to establish a reputation in a much changing side that suffered relegation in 1974, just three years after the magical Alex Murphy era ended, despite a Challenge Cup semi final defeat at the hands of Featherstone Rovers.

In January 1975, with Leigh languishing in the second division, Tommy followed Murphy and moved to Warrington. It was a transfer that ignited his career and set him on the road to cementing his reputation as one of the game's greatest second row forwards.

SADLY MISSED - Tommy Martyn Senior

Like his brother Mick, Tommy was a damaging wide runner but he was also a brilliant passer of a ball, particularly in the tight confines of a game played under the old five yards rule.

Kevin Ashcroft said in tribute: "Tommy's brother Mick was a one club man and a legend in Leigh. Tommy flitted about a bit but once he got settled at Warrington he really showed what he could do. He revolutionised forward play, he would run at you, bang his shoulder down and he'd be off again. And passing? They used to say Tommy could squeeze the ball out of his backside - he was incredible, a magician.

"At Leigh and Warrington they'd always tell you to follow Tommy if he made a break, that was the golden rule. The tries he used to create were incredible. He was a hard player, really hard, in a tough Warrington pack. They might have invented the word 'uncompromising' after him. But off the field he was a gentleman, one of the nicest men you could ever meet. He never strutted about but could look after himself. He never started anything but you didn't mess with Tommy.

"He was at his peak at Warrington. He developed an art of running with the ball, dropping his shoulder, releasing the ball. He was a nightmare to defend against. He was like a horse in a long distance hurdles race, he simply never stopped going, whatever the state of the ground. He had an incredibly economical style, he was like a thoroughbred in a field full of carthorses.

"Tommy was a long distance lorry driver but never missed training or games. He was naturally fit. He hated going off the field and wanted to play every game. He was a delight to play alongside."

Tommy played 220 times for Warrington, scoring 51 tries and kicking one goal, but his most memorable days in Rugby League were still to come. "He'd played at Wembley in the losing Warrington side against Widnes in 1975 and toured in 1979 with Great Britain only to have to return home early due to injury. He'd played for England, yet hadn't won the honours his talents deserved," Ashcroft adds.

Tommy re-joined Leigh in a straight swap deal for Tommy Gittins at the start of the 1981-82 season with Murphy back at the helm at Hilton Park alongside Colin Clarke as coach. It was arguably Leigh's most memorable season - an early Lancashire Cup Final success over Widnes followed by a long, eventful and ultimately successful pursuit of the Holy Grail - the Championship that Leigh had only won once previously, back in 1906.

Tommy Martyn was at his absolute best in that wonderful season; often overshadowed by the brilliant John Woods, Des Drummond, Phil Fox, Terry Bilsbury, Mick Hogan, Steve Donlan and the like in the backs but never under-rated by his team-mates. Together with the likes of fellow forwards Tony Cooke, Ray Tabern, Alf Wilkinson, Ian Potter and Mick McTigue and the brilliant scrum-half Kenny Green he formed the spine of arguably the finest Leigh team of all time.

Come the glorious evening at Whitehaven in April 1982 and the 13-4 victory that sealed Leigh's championship that has gone down in Leigh folklore, the dream season was complete.

GONE, BUT NOT FORGOTTEN - Maurice Gallagher and Wally Tallis *(below, pictured with son Gorden)*

Murphy moved on, but Tommy Martyn remained and in the final game of the 1983-84 season, his last game, he left an enduring legacy. Leigh against Warrington, Tommy's final game, the last game of the season, against his former club. And at Hilton Park, a few hundred yards from his house. Tommy single-handedly destroyed Wire that day, in a quite outstanding display of ball-handling second row play. John Woods, Chris Johnson, Steve Donlan and Des Drummond profited and Leigh won 44-20 but the memory of Tommy's display endures. If you could have a game to cut out and keep in your scrap book that would be the one; so fitting for a final game.

Tommy's son Tommy Junior later lit up Rugby League in his own way- a brilliant outside half who played the game with a smile on his face, his skills honed by countless hours of practice on the terraced streets around his home in Leigh. Tommy's daughter Samantha married Paul Anderson, another fine player, who has played a great part in Leigh's rise to Super League in his role as assistant coach.

GONE, BUT NOT FORGOTTEN -
Alan Rathbone *(above, in action against Hull FC)* and Graham Smith *(left)*

Tommy Martyn Senior played 165 games for Leigh, scoring 23 tries.

"He was one of the best players the town has ever produced and a gentleman," Kevin Ashcroft concluded. "Shy, unobtrusive, unassuming but a genius on the Rugby League field. For all he achieved in the game that Championship season at Leigh was his proudest moment, without a doubt. Another legend of the game has gone, and I don't use the word legend lightly."

Derek Beaumont resumed his popular and informative regular column, originally on the Leigh Observer but now on the club website. "Since returning from Portugal I have been busy shaping our squad with the coaching team," he wrote. "The reality of what we had achieved only really sunk in for me when the fixtures came out.

"We knew we needed to strengthen our backs with the departure of Travis and Greg Worthington to add to the already recruited Dave Thompson. We also knew we needed an extra hooker for Super League to enable rotation and also an

extra middle unit to add to Maria, Vea, Stewart and Green already recruited.

"We had no non-federation trained spots left as this year they are reduced to seven. It doesn't matter if an overseas player has a European passport, they are still non federation trained.

"As a group we scoured around. There wasn't much from Hull KR we fancied and the two players we spoke to from there, Thomas Minns and Adam Walker, we missed out on as Thomas stayed at KR and Adam opted for Saints, which I can understand.

"Jukesy approached Daryl Powell regarding Ben Crooks as they had Michael Shenton coming back, but at first he wasn't interested. I contacted Rads at Wigan regarding Ryan Hampshire and over a few days we were able to agree terms with Wigan and Ryan and that was one down but Ryan was in Australia so we had to be patient to get the ink on the paper.

"Then came the offer of Eloi Pelissier. I spoke to Jukesy, who spoke to the others and did his usual due diligence. It was a no-brainer. I have always liked his running style and toughness. He is a proven Super League player and current French international. The other benefit was he speaks good English and would be a great companion for Maria whose English isn't quite as good.

"So we were still needing a centre and a middle. We weren't as desperate for a middle, as we have as many as last year, so always said if needs be we would wait until the New Year to see what becomes available then.

"There are always players available then, when internal issues cause upsets or squad numbers are issued, leaving some unhappy and disillusioned. But we were really concerned about adding a Super League centre and were continually drawing blanks. I made a call to Cas, with whom I have a good relationship, and again enquired about Ben. Daryl had previously said it may be possible in the New Year but we didn't want to risk that.

"Cas informed me they would speak to Daryl and come back to me. As luck would have it, a week later they informed me that something had come up that could see us get Ben but again he was on holiday, as was Daryl, so again we had to be patient.

"As I went away everyone returned and Jukesy met Ben, selling our club to him and it was all on. We got our man and could relax, happy with our squad, believing we had recruited well and with room to add that middle unit when the right man becomes available."

On commercial matters Derek added: "Whilst I was busy on the recruitment front, Jason Huyton, our Commercial Director, was extremely busy with his own team recruiting sponsors for the playing and training kit.

"Can I place on record what a fantastic acquisition Jason has proved to be. He is extremely professional and hard working, despite being busy with his own business.

"Despite being a shareholding Director he has also increased his company's sponsorship of the Club. When we had our board meeting and he declared his team had sold all properties for the kits

and training and medical kit, even including the socks and over budget, I was, it is fair to say, extremely impressed.

"Yes, we are in Super League, which no doubt makes it easier but even the RFL commented on our budget for the salary cap that we were over estimating what we could achieve there. Mike Norris must have beamed from ear to ear when he informed them we had actually already beaten it!

"So a massive respect to Jason, Amanda and Neil and more importantly to all those businesses who have backed the club in this way. Your support is invaluable.

"Ste Mills is settled as our analyst and is in possession of all the necessary equipment and software he was accustomed to at Huddersfield and Daniel Halliwell of 24/7 Technology should be commended for that. Ste Maden has settled in the overseas players and is a great asset to the club. We are awaiting the arrival of Scott Campbell from the NRL who will head up the Strength and Conditioning department with Nathan and Woody.

"We have also significantly invested in this area with new equipment bringing us right up to Super League standard, including full GPS system for the squad, so when you see the little lump on the players' backs you know what it is."

On 10 November the players met for the start of pre season. "As I arrived into the coaches office the place was buzzing," Derek added. "The off field staff were chunnering away as I added a bit of banter whilst Ayaz from Slaters Menswear amusingly offered his Polos about!

"The players room next door was absolutely buzzing like I have never seen before. The atmosphere was electric with laughter. After welcoming everyone back from their well earned break and applauding our new recruits, we congratulated Gaz and Ticks for finding their way out of Portugal.

"My intention was to break the ice and set the tone for the new lads of the fun, family environment we operate before setting them the expectations of the board. I didn't know we had a couple of internationals in the room, I exclaimed, which saw Hoppy and Hoody look up. I joked with Hoppy whether he had qualified to play for Wales after a caravan holiday in Towyn when he was five, to which very quickly for Hoppy he replied: "It's because my granddad's dog is Welsh!" Quality banter.

"I then asked if there was anybody in the room who didn't know their own country's National Anthem. Hoppy had his hand up, then down, then half up, then eventually decided to put it fully up which was amusing in itself. "Well done for being honest Hoppy," I said. "Hoody, that means you know the Scottish National Anthem, so come on, 'Och I dunnoooo Jimmy' get up here and sing it for the lads."

"He wasn't forthcoming, even when grabbing his hand. The lads were egging him on but he wasn't having it. Then I pulled a bag of sand out of my pocket, waved it at him and said: "I bet you a grand you can't sing it in full!,Äù

"You've never seen Hoody move so quick, perhaps matched only by the speed the lads reached for their phones as Jukesy shouted: ,'You can use your phone for this bit lads!'

"Fair play to Hoody, he nervously set off to a silent room and I have to say he has a voice to rival Ando. He sang it beautifully, with pride and as he stumbled at a certain point, as he passed it he exclaimed: "I've got it!" He ripped off his shirt and beat his chest to enormous cheers and laughter as he belted it out to a finish before sitting down a grand better off.

"He was going to get it off me anyway as a treat for his stand-out performances in the Four Nations which will have certainly increased his value, as we will find out as we look to extend his current contract.

"The place was in uproar and the tone was set. As the room quietened down, I informed the group that they would set their own goals with the coaching staff and whilst I personally thought they were good enough to finish in the top eight there was no pressure to do so.

"As a board our only expectation was to be in Super League in 2018 and how that was achieved was irrelevant. If we have to do that by the Million Pound Game then so be it, Super League survival is the target.

"We discussed how we were prepared as a board and as a coaching group for the worst case scenario and the possibility of being bottom on zero points after the first quarter. This will not phase us, we will be ready for what comes our way.

"We are not under pressure, we want to enjoy the occasions the potential full houses and the fantastic atmospheres we will encounter.

"Jukesy then took over followed by Cookie, Kieron and Nathan and the team set its own standards and goals which will remain private to the group until the appropriate time at the end of the season.

"The remainder of the day and the following day were occupied with testing by the Strength and Conditioning team in state-of-the-art facilities at Bolton University, where young Dave Thompson showed what he may be capable of, setting the marker as the fastest in the club over 40 metres."

Paul Cooke, who extended his contact to the end of 2018 was complimented on his recently published autobiography 'Judas', written in conjunction with Talk Sport presenter Adrian Durham.

"This is the best Rugby League autobiography I have ever read," Derek wrote "The way he breaks down key plays in a game is a real insight for the average fan on the street, not to mention his very truthful and open insight to his turbulent lifestyle.

"Cookie is a real grounded, quality man and having read his book I am even more convinced I have a jewel in the crown. I am really confident at this stage that as a club we are every bit Super League.

"We have a quality, talented board of directors that would cost a significant seven figure sum to employ. We have a great team of employees throughout the business and we operate in a fantastic stadium and sports village with arguably the best playing surface in the game.

"We have a fantastic medical team, a knowledgeable and increased strength and conditioning team with increased equipment and technology.

"We have four fantastic coaches, each with their own specific strengths that I am extremely confident in, supported with all the technology an international team would have, with drone videoing of training sessions and GPS.

"I also believe we have a squad that is worthy of the label of a Super League squad and one I am confident can achieve our goal of Super League survival."

As November neared its end Derek's second column reflected a busy and emotional few weeks, starting with the Remembrance Day Parade when he accompanied Neil Jukes and young supporters Lewis Boardman and Keeley Sandland in laying a wreath on behalf of Leigh Centurions.

"Lewis and Keeley are two fine examples of young people and very apt representatives of the Club," he wrote. " I was extremely proud to have been there and must confess it was my first attendance at the parade. It certainly won't be my last.

"Leigh Centurions is the focal point of this town and it is vital that we show our respect. Lewis and Keeley certainly did us proud in doing that and I thought it was a nice touch from Mike (Latham) to involve them and to demonstrate the club focuses on its youth and the importance of them understanding our history."

Derek Beaumont, Steve Openshaw and Kieron Purtill had a fruitful meeting with Wigan & Leigh College with a view to establishing a Cat 3 academy, the first step towards achieving the Club's long term goals of having academies and scholarships.

BBC Television attended training to do some filming and interviews, all of which were to be screened in a Super League Show preview in December. Angela Powers also commenced filming a mini documentary series for Sky Sports that will follow the Club through to the start of the new campaign. Players and staff also participated with the switching-on of the town's Christmas lights.

Leigh players and staff formed a guard of honour for Tommy Martyn Senior's funeral at St Joseph's. Derek wrote: "The turnout for the funeral was immense and I am sure Marie, Tommy, Sam and Paul would have been extremely proud for Tommy. It seems wrong to say I enjoyed the service but I am going to say it because I did. I thought it was perfect, the music, the hymns the readings.

"The highlight without doubt was the amazingly read eulogy by Mike Latham. It was inspiring to say the least and delivered with such pride and conviction. What an amazing story, starting with when Tommy left home telling only Marie this would be his last ever game. There was humour amongst it and it was a befitting tribute to a very fine man who reached the hearts of many.

"I was unable to attend the wake at Leigh Miners due to having to return to work but I believe that was packed also. The lads had to return to finish off their day's schedule and I had wished I had been able to thank them for their excellent representation, not only of the Club but themselves.

"I called Jukesy on the way back in the car and asked him to pass on my thanks for their impeccable turnout and commitment to do so. I asked him to communicate that it was unfortunate that the first gathering as a squad outside of training was a sad affair but that this should send a clear message as to how important it is to play for this great Club. How those that play with passion, commitment and desire will always be remembered and treasured. I have no doubt Jukesy passed the message as I would have wanted it and that it will deliver an inner strength and perhaps even become something we draw on in the future.

"If we can draw any strength from Tommy Martyn then it will certainly help us on our way. Tommy Martyn rest in peace and watch us from above."

The Australian players trained at LSV prior to the Four Nations Final against New Zealand at Anfield and Derek noted:

"Craig Bellamy, Mal Meninga's assistant, was telling Jukesy and Steve Openshaw just how highly Leigh Centurions were regarded in Australia and that we were up there with the best, most famous English clubs. This backs up what an Australian journalist said to me when he stated that Leigh Centurions are currently the highest profile, most talked about English club in Australia this season. WOW simply WOW."

The Achievers Tee-shirts also arrived and were distributed to 2016 season ticket holders. "They look fab and I hope everyone who has received one feels proud to wear it or looks at it with pride on a regular basis should they frame it," Derek added. "There has been speculation about people missing from it and I simply answer that here. The Achievers were considered those that appeared in the 8s and won the games that ultimately got us into Super League and I make no excuse here for leaving out people who, in my opinion, did not do right by the Club with their actions.

"I am proud of the finished article, as I know our fans are too, based on the feedback to Gillian."

There was more sad news with the passing of their former player Maurice Gallagher at the age of 89. Maurice was one of Leigh's oldest surviving players and signed for the club in December 1947 after impressing in the junior ranks with Leigh St Joseph's.

At 6ft 1 and 13st2 he was an athletically built back row forward though as his career developed he also featured more regularly in the front row. Opportunities for first-team places were limited as Leigh rapidly built up their playing squad in the first season at Kirkhall Lane, buoyed by many five figure attendances in the post war boom years for the sport.

Maurice made his first-team debut at Workington Town in April 1948, proudly and retrospectively earning Heritage Number 575 when the Club's Heritage project was unveiled in 2014. He made a further four appearances before the end of his debut season and two more in 1948-49 before drifting out of first team contention.

After a loan spell at Barrow he moved to Belle Vue Rangers, linking up again with many of his former Leigh team-mates including Nebby Cleworth, Derek Day, Yendle Pugsley, Harry Dagnan and the New Zealand All Black George Beatty. In the summer of 1954 he moved to Rochdale Hornets, going on to play 80 games for them before he was transferred to Warrington in February 1957. He enjoyed a fine spell at Wilderspool, scoring three tries in 44 games before hanging up his boots.

Leigh Centurions Life President Brian Bowman said: "Maurice was a very good player who enjoyed a long professional career. Like many locally born players at the time he didn't get too many opportunities at Leigh and he had to move elsewhere in order to play regular first team football as there was so much competition for places.

"In those days, of course, there were only 13 players for first team duty with no substitutes so it was a far different game than it is today, especially for the forwards, who had to play 80 minutes week in, week out.

"He must have been one of the last surviving players to play for Belle Vue Rangers, who sadly folded in 1955 and he went on to play a lot of games for both Rochdale Hornets and Warrington.

"I knew Maurice for many years and he was a very nice man and a gentleman who retained his interest in the game long after he retired as a player. Like everyone else in Leigh he was delighted that the club achieved promotion to Super League this year. I would like to echo the Club's sentiments and offer my deepest condolences to his family at this sad time."

Leigh Centurions confirmed their two Warm Up games ahead of the 2017 Betfred Super League season, the first a renewal of the Battle of the Borough in the Micky McIlorum Testimonial Game against Wigan Warriors at LSV on Sunday 22 January (3pm). The fixture will also see the presentation of the Arthur Thomas Memorial Trophy presented to the Leigh

Centurions Man of the Match chosen by his family.

Their second and final warm up game will be against Dewsbury Rams at LSV on Sunday 29 January 2017, with a 3pm kick-off. Mr Beaumont said: "This season we only had the opportunity for two warm up matches as we want to ensure we prepare meticulously, so it was important that we got the right fixtures. It is no secret that I am good friends with Mark Sawyer from Dewsbury although that is the case with many Championship chairmen. I have always said neither I nor the club will forget where we come from.

"To that end I wanted to ensure we played a Championship team but at the same time a team that will give us a good hit-out and Neil was confident that Dewsbury would provide that. Glenn Morrison is a good coach and Dewsbury are a progressive club who, with a bit of wind behind their sails in a season, could just crack that top four.

"They always compete very well and are hard to break down so it will be a good test after the Wigan game before having a week off to prepare for the start of Super League. "

With the countdown on to the eagerly awaited Dacia Magic Weekend match-up between Leigh Centurions and Salford Red Devils on 21 May 2017 respective owners Derek Beaumont and Marwan Koukash took the weighty challenge even further.

In a joint statement they revealed: "We are looking to raise some money to be split across two charities close to Rugby League, the Steve Prescott Foundation and Lizzie Jones Foundation.

"There is no doubt we are notably overweight, perhaps due to our busy lifestyles and good living and are similarly out of condition with Marwan just over the 18 and a half stone mark and Derek on the nose of the 19 stone mark.

"We aim to both work hard to reduce our weight to a target weight of 15 and a half stone for the day of the Magic Weekend between our respective clubs.

"We will strip off pitch-side for the "weigh in" and see who has achieved their goals and who has lost the most weight."

The official "weigh in" will be conducted by an official pitch side on the day just prior to kick-off between the clubs. The pair added: "The loser will donate £5,000 to be shared by the chosen charities and in addition to this for every pound in weight either of us is over the target weight we will donate £1,000."

This sees both men with a serious amount of money potentially hanging around their waist lines. In Derek's case this starts out at a whopping £49,000 and Marwan follows closely behind with a substantial £43,000. Both men have been known to be generous to charities both publicly and privately but this challenge sees them try to minimise their exposure.

They are both very driven and single minded individuals so it will be very interesting to see who comes out on top. The pair stated: "One thing is for sure the charities will come out on top as one of us must lose so there is a minimum of £5,000 up for grabs.

"However, at the same time we want to challenge each other to see who can raise the most money between us, so we kind of have two challenges here. We will be looking to our fans and sponsors and even the fans of the wider game to sponsor us to see how much each of us can raise before pooling it to be split between two magnificent charities."

Supporters of both clubs and those in the wider Rugby League community are urged to take part in this challenge. They added: "It would be great if other people out there joined us in the challenge by setting their own goals and obtaining sponsorship to donate to the charities.

"It is a fantastic way to change your lifestyle whilst at the same time raising money for good causes. We would be interested to share the stories of those who get involved and participate helping us to raise as much money as possible."

Anybody wishing to get involved in setting their own challenge to raise money to add to the charities should email: docanddek@leighrl.co.uk so details can be discussed.

Leigh Centurions then revealed their new home playing kit as they have again teamed up with Kukri at a highly successful Commercial Launch at Leigh Sports Village. Leigh Centurions Commercial Director Jason Huyton said: "We are delighted to renew our relationship with Kukri and equally delighted with the design of our home and away kits, the latter which will be revealed shortly .

"The home kit reverts back to the Club's traditional Cherry and White hoops featuring in a modern design and is sure to become a big success with our valued supporters.

"Our home shirt features our principal shirt sponsor CAL Sameday: www.calsameday.co.uk on the front and emblazoned with our other valued sponsors on the shirt and shorts.

The away shirt features our principal away shirt sponsor Slater & Gordon Lawyers www.slatergordon.co.uk.

The other valued sponsors for 2017 are as follows:

The rear top of the shirt sponsors are Palatine Paints: palatine-paints.co.uk and occupying the rear bottom of the shirt are McCauls and Redwaters: www.redwaters.co.uk.

The Collar sponsors are Fitfield: www.fitfield.com and the Chest sponsors are Hilltop: www.hilltop-products.co.uk.

The left shoulder sponsors are Westco: westco.co.uk and the sponsors of the right shoulder are Evans Halshaw: www.evanshalshaw.com.

The front of the shorts are sponsored by McLaughlin's Kitchens: www.mclaughlinskitchens.co.uk and the rear of shorts sponsors are 247 Technology: www.247technology.co.uk and Kingdom Security: www.kingdom.co.uk.

The Trainer/ Doctor/ Physio water carrier kit sponsor is Park Leisure: www.parkleisure.co.uk/ and the training kit sponsor is Regency Glass: http://www.regencyglass.co.uk/.

The 2016-2017 League Express Yearbook, now in its 21st Year and the bible for all Rugby League supporters with its comprehensive look back at the 2016 season named Club Captain Micky

Martyn Ridyard and Atelea Vea launch the 2017 home shirt

Higham as one of its five Personalities of the Year.

2016 was certainly a memorable one both for Higham and Leigh Centurions. In recognising Higham's contributions, Joint Editors Tim Butcher and Daniel Spencer paid tribute to Head Coach Neil Jukes and Owner Derek Beaumont and the Centurions players and backroom staff, acknowledging that Leigh Centurions won promotion back into Super League for the first time since 2005 in style.

They added: "Their smartest signing had arguably been made in May of 2015 when the Centurions paid a sizeable sum to bring Micky Higham home from Warrington.

"It had been a long time away for the former Great Britain hooker who had signed for St Helens from Leigh in November 2000. He went on to win a Super League title with Saints and two Challenge Cups with the Wolves but the 36-year-old put skippering the Centurions to promotion in 2016 right up there with any of his previous illustrious achievements."

The other Personalities of the Year are Castleford Tigers record-breaking winger Denny Solomona, who scored 40 Super League tries, Hull FC's Steve Prescott Man of Steel Danny Houghton, Wakefield

Trinity's Super League Young Player of the Year Tom Johnstone and the broadcaster Mike 'Stevo' Stephenson, who retired after fronting Sky Sports' Rugby League coverage for the past 26 years.

Micky Higham, who was the 2016 Kingstone Press Championship Player of the Year, reflected on his latest award. "It's very humbling to be mentioned in such illustrious company and I am delighted to be named as on the Personalities of the Year," he said. "It's a huge honour and one I accept on behalf of my team-mates and the coaching and backroom staff at Leigh Centurions because 2016 was all about a big team effort.

"The other four Personalities of the Year are all worthy choices in their own right. Denny and Tom are two hugely talented and prolific try-scoring wingers who had great seasons. Danny had another stand-out season with Hull FC and was a fitting choice for Steve Prescott Man of Steel.

"Stevo has had a glittering career in the game as a player, winning international honours and a World Cup with Great Britain and playing at the top level on both sides of the world before embarking on a highly successful career with the microphone.

"Like me he's a member of the hooker's union and I am delighted to be mentioned in the same breath as him and the other nominees. I'm absolutely made up, to be honest."

As the mornings got colder and darker and ice had to be scraped off windscreens the Leigh Centurions squad for 2017 embarked on a gruelling six-week conditioning phase including arduous hill runs and climbs. Briefly there was some respite as some of the players, coaches and directors attended a Champions Joint Celebration Dinner at Leigh Cricket Club to mark both clubs' successes in 2016. Leigh Cricket Club had been crowned champions of the Liverpool & District Competition ECB Premier League, a fantastic achievement.

For sure, though, for Leigh Centurions it was a season to remember, perhaps best summarised in the following way:

A SEASON TO REMEMBER

Leigh Centurions lifted the Kingstone Press Championship League Leaders Shield for the third season in a row and became the first team to be promoted to Super League under the new Super 8s format by finishing second to Leeds Rhinos in the Qualifiers and winning six out of seven games.

AWARD WINNERS

Club Captain Micky Higham was chosen as Championship Player of the Year and Head Coach Neil Jukes was one of three nominees as Championship Coach of the Year (won by Batley's John Kear). Micky Higham was also named as one of the five Personalities of the Year in the prestigious League Express Rugby League 2016-2017 annual, now in its 21st year alongside Mike 'Stevo' Stephenson, Danny Houghton, Denny Solomona and Tom Johnstone.

In the Club awards Dayne Weston was Players' Player of the Year, Coaches' Player of the Year and LCTV Player of the Year. Adam Higson and Micky Higham were the other nominees in each of the first two categories and Greg Worthington and Reni Maitua in the latter category.

Neil Barker was Club Man of the Year and Neil Jukes and Paul Anderson joint winners of the Special Award. Martyn Ridyard's try at Swinton was voted Try of the Year.

A WINNING SEASON

For the third season in succession Leigh lost only one league game and won all 16 home games, 11 in the Championship, 4 in the Qualifiers and one Challenge Cup-tie.

Leigh lost their first game - at Batley - and their last at Leeds. In between they drew at Bradford and lost at Toulouse in the Challenge Cup, winning a total of 28 games.

The sequence was as follows: L1; W2, D1, W7, L1, W19, L1. The sequence of 19 consecutive wins between April and

September 2016 was the second best in Club history, bettered only by the 27 consecutive wins achieved between July 2014 and June 2015. The sequence of 25 consecutive league wins (including Qualifiers) was also the second best in Club history, bettered only by the run of 30 consecutive league wins between September 1985 and August 1986.

In all games Leigh played 32, won 28, drew 1 and lost 3, scoring 1180 points and conceding 627.

ALL TIME RECORDS

Neil Jukes replaced Paul Rowley as Head Coach just before the start of the season and in terms of win percentage (89pc) is the most successful Coach in Leigh's history.

HIGHEST WINNING PERCENTAGE - Neil Jukes

In terms of results it was the second most successful in the Club's history, surpassed only in 2014 when Leigh played 33 games with 31 wins and 2 defeats.

By finishing second in the Qualifiers Leigh were effectively the 10th best team in the country and achieved their highest ranking since finishing 10th in division one in 1986-87.

MILESTONES

Dayne Weston made most appearances (31) and Cory Paterson was top try-scorer with 18, becoming the first forward to top the Club's try charts since Micky Higham in 2000.

Martyn Ridyard topped the Club's goals and points charts for the fifth season in a row, a feat only previously achieved by Jimmy Ledgard in the 1950s.

A total of 37 players played in first team games for the Club in 2016 and there were 19 players on debut.

During the season Martyn Ridyard passed 200 appearances for the Club and ended the season with 1,793pts from 77 tries and 747 goals (including 9 drop-goals) in 217 appearances.

Ridyard moved above Neil Turley into third place in the Club's all-time points table.

Only Jimmy Ledgard (1,043 goals and 2,194pts) and John Woods (997 goals and 2,492pts) have kicked more goals or scored more points for the Club than Ridyard.

Prior to being transferred to Huddersfield Ryan Brierley reached 133 career tries for Leigh, moving to fifth (above Neil Turley) in the all-time list behind Mick Martyn (189), John Woods (152), Bill Kindon (149) and Des Drummond (141).

ATTENDANCE RECORDS

The attendance of 10,556 for the Qualifiers game against Batley was the highest for a Leigh game at Leigh Sports Village and the highest for a Leigh home game since September 1987 when 11,397 saw the home game against Wigan.

The attendance of 14,747 for the Leeds-Leigh Qualifiers game was the highest for a Leeds-Leigh game at Headingley since March 1962.

In a total of 16 home games Leigh had 65,495 spectators, an average of 4,093. This was the highest average attendance for a Leigh season since their Super League season of 2005 when 69,753 spectators watched 15 games (average 4,650).

It was the ninth season in the Club's history that they had been undefeated at home in league games.

SEASON STATISTICS

APPEARANCES (Tries):
Jamie Acton 15 (5); Tom Armstrong 20 (9); Ryan Brierley 3 (3); Mitch Brown 7 (4); Travis Burns 8 (3); Lewis Charnock 2 (1); Rangi Chase 5 (2); Matty Dawson 8 (9); Andrew Dixon 12 (5); Josh Drinkwater 15 (8); Jake Emmitt 15 (2); Ben Evans 3; Brad Fash 8; Lewis Foster 7 (1); Harrison Hansen 29 (6); Eze Harper 3 (1); Micky Higham 26 (7); Adam Higson 30 (14); Gareth Hock 23 (4); Liam Hood 19 (4); Sam Hopkins 27 (13); Liam Kay 18 (11); Reni Maitua 29 (14); Gregg McNally 7 (5); Fuifui Moimoi 20 (4); Richard Owen 2 (1); Cory Paterson 21 (18); Jonny Pownall 8 (4); Ben Reynolds 18 (8); Martyn Ridyard 25 (5); Lee Smith 23 (12); Tom Spencer 10 (1); Danny Tickle 7; Willie Tonga 6 (1); Dayne Weston 31 (6); Richard Whiting 15 (2); Greg Worthington 18 (9).

Goals: Martyn Ridyard 135 plus 2dg; Lee Smith 36; Ben Reynolds 9; Travis Burns 4; Josh Drinkwater 1.

Appearances (tries) on loan from Leigh to other clubs:
Ben Reynolds (Dewsbury) 4 (1) (10 goals); Lewis Foster (Oldham) 7 (1); Eze Harper (Barrow) 12 (11); Tom Spencer (Oldham) 4.

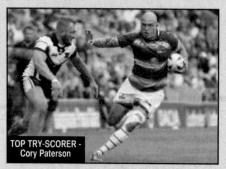

TOP TRY-SCORER - Cory Paterson

Mitch Brown was the last player to receive a Heritage Number in 2016

DEBUTANTS AND NEW HERITAGE NUMBERS

Nineteen players made their Leigh debuts during the season (former clubs in brackets) with Rangi Chase earning Heritage Number 1400. Mitch Brown became the 1418th player to represent the Club since joining the Northern Union in 1895:

1400 Rangi Chase (Salford); 1401 Dayne Weston (Melbourne); 1402 Harrison Hansen (Salford); 1403 Reni Maitua (Featherstone R); 1404 Lee Smith (Hull); 1405 Richard Whiting (Hull, loan); 1406 Cory Paterson (Salford); 1407 Richard Owen (Wakefield, loan); 1408 Eze Harper (Eccles ARL); 1409 Lewis Charnock (St Helens, loan); 1410 Liam Hood (Swinton); 1411 Willie Tonga (Catalans); 1412 Brad Fash (Hull, loan); 1413 Josh Drinkwater (Wests Tigers); 1414 Travis Burns (St Helens, loan); 1415 Ben Evans (Warrington, loan); 1416 Matty Dawson (St Helens); 1417 Danny Tickle (Casteford); 1418 Mitch Brown (Cronulla).

DEPARTURES

Tom Armstrong (Widnes); Sam Barlow (released); Bob Beswick (Toronto); Ryan Brierley (Huddersfield); Rangi Chase (Castleford); Andrew Dixon (Toronto); Jake Emmitt (released); Eze Harper (released); Liam Kay (Toronto); Reni Maitua (retired); Fuifui Moimoi (Toronto); Mathias Pala (released); Jonny Pownall (Toronto); Tom Spencer (London); Greg Worthington (Toronto). Loan players: Travis Burns; Lewis Charnock; Ben Evans; Brad Fash; Richard Owen; Richard Whiting.

SQUAD *(as at 30 November 2016)*

Played in 2016 - Jamie Acton; Mitch Brown; Matty Dawson; Josh Drinkwater; Lewis Foster; Harrison Hansen; Micky Higham; Adam Higson; Gareth Hock; Liam Hood; Sam Hopkins; Gregg McNally; Cory Paterson; Ben Reynolds; Martyn Ridyard; Lee Smith; Danny Tickle; Willie Tonga; Dayne Weston.

New signings yet to make debut:
James Clare (Bradford), Ben Crooks (Castleford - season long loan), James Green (Hull KR); Ryan Hampshire (Wigan); Antoni Maria (Catalans); Eloi Pelissier (Catalans); Glenn Stewart (Catalans); Dave Thompson (Warrington); Atelea Vea (St Helens).

TOWARDS SUPER LEAGUE

As December dawned, Head Coach Neil Jukes was delighted to confirm that Micky Higham will continue as Club Captain for the 2017 Betfred Super League campaign.

After informing the playing and coaching staff at training of the decision to re-appoint Higham, Jukes said: "Every new season brings fresh challenges and there are many decisions to be made. But this was the easiest decision to reach.

"Micky is everything you would want from a Captain both on the playing field, with his efforts, consistency and performance levels and also off the field. He shows the same attributes in training and with the disciplined way he conducts himself around the stadium complex.

"He has the respect of all the coaching staff and all the players and undoubtedly this decision will be well received by all. There's no doubt that Micky played a huge part in what we achieved last season and he is happy to carry the torch leading us into Super League.

"He has earned the right to be Captain of Leigh Centurions on the bigger stage."

Micky Higham said: "When Jukesy gave me a call and asked me to go round again as Captain I immediately felt very proud. It is a huge honour to captain the team again and more so in Super League. It is great to know all the coaches and players are behind me.

"We have a number of natural leaders in the team and there will be times during games when we will need other captains on the field.

"The reality of being in Super League is now hitting home to us. We had some great celebrations on achieving promotion and rightly so, but after three weeks of pre season the intensity levels have been very high.

"The new players that have come into the group have all fitted in and it has been a really good experience so far being back in training.

"Training is longer and more intense and I think all the lads are frustrated that for all their hard work there is no end product at the end of the week in the form of a game.

"Off the field the Club is continuing to have a big involvement in the community and as Captain it is important for me to set the right example. I'm a Leigh lad and I grew up watching the team not only at Hilton Park but at far flung away grounds and I was inspired to want to play for the club by the way the players then interacted with the fans.

"I've no problems giving up a few hours a week going around the town and if I can help inspire someone to want to play for Leigh, keep on playing the game or have an involvement in Rugby League or supporting the team then it makes it worthwhile. It's a very important part of being a professional Rugby League player."

Meanwhile, Club officials including owner Derek Beaumont and Assistant Coach Kieron Purtill had productive meetings with Leigh College's Assistant Principal Michelle Fisher to develop the joint initiative of an Academy side for the 2018 season.

Kieron Purtill said: "This is an important development for the Club and the community and one of the immediate bi-products of achieving Super League status is to build the infrastructure around the playing side. The aim is to create a pathway to our first team but also taking into account the person and providing an education so we can better prepare the player from a rugby point of view and on a personal level for life away from the sport.

"The formation of an academy will strengthen our already excellent links with the local community clubs and as part of that Embed the Pathway sessions with U14s, U15s and U16s players will be delivered together with physical literacy and coach education sessions."

He added: "The re-introduction of a reserves side is to strengthen the pathway between the academy and the first team and also to provide first team squad members with an effective means of maintaining form and fitness or help those coming back from injury. The ultimate goal is to have a team made up primarily of local players and to inspire the next

Martyn Ridyard hosts the Q&A session at the Joint Champions Celebration Christmas Dinner

generation of players and supporters, run a cost effective club and provide an excellent pathway for players in and out of the club.

"Hopefully the Category 3 academy status will be confirmed soon and the College can begin to recruit students using the Leigh Centurions logo and the incentive that they will be monitored by the club. In addition we are looking to forge other links with departments in the College including media, marketing, analysis and many other important skills that combine to make an effective Super League club."

Michelle Fisher, Assistant Principal of Leigh College said "We are delighted to partner with Leigh Centurions. The Academy will be linked to the College's Rugby pathways and our students will have the opportunity to work alongside players and coaches at Leigh Centurions, opening doors to their future careers."

Leigh Centurions Operations Director Steve Openshaw said: "Whilst the efforts of the last few years have now achieved Super League status, the Board have long been aware that focus on long term stability is essential to create a fully sustainable Club.

"Our 2014 Strategic Review highlighted our ambitions for youth development and we fully intend to deliver them, but in order

to do so our primary objective of reaching Super League had to be met first. We shall continue to work hard to maintain that status and certainly do not take it for granted.

"However, it is clear we are now at the next stage of our development as a Club and since Kieron joined us on a full-time basis he has played an integral role in this exciting initiative. Kieron is highly respected and has the skill sets, knowledge, experience and passion to drive it forward.

"We fully understand and agree with our loyal fans that for far too long there has been insufficient opportunity for local youngsters to progress through the Club's ranks. With the new pathway we are establishing, and with the support of everyone involved, including the local community, that should eventually be a thing of the past.

"The opportunities also offered by Leigh College form a key part of this initiative and compliment so many of these ambitions for life not just within rugby but out of it, too. It will take a few years to establish a full pathway from youth to first team as many top youngsters are already with other clubs, but we have to start somewhere and this exciting initiative is one that we know our fans are deeply passionate about.

"To assist the success in this development pathway, the Club have set up a new fundraising partnership with a group of Centurions supporters with the primary intention to raise funds to support youth development."

Leigh Centurions' valued kit sponsors for 2017 were guests of honour of the Club at the exclusive Joint Champions Celebration Christmas Dinner held at Leigh Cricket Club.

The sell-out event was a joint evening of celebration with an excellent three course dinner, entertainment from top party band Madison and an entertaining Q&A hosted by Centurions star Martyn Ridyard and featuring Dayne Weston, Club Captain Micky Higham, Head Coach Neil Jukes and Leigh CC players Mattie McKiernan and Karl Brown (Lancashire CCC).

Special road signs celebrating Leigh Centurions' magnificent return to the Betfred Super League were installed across the town. To mark their achievement in playing in the Super League for the first time since 2005, Wigan Council has installed special plates on the town's boundary signs.

The six signs, which say 'Home of Leigh Centurions and Super League Rugby' have been placed on Atherleigh Way, Manchester Road, St Helens Road/Newton Road, Warrington Road and two on Leigh Road. The signs were requested by Leigh councillor Keith Cunliffe.

Councillor Cunliffe, who represents the Leigh East ward, said: "Leigh Centurions had a fantastic season in 2016 and will be in the Super League next year. This was something that we wanted to recognise and celebrate.

"The signs will now let everyone know who comes into Leigh about this great achievement."

Players Martyn Ridyard and Ben Reynolds came to see one of the signs being installed on Manchester Road. Martyn said: "Seeing the signs go up is a proud moment for the club. We have achieved Super League so hopefully we can maintain it and the signs can stay up."

Ben Reynolds and Martyn Ridyard at the Leigh boundary, in front of one of the new road signs celebrating promotion to Super League

After four weeks of intense conditioning the players and staff enjoyed a brief respite with a trip to Daytona UK at Old Trafford for an afternoon of competitive karting, eventually won by Eloi Pelissier who pipped Derek Beaumont to the crown in an intensely fought last race.

As Christmas came ever closer the last formal event of the year was a hugely successful Q&A evening at LSV when new signings Glen Stewart, James Green, Ryan Hampshire, Eloi Pelissier and Atelea Vea were unveiled to supporters and quizzed by host Martyn Ridyard. To round off the evening Mike Latham interviewed Derek Beaumont, Neil Jukes and Micky Higham and again questions were invited from the floor. The evening was shown on LCTV.

So much to look forward to, so much to reflect upon, 2016 was certainly the Year of the Centurions.

LEAGUE TABLES

SUPER LEAGUE - SUPER 8s

	P	W	D	L	F	A	Pts
Warrington Wolves	30	21	1	8	852	541	43
Wigan Warriors	30	21	0	9	669	560	42
Hull FC	30	20	0	10	749	579	40
St Helens	30	20	0	10	756	641	40
Castleford Tigers	30	15	1	14	830	808	31
Catalans Dragons	30	15	0	15	723	716	30
Widnes Vikings	30	12	0	18	603	643	24
Wakefield Trinity Wildcats	30	10	0	20	571	902	20

SUPER 8s - THE QUALIFIERS

	P	W	D	L	F	A	Pts
Leeds Rhinos	7	6	0	1	239	94	12
Leigh Centurions	7	6	0	1	223	193	12
Huddersfield Giants	7	5	0	2	257	166	10
Hull Kingston Rovers	7	4	0	3	235	142	8
Salford Red Devils	7	3	0	4	208	152	6
London Broncos	7	3	0	4	221	212	6
Batley Bulldogs	7	1	0	6	111	318	2
Featherstone Rovers	7	0	0	7	96	313	0

CHAMPIONSHIP SHIELD

	P	W	D	L	F	A	Pts
Bradford Bulls	30	19	2	9	1077	570	40
Halifax	30	16	1	13	821	682	33
Sheffield Eagles	30	12	0	18	855	843	24
Dewsbury Rams	30	12	0	18	676	809	24
Swinton Lions	30	10	1	19	614	1041	21
Oldham	30	10	0	20	505	918	20
Whitehaven	30	8	1	21	553	918	17
Workington Town	30	7	1	22	597	991	15

LEAGUE 1 - SUPER 8s

	P	W	D	L	F	A	Pts
Toulouse Olympique	21	20	1	0	990	276	41
Rochdale Hornets	21	16	1	4	709	440	33
Barrow Raiders	21	15	1	5	769	375	31
Doncaster	21	14	0	7	683	526	28
York City Knights	21	12	1	8	618	461	25
Keighley Cougars	21	11	0	10	658	514	22
Hunslet Hawks	21	11	0	10	544	550	22
London Skolars	21	8	0	13	470	650	16

LEAGUE 1 SHIELD

	P	W	D	L	F	A	Pts
Newcastle Thunder	20	13	1	6	686	460	27
North Wales Crusaders	20	9	2	9	505	469	20
Coventry Bears	20	8	1	11	446	590	17
Gloucestershire All Golds	20	5	0	15	515	644	10
Oxford	20	4	0	16	356	843	8
South Wales Scorpions	20	2	0	18	274	723	4
Hemel Stags	20	2	0	18	274	976	4

SUPER LEAGUE - REGULAR SEASON

	P	W	D	L	F	A	Pts
Hull FC	23	17	0	6	605	465	34
Warrington Wolves	23	16	1	6	675	425	33
Wigan Warriors	23	16	0	7	455	440	32
St Helens	23	14	0	9	573	536	28
Catalans Dragons	23	13	0	10	593	505	26
Castleford Tigers	23	10	1	12	617	640	21
Widnes Vikings	23	10	0	13	499	474	20
Wakefield Trinity Wildcats	23	10	0	13	485	654	20
Leeds Rhinos	23	8	0	15	404	576	16
Salford Red Devils *	23	10	0	13	560	569	14
Hull Kingston Rovers	23	6	2	15	486	610	14
Huddersfield Giants	23	6	0	17	511	569	12

Six points deducted for salary cap breaches in 2014 & 2015

CHAMPIONSHIP - REGULAR SEASON

	P	W	D	L	F	A	Pts
Leigh Centurions	23	21	1	1	881	410	43
London Broncos	23	17	0	6	702	444	34
Batley Bulldogs	23	15	1	7	589	485	31
Featherstone Rovers	23	15	0	8	595	384	30
Bradford Bulls	23	13	2	8	717	446	28
Halifax	23	13	1	9	615	484	27
Sheffield Eagles	23	8	0	15	583	617	16
Dewsbury Rams	23	8	0	15	486	603	16
Swinton Lions	23	7	1	15	449	813	15
Oldham	23	7	0	16	401	678	14
Workington Town	23	5	1	17	455	756	11
Whitehaven	23	5	1	17	367	720	11

LEAGUE 1 - REGULAR SEASON

	P	W	D	L	F	A	Pts
Toulouse Olympique	14	13	1	0	702	184	27
Rochdale Hornets	14	12	1	1	547	252	25
York City Knights	14	10	1	3	482	256	21
Doncaster	14	10	0	4	499	304	20
Barrow Raiders	14	9	1	4	529	253	19
Keighley Cougars	14	9	0	5	520	368	18
Hunslet Hawks	14	8	0	6	383	374	16
London Skolars	14	8	0	6	354	376	16
Newcastle Thunder	14	7	1	6	404	368	15
North Wales Crusaders	14	5	2	7	336	355	12
Coventry Bears	14	4	1	9	289	460	9
Gloucestershire All Golds	14	3	0	11	334	479	6
South Wales Scorpions	14	1	0	13	176	582	2
Oxford	14	1	0	13	232	648	2
Hemel Stags	14	1	0	13	190	718	2

		2016 Season						Leigh Career								
Name	Date of Birth	A	S	T	G	DG	P	A	S	T	G	DG	P	Debut	Total apps	HN
Acton, Jamie	4/4/92	3	12	5	0	0	20	22	35	6	0	0	24	2014	57	1389
Armstrong, Tom	12/9/89	20	0	9	0	0	36	86	6	53	0	0	212	2011	92	1340
Barlow, Sam	7/3/88	0	0	0	0	0	0	38	13	9	0	0	36	2014	51	1387
Beswick, Bob	8/12/84	3	0	3	0	0	12	94	29	18	0	1	73	2012	123	1353
Brierley, Ryan	12/3/92	3	0	4	0	0	16	99	26	133	40	0	612	2012	125	1354
Brown, Mitch	7/11/87	7	2	3	0	0	16	7	0	4	0	0	16	2016	7	1418
Burns, Travis	6/2/84	6	1	3	4	0	20	6	2	3	4	0	20	2016	2	1414
Charnock, Lewis	2/9/94	1	1	2	0	0	8	1	1	1	0	0	4	2016	5	1409
Chase, Rangi	11/4/86	5	0	2	0	0	8	5	0	2	0	0	8	2016	5	1400
Dawson, Matty	2/10/90	8	3	9	0	0	36	8	0	9	0	0	36	2016	8	1416
Dixon, Andrew	28/2/90	9	3	5	0	0	20	33	5	9	0	0	36	2015	38	1396
Drinkwater, Josh	15/6/92	14	1	8	1	0	34	14	1	8	1	0	34	2016	15	1413
Emmitt, Jake	4/10/88	5	10	2	0	0	8	43	46	15	1	0	62	2010	89	1332
Evans, Ben	30/10/92	1	2	0	0	0	0	1	2	0	0	0	0	2016	3	1415
Fash, Brad	24/1/96	1	7	0	0	0	0	1	7	0	0	0	0	2014	8	1412
Foster, Lewis	21/12/93	1	6	1	0	0	4	1	9	1	0	0	4	2016	10	1391
Hansen, Harrison	26/10/85	15	14	6	0	0	24	15	14	6	0	0	24	2016	29	1402
Harper, Eze	7/12/94	3	0	1	0	0	4	3	0	1	0	0	4	2016	3	1408
Higham, Micky	18/9/80	23	3	7	0	0	28	65	21	36	0	0	144	1999	86	1153
Higson, Adam	19/5/87	30	0	14	0	0	56	116	24	61	0	0	244	2008	140	1310
Hock, Gareth	5/9/83	21	2	4	0	0	16	35	5	9	0	0	36	2015	40	1397
Hood, Liam	6/1/92	7	12	4	0	0	16	7	12	4	0	0	16	2016	19	1410
Hopkins, Sam	17/2/90	4	23	13	0	0	52	57	78	48	0	0	192	2011	135	1347
Kay, Liam	17/12/91	18	0	11	0	0	44	80	2	74	0	0	296	2014	82	1388
Maitua, Reni	11/6/82	24	5	14	0	0	56	24	5	14	0	0	56	2016	29	1403
McNally, Gregg	2/1/91	7	2	5	0	0	20	132	7	88	20	0	392	2012	132	1350
Moimoi, Fuifui	26/9/79	18	2	4	0	0	16	38	7	11	1	0	46	2015	45	1395
Owen, Richard	25/4/90	2	0	1	0	0	4	2	0	1	0	0	4	2016	2	1407
Pala, Mathias	14/6/89	0	0	0	0	0	0	5	0	0	0	0	0	2015	5	1399
Paterson, Cory	14/7/87	21	0	18	0	0	72	21	0	18	0	0	72	2015	21	1406
Pownall, Jonny	22/8/91	8	0	4	0	0	16	90	2	60	0	0	240	2011	92	1346
Reynolds, Ben	15/1/94	14	4	8	0	0	32	19	7	11	15	0	74	2015	26	1398
Ridyard, Martyn	25/7/86	23	2	5	135	2	292	205	12	77	738	9	1793	2009	217	1314
Smith, Lee	8/8/86	23	0	12	0	0	48	23	0	12	36	0	120	2012	23	1404
Spencer, Tom	2/1/91	3	7	1	0	0	4	57	42	14	0	0	56	2016	99	1357
Tickle, Danny	10/3/83	2	5	0	0	0	0	2	5	0	0	0	0	2016	7	1417
Tonga, Willie	8/7/83	6	0	1	0	0	4	6	1	1	0	0	4	2016	6	1411
Weston, Dayne	15/12/86	30	1	6	0	0	24	30	1	6	0	0	24	2016	31	1401
Whiting, Richard	20/12/84	12	3	2	0	0	8	12	3	2	0	0	8	2016	15	1405
Worthington, Greg	17/7/90	18	9	9	0	0	36	41	0	17	0	0	68	2015	41	1394
2016 TOTALS		**416**	**127**	**202**	**135**	**2**	**1180**										

THE 100 CLUB

1201. David Alstead
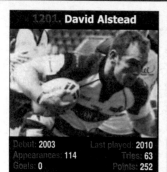
Debut: 2003   Last played: 2010
Appearances: 114   Tries: 63
Goals: 0   Points: 252

1160. Paul Anderson

Debut: 1999   Last played: 2002
Appearances: 103   Tries: 50
Goals: 17   Points: 234

3. Tom Anderton
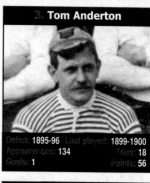
Debut: 1895-96   Last played: 1899-1900
Appearances: 134   Tries: 18
Goals: 1   Points: 56

215. Jack Armstrong

Debut: 1912-13   Last played: 1925-26
Appearances: 177   Tries: 15
Goals: 0   Points: 45

752. Kevin Ashcroft
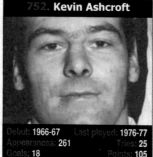
Debut: 1966-67   Last played: 1976-77
Appearances: 261   Tries: 25
Goals: 18   Points: 105

1047. Simon Baldwin
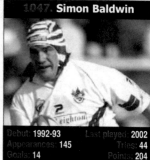
Debut: 1992-93   Last played: 2002
Appearances: 145   Tries: 44
Goals: 14   Points: 204

781. Tony Barrow
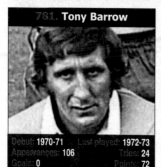
Debut: 1970-71   Last played: 1972-73
Appearances: 106   Tries: 24
Goals: 0   Points: 72

325. Bill Baxter

Debut: 1928-29   Last played: 1937-38
Appearances: 104   Tries: 7
Goals: 42   Points: 105

559. Ken Baxter

Debut: 1946-47   Last played: 1956-57
Appearances: 201   Tries: 48
Goals: 0   Points: 144

112. Herbert Bennett

Debut: 1901-02   Last played: 1910-11
Appearances: 206   Tries: 45
Goals: 2   Points: 139

1353. Bob Beswick

Debut: 2012   Last played: 2015
Appearances: 123   Tries: 18
Goals: 1   Points: 73

840. Terry Bilsbury
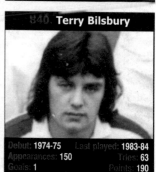
Debut: 1974-75   Last played: 1983-84
Appearances: 150   Tries: 63
Goals: 1   Points: 190

309. Tommy Bithell

Debut: 1926-27   Last played: 1932-33
Appearances: 120   Tries: 26
Goals: 5   Points: 88

250. Albert Blackburn

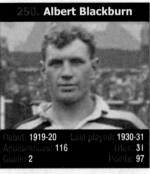

Debut: 1919-20   Last played: 1930-31
Appearances: 116   Tries: 31
Goals: 2   Points: 97

10. George Boardman

Debut: 1895-96   Last played: 1904-05
Appearances: 282   Tries: 9
Goals: 1   Points: 29

128. Jack Blackburn

Debut: 1902-03   Last played: 1907-08
Appearances: 103   Tries: 1
Goals: 0   Points: 3

226. Ernie Boardman

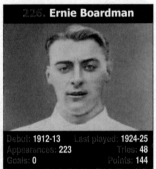

Debut: 1912-13   Last played: 1924-25
Appearances: 223   Tries: 48
Goals: 0   Points: 144

188. Mick Bolewski

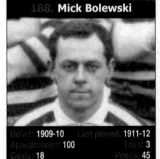

Debut: 1909-10   Last played: 1911-12
Appearances: 100   Tries: 3
Goals: 18   Points: 45

812. Denis Boyd

Debut: 1973-74   Last played: 1983-84
Appearances: 130   Tries: 26
Goals: 0   Points: 78

1176. David Bradbury

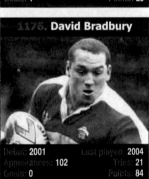

Debut: 2001   Last played: 2004
Appearances: 102   Tries: 21
Goals: 0   Points: 84

1354. Ryan Brierley

Debut: 2012   Last played: 2016
Appearances: 125   Tries: 133
Goals: 42   Points: 612

733. Wilf Briggs

Debut: 1965-66   Last played: 1976-77
Appearances: 112   Tries: 54
Goals: 12   Points: 185

1164. Adam Bristow

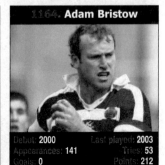

Debut: 2000   Last played: 2003
Appearances: 141   Tries: 53
Goals: 0   Points: 212

209. Joe Cartwright

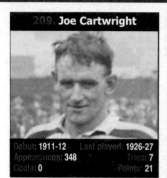

Debut: 1911-12   Last played: 1926-27
Appearances: 348   Tries: 7
Goals: 0   Points: 21

618. Brian Chadwick

Debut: 1951-52   Last played: 1961-62
Appearances: 218   Tries: 48
Goals: 0   Points: 144

756. Dave Chisnall

Debut: 1967-68   Last played: 1976-77
Appearances: 166   Tries: 28
Goals: 0   Points: 84

104. Ellis Clare

Debut: 1900-01   Last played: 1904-05
Appearances: 117   Tries: 1
Goals: 0   Points: 3

155. Ellis Clarkson

Debut: 1904-05   Last played: 1918-19
Appearances: 214   Tries: 10
Goals: 52   Points: 134

779. Geoff Clarkson

Debut: 1970-71   Last played: 1983-84
Appearances: 107   Tries: 9
Goals: 0   Points: 27

726. Keith Clarke

Debut: 1964-65   Last played: 1976-77
Appearances: 104   Tries: 7
Goals: 0   Points: 21

244. Tommy Clarkson

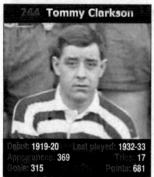

Debut: 1919-20   Last played: 1932-33
Appearances: 369   Tries: 17
Goals: 315   Points: 681

955. Andy Collier

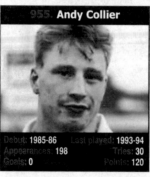

Debut: 1985-86   Last played: 1993-94
Appearances: 198   Tries: 30
Goals: 0   Points: 120

720. Mick Collins

Debut: 1963-64   Last played: 1974-75
Appearances: 408   Tries: 82
Goals: 0   Points: 246

543. Ben Coffey

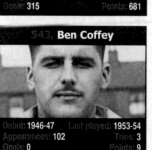

Debut: 1946-47   Last played: 1953-54
Appearances: 102   Tries: 3
Goals: 0   Points: 9

395. Chris Collier

Debut: 1934-35   Last played: 1939-40
Appearances: 107   Tries: 12
Goals: 0   Points: 36

1028. John Costello

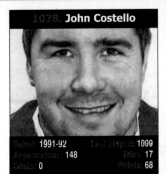

Debut: 1991-92 Last played: 1999
Appearances: 148   Tries: 17
Goals: 0   Points: 68

927. Tony Cottrell

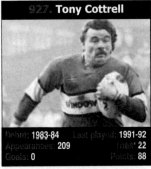

Debut: 1983-84 Last played: 1991-92
Appearances: 209   Tries: 22
Goals: 0   Points: 88

220. Joe Darwell

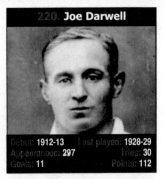

Debut: 1912-13 Last played: 1928-29
Appearances: 297   Tries: 30
Goals: 11   Points: 112

186. Dai Davies

Debut: 1908-09 Last played: 1922-23
Appearances: 259   Tries: 23
Goals: 0   Points: 69

342. Harry (Cocky) Davies

Debut: 1929-30 Last played: 1937-38
Appearances: 137   Tries: 12
Goals: 0   Points: 36

810. John Davies

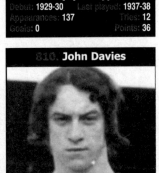

Debut: 1972-73 Last played: 1976-77
Appearances: 115   Tries: 47
Goals: 0   Points: 141

66. Tom Davies

Debut: 1898-99 Last played: 1902-03
Appearances: 140   Tries: 31
Goals: 10   Points: 113

960. Mike Dean

Debut: 1986-87 Last played: 1990-91
Appearances: 109   Tries: 20
Goals: 0   Points: 80

862. Des Drummond

Debut: 1976-77 Last played: 1985-86
Appearances: 280   Tries: 141
Goals: 2   Points: 470

877. Steve Donlan

Debut: 1978-79 Last played: 1984-85
Appearances: 240   Tries: 81
Goals: 49   Points: 337

1117. Stuart Donlan

Debut: 1997 Last played: 2011
Appearances: 194   Tries: 79
Goals: 0   Points: 316

1174. John Duffy

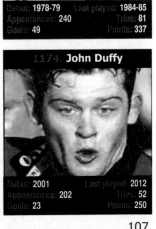

Debut: 2001 Last played: 2012
Appearances: 202   Tries: 52
Goals: 23   Points: 250

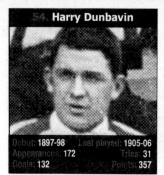

54. Harry Dunbavin

Debut: 1897-98 Last played: 1905-06
Appearances: 172 Tries: 31
Goals: 132 Points: 357

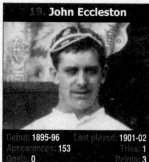

19. John Eccleston

Debut: 1895-96 Last played: 1901-02
Appearances: 153 Tries: 1
Goals: 0 Points: 3

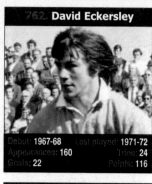

762. David Eckersley

Debut: 1967-68 Last played: 1971-72
Appearances: 160 Tries: 24
Goals: 22 Points: 116

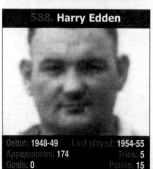

588. Harry Edden

Debut: 1948-49 Last played: 1954-55
Appearances: 174 Tries: 5
Goals: 0 Points: 15

338. Jack Edwards

Debut: 1929-30 Last played: 1938-39
Appearances: 143 Tries: 5
Goals: 9 Points: 33

603. Joe Egan

Debut: 1950-51 Last played: 1954-55
Appearances: 104 Tries: 6
Goals: 1 Points: 20

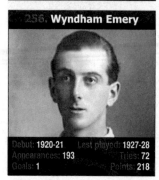

256. Wyndham Emery

Debut: 1920-21 Last played: 1927-28
Appearances: 193 Tries: 72
Goals: 1 Points: 218

719. Terry Entwistle

Debut: 1962-63 Last played: 1968-69
Appearances: 152 Tries: 14
Goals: 1 Points: 44

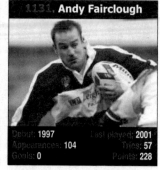

1131. Andy Fairclough

Debut: 1997 Last played: 2001
Appearances: 104 Tries: 57
Goals: 0 Points: 228

648. Brian Fallon

Debut: 1954-55 Last played: 1960-61
Appearances: 217 Tries: 54
Goals: 233 Points: 628

773. Stuart Ferguson

Debut: 1969-70 Last played: 1972-73
Appearances: 112 Tries: 19
Goals: 328 Points: 713

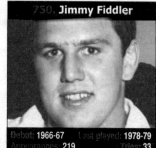

750. Jimmy Fiddler

Debut: 1966-67 Last played: 1978-79
Appearances: 219 Tries: 33
Goals: 327 Points: 737

669. Ray Fisher

Debut: 1957-58   Last played: 1962-63
Appearances: 120   Tries: 23
Goals: 0   Points: 69

357. Mick Flannery
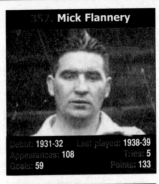
Debut: 1931-32   Last played: 1938-39
Appearances: 108   Tries: 5
Goals: 59   Points: 133

714. Geoff Fletcher
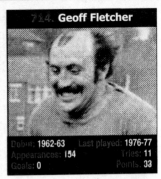
Debut: 1962-63   Last played: 1976-77
Appearances: 154   Tries: 11
Goals: 0   Points: 33

611. Peter Foster

Debut: 1951-52   Last played: 1958-59
Appearances: 236   Tries: 15
Goals: 2   Points: 49

895. Phil Fox

Debut: 1980-81   Last played: 1986-87
Appearances: 196   Tries: 96
Goals: 0   Points: 352

279. Jimmy France
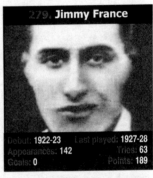
Debut: 1922-23   Last played: 1927-28
Appearances: 142   Tries: 63
Goals: 0   Points: 189

167. Dick Gallop

Debut: 1906-07   Last played: 1913-14
Appearances: 160   Tries: 18
Goals: 0   Points: 54

82. Frank Ganley

Debut: 1899-1900   Last played: 1904-05
Appearances: 125   Tries: 30
Goals: 0   Points: 90

194. Herbert Ganley

Debut: 1909-10   Last played: 1925-26
Appearances: 164   Tries: 29
Goals: 59   Points: 205

644. Jack Gibson

Debut: 1954-55   Last played: 1960-61
Appearances: 111   Tries: 27
Goals: 0   Points: 81

1330. Tommy Goulden
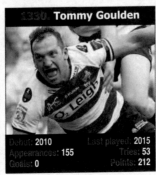
Debut: 2010   Last played: 2015
Appearances: 155   Tries: 53
Goals: 0   Points: 212

702. Tommy Grainey
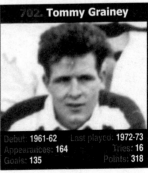
Debut: 1961-62   Last played: 1972-73
Appearances: 164   Tries: 16
Goals: 135   Points: 318

THE 100 CLUB

317. Jimmy Green

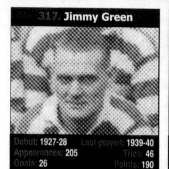

Debut: 1927-28   Last played: 1939-40
Appearances: 205   Tries: 46
Goals: 26   Points: 190

873. Ken Green

Debut: 1977-78   Last played: 1983-84
Appearances: 131   Tries: 16
Goals: 0   Points: 49

331. Mick Griffin

Debut: 1928-29   Last played: 1931-32
Appearances: 119   Tries: 22
Goals: 2   Points: 70

769. Paul Grimes

Debut: 1968-69   Last played: 1978-79
Appearances: 216   Tries: 19
Goals: 0   Points: 57

1101. Alan Hadcroft

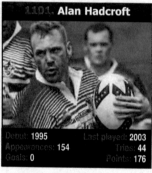

Debut: 1995   Last played: 2003
Appearances: 154   Tries: 44
Goals: 0   Points: 176

345. Fred Harris

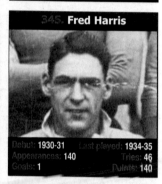

Debut: 1930-31   Last played: 1934-35
Appearances: 140   Tries: 46
Goals: 1   Points: 140

586. Norman Harris

Debut: 1948-49   Last played: 1951-52
Appearances: 118   Tries: 16
Goals: 0   Points: 48

388. George (Bud) Hayes

Debut: 1934-35   Last played: 1938-39
Appearances: 139   Tries: 6
Goals: 11   Points: 40

907. John Henderson

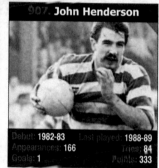

Debut: 1982-83   Last played: 1988-89
Appearances: 166   Tries: 84
Goals: 1   Points: 333

679. Derek Higgs

Debut: 1958-59   Last played: 1969-70
Appearances: 178   Tries: 9
Goals: 0   Points: 27

1310. Adam Higson

Debut: 2008   Last played: 2016
Appearances: 140   Tries: 61
Goals: 0   Points: 244

1252. Chris Hill

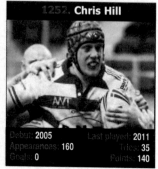

Debut: 2005   Last played: 2011
Appearances: 160   Tries: 35
Goals: 0   Points: 140

992. David Hill

Debut: 1988 Last played: 1990
Appearances: 206 Tries: 50
Goals: 0 Points: 200

804. Mick Hogan

Debut: 1972-73 Last played: 1983-84
Appearances: 296 Tries: 41
Goals: 0 Points: 125

637. Keith Holden

Debut: 1953-54 Last played: 1958-59
Appearances: 142 Tries: 58
Goals: 0 Points: 174

1347. Sam Hopkins

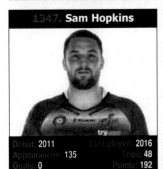

Debut: 2011 Last played: 2016
Appearances: 135 Tries: 48
Goals: 0 Points: 192

649. Joe Hosking

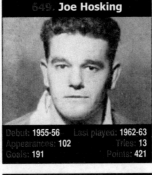

Debut: 1955-56 Last played: 1962-63
Appearances: 102 Tries: 13
Goals: 191 Points: 421

645. Derek Hurt

Debut: 1954-55 Last played: 1963-64
Appearances: 289 Tries: 46
Goals: 51 Points: 240

316. Tommy Hurtley

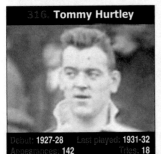

Debut: 1927-28 Last played: 1931-32
Appearances: 142 Tries: 18
Goals: 83 Points: 220

1080. David Ingram

Debut: 1994-95 Last played: 2002
Appearances: 165 Tries: 100
Goals: 3 Points: 406

929. Chris Johnson

964. Ian Jeffrey

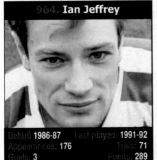

Debut: 1986-87 Last played: 1991-92
Appearances: 176 Tries: 71
Goals: 3 Points: 289

260. Abe Johnson

Debut: 1920-21 Last played: 1931-32
Appearances: 150 Tries: 41
Goals: 165 Points: 453

Debut: 1983-84 Last played: 1989-90
Appearances: 183 Tries: 38
Goals: 467 Points: 1073

THE 100 CLUB

380. Fred Johnson
Debut: 1933-34 Last played: 1937-38
Appearances: 110 Tries: 26
Goals: 6 Points: 90

928. Phil Johnson
Debut: 1983-84 Last played: 1991-92
Appearances: 160 Tries: 28
Goals: 135 Points: 375

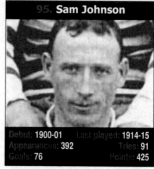

95. Sam Johnson
Debut: 1900-01 Last played: 1914-15
Appearances: 392 Tries: 91
Goals: 76 Points: 425

156. Tom Johnson
Debut: 1905-06 Last played: 1914-15
Appearances: 238 Tries: 56
Goals: 2 Points: 172

848. Clive Jones
Debut: 1974-75 Last played: 1978-79
Appearances: 112 Tries: 11
Goals: 0 Points: 33

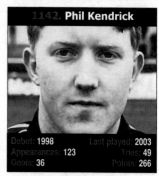

1142. Phil Kendrick
Debut: 1998 Last played: 2003
Appearances: 123 Tries: 49
Goals: 36 Points: 266

323. Jack Kenny
Debut: 1928-29 Last played: 1938-39
Appearances: 117 Tries: 44
Goals: 0 Points: 132

946. John Kerr
Debut: 1985-86 Last played: 1989-90
Appearances: 120 Tries: 54
Goals: 0 Points: 216

553. Ted Kerwick
Debut: 1946-47 Last played: 1952-53
Appearances: 202 Tries: 71
Goals: 0 Points: 213

587. Bill Kindon
Debut: 1948-49 Last played: 1959-60
Appearances: 259 Tries: 149
Goals: 0 Points: 447

606. Frank Kitchen
Debut: 1950-51 Last played: 1956-57
Appearances: 107 Tries: 79
Goals: 0 Points: 237

693. Tony Leadbetter
Debut: 1960-61 Last played: 1965-66
Appearances: 133 Tries: 44
Goals: 0 Points: 132

574. Jimmy Ledgard

Debut: 1947-48   Last played: 1957-58
Appearances: 334   Tries: 36
Goals: 1043   Points: 2194

136. Aaron Lee

Debut: 1903-04   Last played: 1912-13
Appearances: 264   Tries: 12
Goals: 0   Points: 36

680. Gordon Lewis

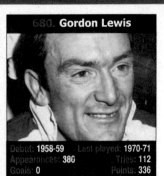

Debut: 1958-59   Last played: 1970-71
Appearances: 386   Tries: 112
Goals: 0   Points: 336

283. Jimmy Leyland

Debut: 1923-24   Last played: 1931-32
Appearances: 250   Tries: 7
Goals: 0   Points: 21

1073. Tau Liku

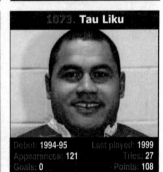

Debut: 1994-95   Last played: 1999
Appearances: 121   Tries: 27
Goals: 0   Points: 108

1342. Stuart Littler

Debut: 2011   Last played: 2014
Appearances: 101   Tries: 32
Goals: 0   Points: 128

192. Jimmy Lowe

Debut: 1909-10   Last played: 1918-19
Appearances: 120   Tries: 14
Goals: 0   Points: 42

831. Dave Macko

Debut: 1973-74   Last played: 1978-79
Appearances: 103   Tries: 30
Goals: 0   Points: 90

14. Bob MacMasters

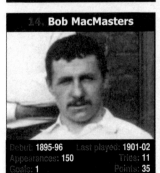

Debut: 1895-96   Last played: 1901-02
Appearances: 150   Tries: 11
Goals: 1   Points: 35

1213. Ste Maden

Debut: 2004   Last played: 2014
Appearances: 210   Tries: 73
Goals: 0   Points: 292

180. Harry Marsh

Debut: 1908-09   Last played: 1919-20
Appearances: 134   Tries: 10
Goals: 0   Points: 30

640. Mick Martyn

Debut: 1954-55   Last played: 1967-68
Appearances: 329   Tries: 189
Goals: 0   Points: 567

792. Tommy Martyn Senior

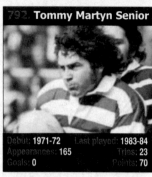

Debut: 1971-72   Last played: 1983-84
Appearances: 165   Tries: 23
Goals: 0   Points: 70

807. John McAtee

Debut: 1972-73   Last played: 1978-79
Appearances: 148   Tries: 30
Goals: 0   Points: 90

1216. Dave McConnell

Debut: 2004   Last played: 2010
Appearances: 112   Tries: 28
Goals: 0   Points: 112

608. Bill McFarlane

Debut: 1950-51   Last played: 1958-59
Appearances: 138   Tries: 25
Goals: 0   Points: 75

1350. Gregg McNally

Debut: 2012   Last played: 2016
Appearances: 132   Tries: 88
Goals: 20   Points: 392

18. Jimmy Molyneux

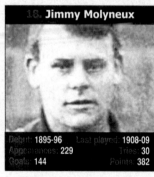

Debut: 1895-96   Last played: 1908-09
Appearances: 229   Tries: 30
Goals: 144   Points: 382

371. Bob Muntford

Debut: 1932-33   Last played: 1948-49
Appearances: 217   Tries: 4
Goals: 8   Points: 28

214. Walter Mooney

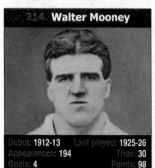

Debut: 1912-13   Last played: 1925-26
Appearances: 194   Tries: 30
Goals: 4   Points: 98

755. Alex Murphy

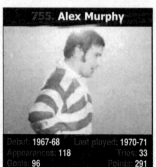

Debut: 1967-68   Last played: 1970-71
Appearances: 118   Tries: 33
Goals: 96   Points: 291

721. Mick Murphy

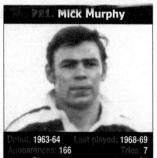

Debut: 1963-64   Last played: 1968-69
Appearances: 166   Tries: 7
Goals: 0   Points: 21

286. Bert Myers

Debut: **1924-25** Last played: **1929-30**
Appearances: **130** Tries: **15**
Goals: **1** Points: **47**

124. Bob Neville

Debut: **1902-03** Last played: **1913 14**
Appearances: **238** Tries: **88**
Goals: **0** Points: **264**

1148. Paul Norman

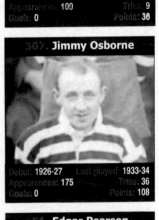

Debut: **1998** Last played: **2004**
Appearances: **100** Tries: **9**
Goals: **0** Points: **36**

1071. Jason O'Loughlin

Debut: **1994-95** Last played: **1998**
Appearances: **115** Tries: **19**
Goals: **19** Points: **111**

132. Paddy O'Neill

Debut: **1902-03** Last played: **1910-11**
Appearances: **211** Tries: **15**
Goals: **11** Points: **67**

307. Jimmy Osborne

Debut: **1926-27** Last played: **1933-34**
Appearances: **175** Tries: **36**
Goals: **0** Points: **108**

617. Stan Owen

Debut: **1951-52** Last played: **1963-64**
Appearances: **415** Tries: **44**
Goals: **0** Points: **132**

564. Charlie Pawsey

Debut: **1947-48** Last played: **1954-55**
Appearances: **216** Tries: **27**
Goals: **0** Points: **81**

902. Ian Potter

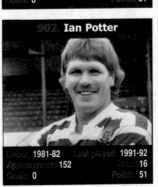

Debut: **1981-82** Last played: **1991-92**
Appearances: **152** Tries: **16**
Goals: **0** Points: **51**

51. Edgar Pearson

Debut: **1897-98** Last played: **1908-09**
Appearances: **232** Tries: **7**
Goals: **2** Points: **25**

313. Dicky Prescott

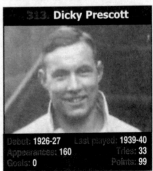

Debut: **1926-27** Last played: **1939-40**
Appearances: **160** Tries: **33**
Goals: **0** Points: **99**

890. Derek Pyke

Debut: 1979-80 Last played: 1987-88
Appearances: 220 Tries: 27
Goals: 0 Points: 102

304. Ted Richardson

Debut: 1925-26 Last played: 1936-37
Appearances: 200 Tries: 11
Goals: 0 Points: 33

1314. Martyn Ridyard

Debut: 2009 Last played: 2016
Appearances: 217 Tries: 77
Goals: 747 Points: 1793

449. Peter Riley

Debut: 1938-39 Last played: 1951-52
Appearances: 245 Tries: 30
Goals: 0 Points: 90

694. Bev Risman

Debut: 1960-61 Last played: 1965-66
Appearances: 140 Tries: 31
Goals: 241 Points: 575

69. Billy Roberts

Debut: 1898-99 Last played: 1905-06
Appearances: 234 Tries: 1
Goals: 0 Points: 3

70. Jimmy Roberts

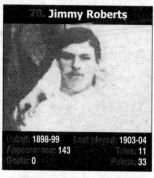

Debut: 1898-99 Last played: 1903-04
Appearances: 143 Tries: 11
Goals: 0 Points: 33

634. Bill Robinson

Debut: 1953-54 Last played: 1967-68
Appearances: 395 Tries: 26
Goals: 0 Points: 78

537. Jimmy Rowe

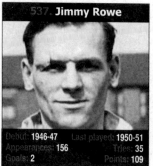

Debut: 1946-47 Last played: 1950-51
Appearances: 156 Tries: 35
Goals: 2 Points: 109

788. Allan Rowley

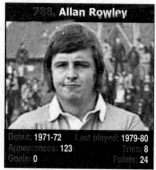

Debut: 1971-72 Last played: 1979-80
Appearances: 123 Tries: 8
Goals: 0 Points: 24

1052. Paul Rowley

Debut: 1992-93 Last played: 2007
Appearances: 198 Tries: 70
Goals: 2 Points: 282

978. David Ruane

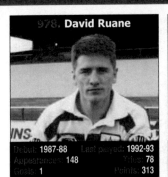

Debut: 1987-88 Last played: 1992-93
Appearances: 148 Tries: 78
Goals: 1 Points: 313

436. Ces Ryan

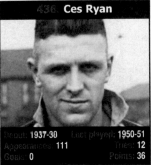

Debut: 1937-30 Last played: 1950-51
Appearances: 111 Tries: 12
Goals: 0 Points: 36

797. Cliff Sayer

Debut: 1971-72 Last played: 1977-78
Appearances: 149 Tries: 25
Goals: 0 Points: 75

116. Billy Smith

Debut: 1901-02 Last played: 1909-10
Appearances: 111 Tries: 46
Goals: 0 Points: 138

794. Mick Stacey

Debut: 1971-72 Last played: 1981-82
Appearances: 223 Tries: 72
Goals: 236 Points: 688

989. Tim Street

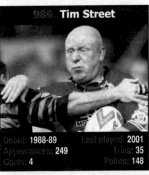

Debut: 1988-89 Last played: 2001
Appearances: 249 Tries: 35
Goals: 4 Points: 148

364. Billy Stringman

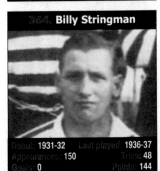

Debut: 1931-32 Last played: 1936-37
Appearances: 150 Tries: 48
Goals: 0 Points: 144

892. Ray Tabern

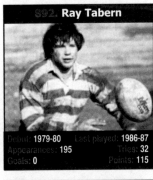

Debut: 1979-80 Last played: 1986-87
Appearances: 195 Tries: 32
Goals: 0 Points: 115

596. Walt Tabern

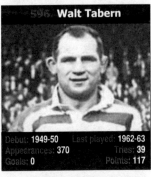

Debut: 1949-50 Last played: 1962-63
Appearances: 370 Tries: 39
Goals: 0 Points: 117

1242. James Taylor

Debut: 2005 Last played: 2013
Appearances: 183 Tries: 24
Goals: 0 Points: 96

854. John Taylor

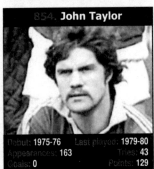

Debut: 1975-76 Last played: 1979-80
Appearances: 163 Tries: 43
Goals: 0 Points: 129

863. Kevin Taylor

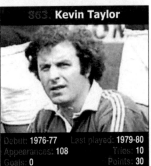

Debut: 1976-77 Last played: 1979-80
Appearances: 108 Tries: 10
Goals: 0 Points: 30

THE 100 CLUB

13. Peter Taylor
Debut: 1895-96   Last played: 1900-01
Appearances: 126   Tries: 5
Goals: 0   Points: 15

254. Emlyn Thomas
Debut: 1920-21   Last played: 1925-26
Appearances: 200   Tries: 26
Goals: 2   Points: 82

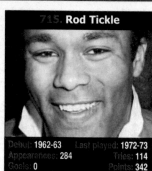

715. Rod Tickle
Debut: 1962-63   Last played: 1972-73
Appearances: 284   Tries: 114
Goals: 0   Points: 342

1172. Neil Turley
Debut: 2001   Last played: 2005
Appearances: 124   Tries: 132
Goals: 503   Points: 1519

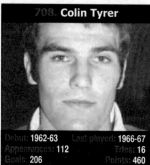

708. Colin Tyrer
Debut: 1962-63   Last played: 1966-67
Appearances: 112   Tries: 16
Goals: 206   Points: 460

293. Alf Unsworth
Debut: 1924-25   Last played: 1933-34
Appearances: 108   Tries: 12
Goals: 18   Points: 72

735. Joe Walsh
Debut: 1965-66   Last played: 1977-78
Appearances: 353   Tries: 128
Goals: 0   Points: 384

766. Derek Watts
Debut: 1968-69   Last played: 1971-72
Appearances: 113   Tries: 14
Goals: 0   Points: 42

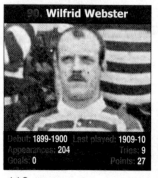

90. Wilfrid Webster
Debut: 1899-1900   Last played: 1909-10
Appearances: 204   Tries: 9
Goals: 0   Points: 27

724. Bob Welding
Debut: 1963-64   Last played: 1969-70
Appearances: 159   Tries: 15
Goals: 0   Points: 45

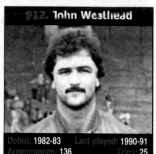

912. John Westhead
Debut: 1982-83   Last played: 1990-91
Appearances: 136   Tries: 25
Goals: 0   Points: 100

144. Sam Whittaker
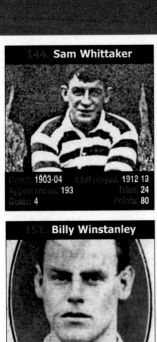
Debut: 1903-04 Last played: 1912-13
Appearances: 193   Tries: 24
Goals: 4   Points: 80

1145. Dave Whittle
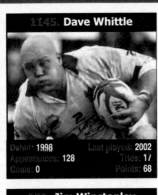
Debut: 1998   Last played: 2002
Appearances: 128   Tries: 17
Goals: 0   Points: 68

811. Alf Wilkinson
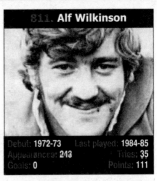
Debut: 1972-73 Last played: 1984-85
Appearances: 243   Tries: 35
Goals: 0   Points: 111

151. Billy Winstanley

Debut: 1904-05 Last played: 1910-11
Appearances: 171   Tries: 19
Goals: 0   Points: 57

233. Jim Winstanley
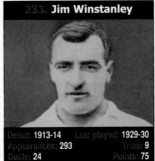
Debut: 1913-14 Last played: 1929-30
Appearances: 293   Tries: 9
Goals: 24   Points: 75

297. Billy Wood

Debut: 1925-26 Last played: 1930-31
Appearances: 164   Tries: 32
Goals: 0   Points: 96

557. Jack Wood

Debut: 1946-47 Last played: 1953-54
Appearances: 102   Tries: 78
Goals: 37   Points: 308

164. Herbert Woods

Debut: 1906-07 Last played: 1913-14
Appearances: 173   Tries: 1
Goals: 0   Points: 3

858. John Woods

Debut: 1976-77 Last played: 1992-93
Appearances: 349   Tries: 152
Goals: 997   Points: 2492

249. Albert Worrall

Debut: 1919-20 Last played: 1937-38
Appearances: 503   Tries: 46
Goals: 0   Points: 138

HONOURS

CHAMPIONSHIP WINNERS

Season 1905-06: Herbert Bennett, Bob Berry, Jack Blackburn, Phil Brady, Jim Buckley, Arthur Burgess, Ellis Clarkson, Harry Dunbavin (c), Dick Higson, Sam Johnson, Tom Johnson, Aaron Lee, Bobby Messer, William Naughton, Bob Neville, Paddy O'Neill (c), John Orrell, Billy Roberts, Horace Roscoe, Tom Shaughnessy, Dick Silcock, Billy Smith, Jim Threlfall, Bill Unsworth, Wilf Webster, Sam Whittaker, Billy Winstanley (no1), Billy Winstanley (no2).

Season 1981-82: Gary Ainsworth, Geoff Aspinall, Terry Bilsbury, Eric Chisnall, Geoff Clarkson, Tony Cooke, Steve Donlan, Des Drummond, David Dunn, Phil Fox, Ken Green, Mick Hogan, Roy Howarth, Mick McTigue, Tommy Martyn, Sean Mellor, Steve Mills, Billy Platt, Ian Potter, Derek Pyke, Mick Stacey, Ray Tabern, Steve Tomlinson, Alf Wilkinson, John Woods (c), Graham Worgan.

SECOND DIVISION CHAMPIONSHIP WINNERS

Season 1977-78: Terry Bilsbury, Dennis Boyd, Des Drummond, Alan Fairhurst, Jimmy Fiddler, Tony Garrity, Tommy Gittins, Ken Green, Paul Grimes, Steve Grimshaw, Mick Hogan, Clive Jones, John McAtee, Dave Macko, John Mantle (c), Ged Marsh, Maurice Platt, Alan Prescott, Alan Rathbone, Alan Riding, Allan Rowley, Cliff Sayer, Mick Stacey, John Taylor, Kevin Taylor, Joe Walsh, Alf Wilkinson, John Woods, Graham Worgan, Mal Yates.

Season 1985-86: Gary Ainsworth, Wayne Atherton, Darren Beazant, Simon Brockwell, Danny Campbell, Jeff Clarke, Trevor Cogger, Andy Collier, Tony Cottrell, Mike Davis, Des Drummond, Phil Fox, Bryan Gelling, Steve Halliwell, Paul Hardman, John Henderson, Bob Henson, Roy Howarth, Gary Hughes, Chris Johnson, Phil Johnson, John Kerr, Tony Manfredi, Peter Mayoh, David O'Toole, Derek Pyke (c), Darren Ramsdale, Colin Riding, Ray Tabern, David Taylor, Mark Thomas, Gary Walkden, John Westhead.

Season 1988-89: Craig Burrill, Andy Collier, Mark Cooper, Tony Cottrell, Mick Dean, Jason Donohue, Brian Dunn, Adrian Earner, Andy Evans, Dave Evans, Stuart Evans, John Henderson, David Hill, Mike Holliday, Ian Jeffrey, Chris Johnson, Phil Johnson, John Kerr, Mark Knight, Shaun Lang, Barrie Ledger, Neil McCulloch, George Mann, Sean Mellor, Robert Moimoi, David O'Toole, Ivor Owen, Steve Peters, Alan Platt (c), Peter Ropati, Mick Round, David Ruane, Tim Street, Carl Webb, John Westhead.

LEAGUE LEADERS (SUMMER ERA)

Premiership 2001: Paul Anderson, Simon Baldwin, Radney Bowker, David Bradbury, Liam Bretherton, Adam Bristow (c), Alan Cross, John Duffy, Andy Fairclough (c), Jamie Gass, Alan Hadcroft, John Hamilton, David Ingram, Jason Johnson, David Jones, Phil Kendrick, Andy Leathem, Chris Morley, Paul Norman, Kieron Purtill, Martin Roden, Lee Sanderson, Tim Street, Simon Svabic, Willie Swann, Neil Turley, Michael Watts, Dave Whittle.

National League One 2004: David Alstead, Radney Bowker, David Bradbury, Mike Callan, Dale Cardoza, Mick Coates, Ben Cooper, Heath Cruckshank, John Duffy, Mick Govin, Danny Halliwell, Luke Isakka, Andrew Isherwood, Phil Jones, Ian Knott (c), Simon Knox, David Larder, Steve Maden, Richard Marshall, Tommy Martyn, Dave McConnell, Mark McCully, Damian Munro, Paul Norman, Chris Percival, Dan Potter, Gary Rourke, Paul Rowley (c), Rob Smyth, Matt Sturm, Willie Swann, Neil Turley, Craig Weston, Oliver Wilkes.

Championship 2014: Jamie Acton, Tom Armstrong, Martin Aspinwall, Sam Barlow, Anthony Bate, Bob Beswick, Ryan Brierley, Alex Brown, Ryan Duffy, Jake Emmitt, Lewis Foster, Tommy Goulden, Kurt Haggerty, Chris Hankinson, Adam Higson, Sam Hopkins, Liam Kay, Stuart Littler, Steve Maden, Gregg McNally, Sean Penkywicz, Cameron Pitman, Michael Platt, Jonny Pownall, Martyn Ridyard, Matt Sarsfield, Tom Spencer, Andy Thornley, Jonny Walker, Oliver Wilkes (c).

Championship 2015: Jamie Acton, Tom Armstrong, Martin Aspinwall, Sam Barlow, Bob Beswick, Ryan Brierley, Andrew Dixon, Jake Emmitt, Lewis Foster, Tommy Goulden, Kurt Haggerty, Mickey Higham, Adam Higson, Gareth Hock, Sam Hopkins, Liam Kay, Gregg McNally, Fuifui Moimoi, Mathias Pala, Sean Penkywicz, Michael Platt, Jonny Pownall, Ben Reynolds, Martyn Ridyard, Matt Sarsfield, Tom Spencer, Jonny Walker, Oliver Wilkes (c), Greg Worthington.

Championship 2016: Jamie Acton, Tom Armstrong, Ryan Brierley, Travis Burns, Lewis Charnock, Rangi Chase, Matty Dawson, Andrew Dixon, Jake Emmitt, Ben Evans, Brad Fash, Lewis Foster, Harrison Hansen, Eze Harper, Micky Higham (c), Adam Higson, Gareth Hock, Liam Hood, Sam Hopkins, Liam Kay, Reni Maitua, Gregg McNally, Fuifui Moimoi, Richard Owen, Cory Paterson, Jonny Pownall, Ben Reynolds, Martyn Ridyard, Lee Smith, Tom Spencer, Danny Tickle, Willie Tonga, Dayne Weston, Richard Whiting, Greg Worthington.

Club Records

LEIGH IN CUP FINALS

1901: South West Lancashire & Border Towns Cup Final, Mon 29 Apr 2001, drew 0-0 against Warrington at Springfield Park, Wigan (6,000). Team: Edgar Pearson (c); Tom Davies, Sam Johnson, Tom Kight, Frank Ganley; Harry Dunbavin, Jimmy Molyneux; Bob MacMasters, George Boardman, Billy Roberts, Jimmy Roberts, Wilf Webster, John Eccleston, Ellis Clare, Jack Ramsdale. Note-Warrington failed to turn up for the replay at Widnes the following day and Leigh were awarded the Cup due to Warrington's default.

1905: The first Lancashire Cup Final, Sat 2 Dec 1905, drew 0-0 against Wigan at Wheater's Field, Broughton (16,000). Team: Ellis Clarkson; Sam Johnson, Tom Johnson, Herbert Bennett, Bob Neville; Harry Dunbavin (c), Sam Whittaker; Paddy O'Neill, Bob Berry, Jack Blackburn, Wilf Webster, Aaron Lee, Dick Silcock, Billy Winstanley (no2), Billy Roberts. Replay, Mon 11 Dec 1905, lost 0-8 to Wigan at Wheater's Field, Broughton (7,000). Team: same as for first game except Phil Brady for Tom Johnson, Billy Winstanley (no1) for Silcock.

1909: Lancashire Cup Final, Sat 27 Nov 1909, lost to Wigan 5-22 at Wheater's Field, Broughton (12,000). Team: Ellis Clarkson; Sam Johnson (t), Dai Davies, Dan Isherwood (c), Tom Johnson; Mick Bolewski, Frank Battersby (g); Paddy O'Neill, Aaron Lee, Dick Gallop, Herbert Woods, Edward Jones, Harry Marsh.

1920: Lancashire Cup Final, Sat 4 Dec 1920, lost to Broughton Rangers 3-6 at Salford (18,000). Team: Tommy Clarkson; George Higham (t), Dai Price, Wyndham Emery, Stanley Rowe; Bert Ganley; Emlyn Thomas; Jim Winstanley, Joe Cartwright, Jack Prosser, Joe Darwell, Fred Coffey, Dai Davies.

1921: Challenge Cup Final, Sat 30 Apr 1921, beat Halifax 13-0 at The Cliff, Broughton (25,000). Team: Tommy Clarkson (2g); Fred Hurst, Peter Heaton, Emlyn Thomas (2t), Cyril Braund; Billy Parkinson (t), Walter Mooney (c); Jim Winstanley, Joe Cartwright, Jack Prosser, Joe Darwell, Fred Coffey, Ernie Boardman.

1922: Lancashire Cup Final, Sat 25 Nov 1922, lost to Wigan 2-20 at Salford (20,000). Team: Tommy Clarkson (g); Abe Johnson, Wyndham Emery, Emlyn Thomas, Reg Taylor; Bert Ganley, Walter Mooney (c); Jim Winstanley, Joe Cartwright, Albert Worrall, Dai Davies, Jack Armstrong, Ernie Boardman.

1949: Lancashire Cup Final, Sat 29 Oct 1949, lost to Wigan 7-20 at Warrington (34,000). Team: Jimmy Ledgard (c) (2g); Jack Wood, Ted Kerwick, Norman Harris, Nebby Cleworth (t); Jimmy Rowe, Peter Riley; Alf Edge, Terry Stephens, Reg Wheatley, Ces Ryan, Charlie Pawsey, Jeff Burke.

1951: Lancashire Cup Final, Sat 27 Oct 1951, lost to Wigan 6-14 at Swinton (33,230). Team: Jimmy Ledgard; Bill Kindon, Trevor Allan, Norman Harris (t), Frank Morgan (t); Ted Kerwick, Ken Baxter; Harry Edden, Joe Egan (c), Jeff Burke, Charlie Pawsey, Walt Tabern, Peter Foster.

1952: Lancashire Cup Final, Sat 29 Nov 1952, beat St Helens 22-5 at Swinton (34,000). Team: Jimmy Ledgard (5g); Brian Chadwick (t), Trevor Allan (t), Ted Kerwick, Frank Kitchen (2t); Ken Baxter, Tommy Bradshaw; Harry Edden, Joe Egan (c), Stan Owen, Charlie Pawsey, Rex Mossop, Peter Foster.

1955: Lancashire Cup Final, Sat 15 Oct 1955, beat Widnes 26-9 at Wigan (26,509). Team: Jimmy Ledgard (c) (7g); Bill Kindon (t), Don Gullick (t), Albert Moore, Malcolm Davies; Jack Fleming, Brian Chadwick; John Barton (t), Walt Tabern, Stan Owen (t), Derek Hurt, Mick Martyn, Peter Foster.

1955: ITA Trophy Final, Wed 16 Nov 1955, lost to Warrington 18-43 at Queens Park Rangers FC (3,500). Team: Jimmy Ledgard (c) (3g); Keith Holden (t), Bob Wilson (t), Jim Murphy, Jack Gibson (t); Albert Moore, Tom O'Brien; Bill Robinson, Martin Dickens (t), Stan Owen, Peter Davies, Jack Crook, Jack McFarlane.

1963: Lancashire Cup Final, Sat 26 Oct 1963, lost to St Helens 4-15 at Swinton (21,321). Team: Bev Risman (c); Colin Tyrer (2g), Gordon Lewis, Mick Collins, Tony Leadbetter; Austin Rhodes, Terry Entwistle; Bill Robinson, John Lewis, Stan Owen, Mick Murphy, Mick Martyn, Derek Hurt.

1968: BBC2 Floodlit Trophy Final, Tue 16 Jan 1968, lost to Castleford 5-8 at Leeds (9,525). Team: Tom Grainey; Rod Tickle (t), Gordon Lewis, Mick Collins, Joe Walsh; Terry Entwistle, Alex Murphy (c); Alan Whitworth, Kevin Ashcroft, Harry Major, Bob Welding, Mick Murphy, Laurie Gilfedder (t).

1969: Lancashire Cup Final, Sat 1 Nov 1969, lost to Swinton 2-11 at Wigan (13,532). Team: Tom Grainey; Rod Tickle, Tom Warburton, Mick Collins, Harold Stringer; David Eckersley, Alex Murphy (c) (g); Dave Chisnall, Kevin Ashcroft, Derek Watts, Bob Welding, Jimmy Fiddler, Geoff Lyon. Sub: Dennis Brown.

1969: BBC2 Floodlit Trophy Final, Tue 16 Dec 1969, beat Wigan 11-6 at Wigan (12,234). Team: Stuart Ferguson (3g); Rod Tickle (t), Stan Dorrington, Mick Collins, Joe Walsh; David Eckersley, Alex Murphy (c) (g); Dave Chisnall, Kevin Ashcroft, Derek Watts, Bob Welding, Paul Grimes, Geoff Lyon. Sub: Gordon Lewis.

1970: Lancashire Cup Final, Sat 28 Nov 1970, beat St Helens 7-4 at Swinton (10,776). Team: Stuart Ferguson (2g); Rod Tickle, Mick Collins, Les Chisnall, Joe Walsh; David Eckersley (t), Alex Murphy (c); Dave Chisnall, Kevin Ashcroft, Derek Watts, Paul Grimes, Geoff Clarkson, Mick Mooney. Sub: Tommy Canning.

1971: Challenge Cup Final, Sat 15 May 1971, beat Leeds 24-7 at Wembley Stadium (85,514). Team: David Eckersley (t, g); Stuart Ferguson (5g), Stan Dorrington (t), Mick Collins, Joe Walsh; Tony Barrow, Alex Murphy (c) (2g); Derek Watts, Kevin Ashcroft, Jimmy Fiddler (g), Paul Grimes, Geoff Clarkson, Peter Smethurst. Sub: Les Chisnall.

1972: BBC2 Floodlit Trophy Final, Tue 19 Dec 1972, beat Widnes 5-0 at Wigan (4,872). Team: Mick Hogan; Graeme Lawson (t), John Atkin, Mick Collins, Mick Stacey; Tony Barrow (c), Cliff Sayer; Paul Grimes, Derek Clarke, Geoff Fletcher, Jimmy Fiddler (g), Frank Barrow, Tommy Martyn. Subs: Alan Riding, Roy Lester.

1976: BBC2 Floodlit Trophy Final, Tue 14 Dec 1976, lost to Castleford 4-12 at Leigh (5,417). Team: Mick Hogan; Alan Prescott, Mick Stacey, John Woods, Joe Walsh (t); John Taylor, Cliff Sayer; Dave Chisnall, Kevin Ashcroft (c) (dg), Geoff Fletcher, Dave Macko, Paul Grimes, Denis Boyd.

1981: Lancashire Cup Final, Sat 26 Sep 1981, beat Widnes 8-3 at Wigan (9,011). Team: Mick Hogan; Des Drummond, Terry Bilsbury (t), Stuart Donlan (dg), Graham Worgan; John Woods (c) (2g), Ken Green; Alf Wilkinson, Ray Tabern, Tony Cooke, Tommy Martyn, Geoff Clarkson, Mick McTigue. Sub: Billy Platt.

2000: Trans Pennine Cup Final, Wed 12 Apr 2000, lost to Dewsbury 8-10 at Dewsbury (2,465). Team: Stuart Donlan; Paul Wingfield (2g), Paul Anderson, Alan Cross, Alan Hadcroft; Andy Fairclough (c), Kieron Purtill; Tim Street, Anthony Murray (t), Dave Whittle, Simon Baldwin, Heath Cruckshank, Adam Bristow. Subs: Safraz Patel, Chris Causey, Paul Norman, Radney Bowker.

2000: Premiership Grand Final, Sat 29 Jul 2000, lost to Dewsbury 12-13 at Bury FC (8,487). Team: Stuart Donlan; David Ingram, Paul Anderson, Andy Fairclough (c), Alan Cross; Liam Bretherton (2g), Kieron Purtill; Tim Street, Mick Higham (2t), Andy Leathem, Simon Baldwin, Heath Cruckshank, Adam Bristow. Subs: James Arkwright, Paul Norman, Dave Whittle.

2001: Trans Pennine Cup Final, Wed 30 May 2001, beat Keighley 36-0 at Keighley (2,626). Team: Neil Turley (2t); David Ingram, Paul Anderson (2t), Andy Fairclough (c), Michael Watts; Simon Svabic (4g), Willie Swann (t); Tim Street, John Hamilton, Dave Whittle, Simon Baldwin (t), Phil Kendrick, Adam Bristow. Subs: Andy Leathem, David Bradbury, John Duffy, Liam Bretherton (t).

2002: Premiership Grand Final, Sun 12 Oct 2002, lost to Huddersfield Giants 16-38 at Widnes (9,051). Team: Neil Turley (2g); Leon Felton, Jon Roper, Dale Cardoza (t), Oliver Marns (t); Willie Swann, Bobbie Goulding; Vila Matautia, Paul Rowley, David Bradbury, Simon Baldwin, Andrew Isherwood, Adam Bristow (c). Subs: Gareth Price, John Duffy, John Hamilton (t), Dave Whittle.

2003: National League Cup Final, Sun 6 Jul 2003, lost to Salford 19-36 at Rochdale (6,486). Team: Neil Turley (t, g, dg); Damian Munro (t), Alan Hadcroft, Phil Kendrick, Leroy Rivett (t); Patrick Weisner, John Duffy; Sonny Nickle, Paul Rowley, Rob Ball, Sean Richardson, Bryan Henare, Adam Bristow (c). Subs: David Bradbury, Dale Cardoza, Willie Swann (t), Paul Norman.

2003: National League One Grand Final, Sun 5 Oct 2003, lost to Salford 14-31 at Widnes (9,186). Team: Neil Turley (g); Damian Munro, Alan Hadcroft, Danny Halliwell (t), Leroy Rivett; John Duffy, Tommy Martyn; Sonny Nickle, Patrick Weisner, Paul Norman, Sean Richardson (t), Willie Swann (t), Adam Bristow (c). Subs: David Bradbury, Lee Sanderson, Bryan Henare, Ricky Bibey.

2004: National League Cup Final, Sun 18 Jul 2004, beat Hull KR 42-14 at Rochdale (4,383). Team: Neil Turley (t, 6g, dg); Dan Potter, Danny Halliwell (2t), Ben Cooper (t), Rob Smyth; John Duffy, Tommy Martyn (t, dg); Simon Knox (2t), Paul Rowley, Matt Sturm, David Larder, Oliver Wilkes, Ian Knott (c). Subs: Dave McConnell, Willie Swann, Richard Marshall, Heath Cruckshank.

2004: National League One Grand Final, Sun 10 Oct 2004, beat Whitehaven 32-16 (after extra time) at Widnes (11,005). Team: Neil Turley (t, 6g, 2dg); Rob Smyth, Danny Halliwell, Ben Cooper (2t), David Alstead; John Duffy, Tommy Martyn (t, dg); Simon Knox, Paul Rowley (dg), Matt Sturm, David Larder, Oliver Wilkes, Ian Knott (c). Subs: Dave McConnell, Heath Cruckshank, Richard Marshall, Willie Swann.

2006: National League Cup Final, Sun 16 Jul 2006, beat Hull KR 22-18 at Blackpool FC (7,547). Team: Scott Grix (t); Dean Gaskell, Adam Hughes, Danny Halliwell, Lee Greenwood; Mick Govin (3g), Aaron Heremaia; Ricky Bibey, Paul Rowley (c) (t), Dana Wilson (t), Chris Hill, Tere Glassie (t), Robert Roberts. Subs: Carl Forber, Danny Speakman, James Taylor, Warren Stevens.

2011: Northern Rail Cup Final, Sun 17 Jul 2011, beat Halifax 20-16 at Blackpool FC (8,820). Team: Stuart Donlan (c); Steve Maden, Stuart Littler, Mick Nanyn (2g), Dean McGilvray; Martyn Ridyard, Jamie Ellis (2t); Chris Hill (t), John Duffy, David Mills, Andy Thornley, Tommy Goulden, James Taylor. Subs: Robbie Hunter-Paul, Stephen Nash, Tom Armstrong (t), Adam Higson.

2013: Northern Rail Cup Final, Sat 20 Jul 2013, beat Sheffield Eagles 43-28 at Halifax (4,179). Team: Gregg McNally; Steve Maden, Stuart Littler (2t), Matt Gardner, Jonny Pownall; Martyn Ridyard (7g), Ryan Brierley (t, dg); Michael Ostick, Bob Beswick, Tom Spencer (t), Simon Finnigan, Tommy Goulden (t), Sam Hopkins. Subs: Sean Penkywicz (t), Andy Thornley, Anthony Bate (t), Rob Parker (c).

2014: Championship Grand Final, Sun 5 Oct 2014, beat Featherstone Rovers 36-12 at Leeds (9,164). Team: Gregg McNally (t); Adam Higson (t), Michael Platt, Tom Armstrong (t), Liam Kay; Martyn Ridyard (6g), Ryan Brierley (t); Jake Emmitt, Sean Penkywicz, Oliver Wilkes (c), Matt Sarsfield (t), Kurt Haggerty, Sam Barlow (t). Subs: Bob Beswick, Jamie Acton, Martin Aspinwall, Jonny Walker.

TEAM RECORDS

HIGHEST SCORES FOR

92-2 v Keighley (h) 30 Apr 1986
88-2 v Runcorn H (a) 15 Jan 1989
84-12 v York (a) 8 Mar 2001
84-1 v York (h) 1 Jul 2001
82-0 v Gateshead
(away game staged at Leigh) 21 Aug 2002
82-6 v Lokomotiv Moscow (h) 8 Mar 2009
80-8 v Highfield (a) 11 Sep 1994
80-0 v Strela Kazan (h) 12 Mar 2006
78-18 v Dewsbury (h) 24 Aug 2003
78-10 v Chorley (a) 4 Apr 2004
76-6 v Mansfield M (h) 13 Oct 1985
75-3 v Doncaster (h) 28 Mar 1976
75-20 v Featherstone R (a) 11 Jul 2004
74-24 v Rochdale H (a) 9 May 2004
74-0 v London S (a) 23 Apr 2006
74-6 v London S (h) 15 Feb 2009
74-6 v Wigan St Patrick's
(away tie staged at Leigh) 14 Mar 2014
72-6 v Doncaster (h) 6 Jun 1999
72-6 v Hunslet H (h) 8 Jul 2015
72-22 v Rochdale H (a) 27 Jul 2014
71-14 v Lancashire County Amateurs (h) 27 Aug 1955
70-0 v Ryedale-York (h) 12 Jan 1992
70-0 v Workington T (h) 31 Jan 2001
70-2 v Batley (a) 24 Nov 1985

HIGHEST SCORES AGAINST

4-94 v Workington T (a) 26 Feb 1995
22-78 v Batley (a) 26 Mar 1995
4-78 v St Helens (h) 4 Sep 2005
20-76 v Hull (a) 14 Aug 2005
0-74 v Leeds (h) 7 Aug 2005
6-74 v Barrow (a) 25 Jul 2009
6-70 v Castleford (a) 20 Feb 1994
16-70 v Hull (a) 24 Apr 1994
16-70 v London B (a) 29 May 2005

HIGHEST SCORING DRAWS

36-36 v Bradford B (a) 19 Jul 2015
32-32 v Bradford B (a) 28 Feb 2016
28-28 v Featherstone R (a) 25 Apr 2011
24-24 v Castleford (h) 23 Apr 1985
22-22 v Wigan (h) 26 Aug 1959
22-22 v Hull (h) 17 Apr 2005
21-21 v Hull KR (h) 22 Mar 1981

SEQUENCES OF CONSECUTIVE WINS AND DEFEATS

ALL MATCHES

MOST CONSECUTIVE WINS

27 Jul 2014 to Jun 2015
19 Apr to Sep 2016
16 Feb to Jun 2014
14 Nov 1981 to Feb 1982
14 Mar to May 1986
13 Aug to Oct 1969
13 Apr to Jun 2001

WITHOUT DEFEAT
(excluding above)
13 Dec 1952 to Mar 1953 (W 11, D 2)
13 Dec 2001 to Mar 2002 (W 11, D 1, A 1)
13 Feb 2011 to May 2011 (W 12, D 1)

MOST CONSECUTIVE DEFEATS

18 Apr 1940 to Mar 1941
17 May 2005 to Sep 2005
14 Mar to Oct 1913
13 Jan to Mar 1937

WITHOUT A WIN
(excluding above)
21 Jan to Sep 1937 (D 1, L 20)
14 Dec 1899 to Mar 1900 (D 5, L 9)

LEAGUE MATCHES ONLY

MOST CONSECUTIVE WINS

30 Sep 1985 to Aug 1986
25 (including Qualifiers) Feb to Sep 2016
22 Jul 2014 to Jun 2015
18 Feb to Jul 2014
13 Jan to Sep 1989
12 Nov 1981 to Feb 1982
12 Apr to Jun 2001

MOST CONSECUTIVE DEFEATS

16 May to Sep 2005
15 Apr to Dec 1940
13 Mar to Oct 1913

MISCELLANY

● Leigh have remained undefeated at home in league games in nine seasons: 1969-70, 1970-71, 1977-78, 1981-82, 1985-86, 1988-89, 2014, 2015, 2016.
● From Dec 1968 to Aug 1971 Leigh remained undefeated in 44 consecutive home league matches (excluding one abandoned match)
● From 11 Jan 1976 to 16 Sep 1990 Leigh were undefeated in 48 consecutive home Second Division fixtures (W 47, D1) including a run of 46 consecutive wins.

PLAYER RECORDS

CAREER

MOST APPEARANCES *(300 and over)*
503	Albert Worrall
415	Stan Owen
408	Mick Collins
395	Bill Robinson
392	Sam Johnson
386	Gordon Lewis
370	Walt Tabern
369	Tommy Clarkson
353	Joe Walsh
349	John Woods
348	Joe Cartwright
334	Jimmy Ledgard
329	Mick Martyn

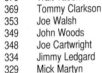
Albert Worrall

MOST TRIES *(100 and over)*
189	Mick Martyn
152	John Woods
149	Bill Kindon
141	Des Drummond
133	Ryan Brierley
132	Neil Turley
128	Joe Walsh
114	Rod Tickle
112	Gordon Lewis
100	David Ingram

Mick Martyn

MOST GOALS *(300 and over)*
1043	Jimmy Ledgard
997	John Woods
747	Martyn Ridyard
503	Neil Turley
467	Chris Johnson
337	Jimmy Fiddler
328	Stuart Ferguson
315	Tommy Clarkson

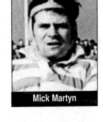
Jimmy Ledgard

MOST POINTS *(1,000 and over)*
2492	John Woods
2194	Jimmy Ledgard
1793	Martyn Ridyard
1519	Neil Turley
1073	Chris Johnson

John Woods

SEASON

MOST TRIES
55	Neil Turley, 2001
49	Steve Halliwell, 1985-86
43	Ryan Brierley, 2014
37	Ryan Brierley, 2015
36	Bill Kindon, 1956-57
36	Liam Kay, 2015
34	Malcolm Davies, 1954-55
34	Barrie Ledger, 1988-89
34	Jamie Ellis, 2011

MOST GOALS
187	Neil Turley, 2004
173	Chris Johnson, 1985-86
167	Martyn Ridyard, 2014
166	Stuart Ferguson, 1970-71
165	Jimmy Ledgard, 1954-55
159	Martyn Ridyard, 2015
156	Simon Svabic, 2001
155	Neil Turley, 2002

Neil Turley

MOST POINTS
468	Neil Turley, 2004
426	Neil Turley, 2002
400	Chris Johnson, 1985-86
394	Mick Nanyn, 2011
356	Stuart Ferguson, 1970-71
355	John Woods, 1983-84

MATCH

MOST TRIES
6	Jack Wood v York, 4 Oct 1947
6	Neil Turley v Workington T, 31 Jan 2001
5	Billy Smith v Liverpool C, 15 Dec 1906
5	Billy Smith v Keighley, 25 Apr 1908
5	Joe Houghton v Bramley, 16 Oct 1926
5	Jack Wood v Liverpool S, 31 Aug 1949
5	Rod Tickle v Liverpool C, 12 Apr 1968
5	John Davies v Blackpool B, 21 Apr 1973
5	Des Drummond v Carlisle, 20 Nov 1983
5	Phil Fox v Batley, 24 Nov 1985
5	Steve Halliwell v Keighley, 30 Apr 1986
5	Neil Turley v Chorley, 7 Jan 2001
5	Neil Turley v Featherstone R, 24 Jun 2001
5	Eric Andrews v Gateshead, 21 Aug 2002
5	Neil Turley v Swinton, 23 Mar 2003
5	Neil Turley v Chorley, 4 Apr 2004
5	Ryan Brierley v Barrow, 23 Feb 2014
5	Liam Kay v Barrow, 15 Jun 2014
5	Gregg McNally v Hunslet, 8 Jul 2015
5	Liam Kay v Doncaster, 26 Jul 2015

PLAYER RECORDS

(continued)

MOST GOALS

15	Mick Stacey v Doncaster, 28 Mar 1976
14	Chris Johnson v Keighley, 30 Apr 1986
14	Simon Svabic v York, 8 Mar 2001
13	John Woods v Blackpool B, 11 Sep 1977

MOST POINTS

42	Neil Turley v Chorley, 4 Apr 2004
38	John Woods v Blackpool B, 1 Sep 1977
38	John Woods v Ryedale-York, 12 Jan 1992
38	Neil Turley v Swinton, 23 Mar 2003
36	Mick Stacey v Doncaster, 28 Mar 1976
36	Simon Svabic v York, 8 Mar 2001
36	Neil Turley v Chorley, 7 Jan 2001

GROUNDS

MATHER LANE

First match: 7 Sep 1889 v Aspull
First match (Northern Union): 7 Sep 1895 v Leeds
Last match: 27 Apr 1940 v St Helens
Attendance record: 25,000 Wigan v St Helens
(RL Challenge Cup Semi-Final Replay) 2 Apr 1930
Attendance record for a game involving Leigh:
21,500 v Rochdale H, 3 Nov 1920

CHARLES STREET

First match: 14 Sep 1946 v St Helens
Last match: 10 May 1947 v Wigan
Attendance record: 13,000 v Warrington, 26 Apr 1947

KIRKHALL LANE
(renamed HILTON PARK in 1959)

First match: 30 Aug 1947 v St Helens
Last match: 7 Sep 2008 v Whitehaven
Attendance record: 31,326 v St Helens, 14 Mar 1953

LEIGH SPORTS VILLAGE

First official match: 15 Feb 2009 v London S *(nb. First
game was a friendly, Leigh v Salford on 28 Dec 2008)*
Attendance record:
10,544, Cook Islands v Tonga (World Cup) 5 Nov 2013
Attendance record for a game involving Leigh:
10,556 v Batley B, 17 Sep 2016

SEQUENCES

CONSECUTIVE CLUB APPEARANCES

179	Steve Donlan, Feb 1980 to Oct 1984
136	Albert Worrall, Apr 1926 to Jan 1930
102	Tom Anderton, Jan 1896 to Jan 1899

TRIES IN CONSECUTIVE CLUB GAMES

11	Mick Martyn, Jan to Mar 1959 (1-1-1-3-1-1-1-2-1-2-1)
9	Liam Kay, Feb to Apr 2015 (1-2-1-4-2-1-3-2-1)
8	Steve Halliwell, Apr to May 1986 (2-1-2-5-4-1-2-4)

GOALS IN CONSECUTIVE CLUB GAMES

53	Stuart Ferguson, Apr 1970 to Aug 1971
45	John Woods, Apr 1977 to Sep 1978
35	Jimmy Fiddler, Feb 1973 to Jan 1974

POINTS IN CONSECUTIVE CLUB GAMES

As goals in consecutive club games (above)

INTERNATIONAL GAMES AT LEIGH GROUNDS

19 Nov 1954, Australia 18-5 New Zealand
(International friendly) at Kirkhall Lane (6,000);
19 Oct 1955, Other Nationalities 32-9 France
(European Championship) at Kirkhall Lane (7,289);
29 Oct 1956, Australia 19-15 Rugby League XIII
(International Friendly) at Kirkhall Lane (7,811);
18 Mar 1964, Great Britain 39-0 France
(Test Match) at Hilton Park (4,750);
24 Nov 1979, Great Britain 14-2 France
(Under-24s International) at Hilton Park (4,077);
5 Mar 1983, Great Britain 24-10 France
(Colts International) at Hilton Park (1,024);
18 Oct 1995, Cook Islands 58 Russia 20
(Emerging Nations World Cup) at Hilton Park (1,921);
12 Jun 2010, England 60-6 France
(International) at Leigh Sports Village (7,951);
4 Dec 2010, England Academy 38-30 Australian Schoolboys
(Academy International) at Leigh Sports Village (732);
10 Dec 2010,
England Academy 34-22 Australian Schoolboys
(Academy International) at Leigh Sports Village (980);
15 Oct 2011, England Knights 38-18 France
(International Friendly) at Leigh Sports Village (2,071);
29 Oct 2011, England 42-4 Wales
(Four Nations) at Leigh Sports Village (10,377);
5 Nov 2013, Tonga 22-16 Cook Islands
(World Cup) at Leigh Sports Village (10,544).
6 Dec 2014, England Academy 18-22 Australian Schoolboys
(Academy International) at Leigh Sports Village (1,583);
12 Dec 2014,
England Academy 28-14 Australian Schoolboys
(Academy International) at Leigh Sports Village (1,197);
24 Oct 2015, England 84-4 France
(International Friendly) at Leigh Sports Village (8,380).
5 Nov 2016, Italy 76-0 Russia
(World Cup Qualifier) at Leigh Sports Village (450).

No.	Season	P	W	D	A	L	F	A	MOST APPEARANCES (ever presents in Bold)	TOP TRIES	TOP GOALS	TOP POINTS
1	1895-96	42	21	4	0	17	214	269	Boardman 41, Coop 41	Wallwork 9	Coop 21	Coop 55
2	1896-97	28	11	5	0	12	109	160	**Anderton 28, Coop 28, R Taylor 28**	Anderton 5	Coop 13	Coop 37
3	1897-98	30	13	3	0	14	248	195	**Anderton 30**	Dunbavin 12	Dunbavin 21	Dunbavin 78
4	1898-99	31	21	0	0	10	214	154	Boardman 30, Dunbavin 30, Pearson 30	Molyneux 11	Dunbavin 19	Molyneux 67
5	1899-1900	29	9	5	0	15	133	236	**T Davies 29**	Caldecott 9	Molyneux 18	Molyneux 39
6	1900-01	31	15	3	0	13	218	161	Boardman 30, S Johnson 30, Ramsdale 30	Ganley 11	Dunbavin 15, Towers 15	Dunbavin 45
7	1901-02	34	12	1	0	21	183	208	T Davies 32, Pearson 32	T Davies 9	Dunbavin 14	Dunbavin 34
8	1902-03	37	13	6	0	18	143	194	**Ganley 37, S Johnson 37**	Ganley 6	S Johnson 13	S Johnson 35
9	1903-04	37	11	5	0	21	186	266	Bennett 36, Blackburn 36, Boardman 36	Bennett 9	S Johnson 16	S Johnson 47
10	1904-05	36	15	3	0	18	168	214	**S Johnson 36**	S Johnson 14	Dunbavin 13	S Johnson 48
11	1905-06	37	27	3	0	7	268	159	**Berry 37**	Neville 13	Dunbavin 41	Dunbavin 88
12	1906-07	30	12	1	0	17	341	352	**Lee 30**	Smith 24	Molyneux 21	Smith 72
13	1907-08	37	16	1	0	20	357	431	**Winstanley 37**	Neville 17	Molyneux 23	Molyneux 55
14	1908-09	34	13	1	0	20	249	366	Lee 32	S Johnson 7, T Johnson 7, Neville 7	S Johnson 17	S Johnson 55
15	1909-10	37	18	5	0	14	269	255	Woods 35	T Johnson 11	Battersby 22	Battersby 50
16	1910-11	34	13	0	0	21	233	380	Bolewski 32	S Johnson 10	Ganley 17	Ganley 49
17	1911-12	36	18	1	0	17	340	365	Lee 35	T Johnson 15	Ganley 34	Ganley 89
18	1912-13	32	8	0	0	24	162	360	Cartwright 31, Roberts 31	Roberts 9	Prescott 6	Roberts 33
19	1913-14	33	11	0	0	22	173	361	D Davies 32	Boardman 6	Prescott 22	Prescott 44
20	1914-15	33	14	0	0	19	252	194	**Boardman 33, Keegan 33, Marsh 33**	Keegan 11	Winstanley 19	Winstanley 47

Competitive games suspended for the duration of the war

No.	Season	P	W	D	A	L	F	A	MOST APPEARANCES (ever presents in Bold)	TOP TRIES	TOP GOALS	TOP POINTS
21	1918-19	13	8	2	0	3	104	43	**Davies 13, Grundy 13, Keegan 13, Mooney 13, O'Neill 13**	Keegan 7	Whalley 10	Keegan 21
22	1919-20	30	12	2	0	16	175	242	Darwell 28	Boardman 5	Clarkson 35	Clarkson 70
23	1920-21	44	18	6	0	20	251	345	Prosser 38, E Thomas 38	Emery 9	Clarkson 34	Clarkson 68
24	1921-22	40	21	4	0	15	322	275	W Parkinson 37	Taylor 19	Clarkson 33	Clarkson 66
25	1922-23	36	25	0	0	11	403	304	Clarkson 35, Worrall 35	Taylor 24	Clarkson 31	Johnson 73
26	1923-24	37	20	3	0	14	415	289	France 36, Johnson 36	France 30	Johnson 29	Johnson 103
27	1924-25	36	13	1	0	22	328	446	**Cartwright 36**	H Thomas 18	Johnson 42	Johnson 108
28	1925-26	35	9	2	0	24	292	468	**France 35**	Emery 16	Johnson 15	Emery 48
29	1926-27	39	23	1	0	15	425	383	**Worrall 39**	Baldwin 23	Clarkson 31	Baldwin 69
30	1927-28	38	21	0	1	16	325	273	**Clarkson 38, Worrall 38**	Emery 11	Clarkson 50	Clarkson 106
31	1928-29	37	18	3	0	16	313	294	**Worrall 37**	Houghton 11, Kenny 11	Clarkson 30	Clarkson 63
32	1929-30	36	16	0	0	20	379	333	Worrall 35	Kenny 24	Clarkson 28	Kenny 72
33	1930-31	40	11	3	0	26	262	527	Griffin 35, Rudd 35	Griffin 7	Hurtley 18	Hurtley 45
34	1931-32	44	16	3	0	25	412	566	Worrall 41	Green 11, Harris 11, Tolan 11	Johnson 48	Johnson 105
35	1932-33	40	15	0	0	25	370	658	Worrall 38	Stringman 11	Baxter 40	Baxter 80
36	1933-34	41	15	2	0	24	498	570	Stringman 40	Stringman 22	Meadows 28	Stringman 66

127

Seasonal Summaries

No.	Season	P	W	D	A	L	F	A	MOST APPEARANCES (ever presents in Bold)	TOP TRIES	TOP GOALS	TOP POINTS
37	1934-35	40	13	0	0	27	311	665	Stringman 39	Harris 10, Walsh 10	Walsh 33	Walsh 96
38	1935-36	42	12	2	0	28	285	536	Hutchinson 40	Stringman 9	Farrington 51	Farrington 102
39	1936-37	41	5	5	0	31	248	658	Collier 39	Thompson 8	Farrington 41	Farrington 85
40	1937-38	40	8	3	0	29	243	646	T Winnard 38	Lomas 16	Thompson 17	Lomas 48
41	1938-39	43	7	3	1	32	253	732	Hart 39	Hewitt 6, Riley 6	Wade 27	Wade 54
42	1939-40	28	6	3	0	19	212	461	**Ord 28**	Riley 5	Wade 24	Wade 48
43	1940-41	14	0	0	0	14	70	464	**Cheetham 14**	Blakeley 2, Cheetham 2, Grimes 2, Murphy 2	Fields 7	Fields 14

The Club closed down and re-formed in 1946

No.	Season	P	W	D	A	L	F	A	MOST APPEARANCES (ever presents in Bold)	TOP TRIES	TOP GOALS	TOP POINTS
44	1946-47	42	23	1	0	18	367	286	**Ryan 42**	Kerwick 9, Riley 9, Rowe 9	Ackers 29	Ackers 58
45	1947-48	42	20	1	0	21	414	525	Daley 38, Riley 38	Wood 18	Wood 31	Wood 116
46	1948-49	43	17	5	0	21	415	399	Riley 42	Wood 23	Ledgard 55	Ledgard 116
47	1949-50	42	28	1	0	13	569	319	Kerwick 41	Wood 31	Ledgard 92	Ledgard 202
48	1950-51	43	27	2	0	14	541	365	N Harris 38	Kindon 22	Breare 53	Breare 112
49	1951-52	47	31	2	0	14	596	469	Ledgard 43	Kindon 16	Ledgard 125	Ledgard 262
50	1952-53	47	31	3	0	13	735	475	Mossop 44	Allan 30	Ledgard 116	Ledgard 247
51	1953-54	42	23	0	0	19	625	502	Ledgard 36	Kitchen 25	Ledgard 104	Ledgard 217
52	1954-55	42	29	2	0	11	831	449	W McFarlane 39	M Davies 34	Ledgard 165	Ledgard 345
53	1955-56	43	26	2	0	15	811	703	Ledgard 38, Owen 38	Kindon 24	Ledgard 148	Ledgard 320
54	1956-57	45	22	2	0	21	776	670	Foster 40	Kindon 36	Hosking 80	Hosking 172
55	1957-58	41	25	0	0	16	655	481	Foster 38	Martyn 24	Ledgard 101	Ledgard 208
56	1958-59	45	22	1	0	22	647	604	Owen 42, Robinson 42, Tabern 42	Martyn 28	Hosking 69	Hosking 156
57	1959-60	44	23	5	0	16	663	578	Fallon 40	Lewis 14	Fallon 111	Fallon 246
58	1960-61	40	28	0	0	12	642	345	Chadwick 37, Hurt 37	Martyn 22	Fallon 69	Fallon 156
59	1961-62	42	19	1	0	22	446	604	Owen 41	Davies 7	Botha 82	Botha 164
60	1962-63	36	15	0	0	21	454	479	Martyn 30	Martyn 19	Rhodes 37, Risman 37	Risman 98
61	1963-64	42	23	4	0	15	608	409	Entwistle 41, Leadbetter 41, Martyn 41	Martyn 22	Tyrer 61	Tyrer 134
62	1964-65	37	19	1	0	17	466	379	Tickle 36	Tickle 19	Risman 100	Risman 215
63	1965-66	42	18	1	0	23	390	507	Tickle 41	Tickle 15	Tyrer 31	Tyrer 65
64	1966-67	39	17	3	0	19	465	553	**Collins 39**	Briggs 13	Tyrer 79	Tyrer 176
65	1967-68	43	27	1	0	15	526	337	Lewis 42	Tickle 20	Gilfedder 63	Gilfedder 138
66	1968-69	43	22	5	1	15	574	486	**Collins 43**	Tickle 14	Warburton 48	Warburton 132
67	1969-70	48	31	4	0	13	714	439	D Chisnall 46	Tickle 20	Ferguson 56	Ferguson 112
68	1970-71	48	38	0	0	10	804	467	**Ferguson 48**	Walsh 17	Ferguson 166	Ferguson 356
69	1971-72	44	21	0	0	23	498	520	Eckersley 41	Ferguson 11	Ferguson 103	Ferguson 239
70	1972-73	44	24	2	0	18	582	510	Collins 43	J Davies 15	Fiddler 95	Fiddler 208
71	1973-74	39	11	0	0	28	492	794	Fiddler 36	J Davies 11, Fiddler 11, Stacey 11	Fiddler 110	Fiddler 253
72	1974-75	36	16	1	0	19	439	496	Sayer 34	Walsh 12	Stacey 46	Stacey 107
73	1975-76	34	23	1	0	10	688	310	**Ashcroft 34, Hogan 34, Stacey 34**	Briggs 23	Stacey 137	Stacey 331
74	1976-77	43	17	1	0	25	542	810	Woods 39	Walsh 13	Woods 90	Woods 193
75	1977-78	34	25	0	0	9	677	333	**K Taylor 34, Woods 34**	Drummond 19	Woods 140	Woods 328
76	1978-79	40	18	2	0	20	528	688	Platt 39	Drummond 13	Woods 86	Woods 201
77	1979-80	43	23	1	0	19	596	487	Drummond 42	Woods 22	Woods 82	Woods 228
78	1980-81	38	17	1	1	19	526	515	**Donlan 38**	Drummond 17	Woods 86	Woods 213
79	1981-82	41	31	2	0	8	776	449	**Donlan 41**	Woods 18	Woods 147	Woods 347

No.	Season	P	W	D	A	L	F	A	MOST APPEARANCES (ever presents in Bold)	TOP TRIES	TOP GOALS	TOP POINTS
80	1982-83	36	15	3	0	18	561	511	**Donlan 36, Potter 36**	Drummond 19	Tomlinson 63	Tomlinson 135
81	1983-84	38	18	0	1	19	832	721	**Donlan 38**	Woods 27	Woods 124	Woods 355
82	1984-85	36	11	2	0	23	649	864	Cottrell 34, Pyke 34	Fox 13, Taylor 13	Woods 66	Woods 174
83	1985-86	43	39	0	0	4	1436	515	Fox 42, C Johnson 42	Halliwell 49	C Johnson 173	C Johnson 400
84	1986-87	38	18	1	0	19	694	703	**McCulloch 38**	Henderson 27	C Johnson 86	C Johnson 174
85	1987-88	31	11	0	0	20	504	655	**McCulloch 31**	Kerr 12	C Johnson 41	C Johnson 88
86	1988-89	35	29	0	0	6	1084	445	**D Ruane 35**	Ledger 34	C Johnson 117	C Johnson 279
87	1989-90	30	10	1	0	19	514	733	**Jeffrey 30**	Ruane 13	C Johnson 50	C Johnson 100
08	1990-91	36	22	1	0	13	866	506	**Ropati 36**	Ruane 18, Topping 18	Topping 75	Topping 214
89	1991-92	33	22	0	0	11	703	506	**A Ruane 33**	Topping 16	Woods 74	Woods 178
90	1992-93	32	12	2	0	18	541	751	**D Ruane 32**	D Ruane 14	Platt 27	Platt 78
91	1993-94	33	3	1	0	29	414	1020	Rowley 32	Hanger 14	Clarke 26	Clarke 64
92	1994-95	35	15	0	0	20	728	989	Hill 26	Sarsfield 13	Blakeley 51	Blakeley 121
93	1995-96	21	16	0	0	5	608	354	O'Loughlin 20, Stazicker 20	Davies 13	Wilkinson 81	Wilkinson 175
94	1996	25	12	0	0	13	688	560	**Hill 25**	Ingram 23	Purtill 90	Purtill 224
95	1997	34	24	0	0	10	929	723	**Liku 34, O'Loughlin 34**	Purtill 21	Purtill 107	Purtill 298
96	1998	32	7	0	0	25	560	1126	**Costello 32**	Murray 12	Wingfield 61	Wingfield 138
97	1999	32	23	0	0	9	898	583	**Street 32, Whittle 32**	Murray 20	Wingfield 75	Wingfield 169
98	2000	34	24	0	0	10	983	573	**Anderson 34, Bristow 34, Street 34, Whittle 34**	Higham 22	Wingfield 99	Wingfield 230
99	2001	35	30	0	0	5	1287	409	Bretherton 32, Bristow 32, Hamilton 32, Svabic 32	Turley 55	Svabic 156	Svabic 341
100	2002	42	30	1	1	10	1488	754	Bristow 39	Turley 29	Turley 155	Turley 426
101	2003	36	26	1	0	9	1265	677	**Bristow 36, Richardson 36**	Munro 32	Turley 127	Turley 326
102	2004	33	28	0	0	5	1330	638	Cruckshank 30, Wilkes 30	Turley 26	Turley 187	Turley 468
103	2005	31	4	1	0	26	524	1284	**Leafa 31, Stapleton 31**	Wilshere 10	Jones 37	Jones 110
104	2006	31	23	0	0	8	1049	515	Hill 29	L Greenwood 24	O'Neill 60	Forber 124
105	2007	28	13	0	0	15	738	721	Rivett 27	M Greenwood 16	Couturier 61	Couturier 158
106	2008	28	17	0	0	11	725	616	Doran 27, Taylor 27, Watson 27	Alstead 16	Watson 65	Watson 148
107	2009	27	13	0	0	14	662	750	**Hill 27**	Durbin 13	Mort 74	Mort 192
108	2010	30	18	1	0	11	866	595	**Maden 30**	Nanyn 20	Nanyn 103	Nanyn 286
109	2011	31	26	1	0	4	1180	557	**Ellis 31, Littler 31**	Ellis 35	Nanyn 145	Nanyn 394
110	2012	31	22	0	0	9	1024	623	**Ridyard 31**	Brierley 25	Ridyard 133	Ridyard 321
111	2013	34	23	0	0	11	974	678	**Littler 34**	Brierley 25	Ridyard 123	Ridyard 280
112	2014	33	31	0	0	2	1274	513	**Brierley 33**	Brierley 43	Ridyard 167	Ridyard 344
113	2015	34	25	1	0	8	1264	668	Brierley 33, McNally 33	Brierley 37	Ridyard 159	Ridyard 345
114	2016	32	28	1	0	3	1180	627	Weston 31	Paterson 18	Ridyard 137	Ridyard 292

GRAND TOTALS

Played	4166
Won	2121
Drawn	171
Abandoned	6
Lost	1868
Points For	63456
Points Against	56663

REPRESENTATIVE HONOURS

The following list details representative honours earned by Leigh players since the Northern Union was founded in 1895.

1895-96: Lancashire- Tom Anderton, Tom Coop, Tom Smith, Peter Taylor.

1896-97: Lancashire- Tom Coop; The Rest- George Boardman.

1897-98: Lancashire- George Boardman, Peter Taylor; The Rest- Harry Dunbavin, Peter Taylor.

1898-99: Lancashire- Peter Taylor; The Rest- Harry Dunbavin, Jimmy Molyneux, Jimmy Roberts (ex Tyldesley), Peter Taylor.

1899-1900: Lancashire- Peter Taylor.

1900-01: The Rest- Bob MacMasters.

1901-02: Lancashire- Jimmy Roberts.

1902-03: Lancashire- George Boardman.

1903-04: Lancashire- George Boardman; Cheshire- Jimmy Molyneux.

1904-05: Lancashire- Paddy O'Neill; Cheshire: Harry Dunbavin, Sam Johnson.

1905-06: England- Dick Silcock; Lancashire- Paddy O'Neill, Dick Silcock.

1906-07: Lancashire- Sam Johnson, Paddy O'Neill.

1907-08: None.

1908-09: Lancashire- Ellis Clarkson, Dick Gallop, Bob Neville, Paddy O'Neill, Billy Smith, Billy Winstanley.

1909-10: The first Northern Union Tour of Australia and New Zealand (1910)- Billy Winstanley; Lancashire- Ellis Clarkson, Dick Gallop, Paddy O'Neill; Tour trials: Sam Johnson, Billy Winstanley.

1910-11: England- Billy Winstanley, Lancashire- Mick Rolowoki, Billy Winstanley; Tourists- Billy Winstanley.

1911-12: Lancashire- Bert Ganley, Tom Johnson, Aaron Lee.

1912-13: Lancashire- Tom Johnson, Aaron Lee.

1913-14: Tour trial- Joe Cartwright.

1914-15: None.

1918-19: None.

1919-20: Northern Union Tour of Australia and New Zealand (1920)- Joe Cartwright; Lancashire- Joe Cartwright, Walter Mooney; Tour trials: Joe Cartwright, Joe Darwell.

1920-21: England- Joe Cartwright; Other Nationalities- Wyndham Emery.

1921-22: Great Britain- Joe Cartwright; England- Joe Cartwright, Tommy Clarkson; Lancashire- Joe Cartwright, Tommy Clarkson; Lancashire League- Tommy Clarkson, Wyndham Emery, Jim Winstanley.

1922-23: England- Joe Cartwright, Tommy Clarkson, Joe Darwell; Wales- Wyndham Emery; Lancashire: Joe Cartwright, Tommy Clarkson, Joe Darwell.

1923-24: Great Britain Tour of Australia and New Zealand (1924)- Joe Darwell, Walter Mooney; England: Joe Cartwright, Joe Darwell; Lancashire- Joe Cartwright, Joe Darwell, Abe Johnson; Tour trials- Joe Cartwright, Joe Darwell, Abe Johnson.

1924-25: Lancashire- Joe Darwell.

1925-26: None.

1926-27: Lancashire- Tommy Bithell, Billy Wood.

1927-28: Lancashire- Billy Wood; Tour trials: Billy Wood, Albert Worrall.

1928-29: Lancashire- Billy Wood.

1929-30: Lancashire- Billy Wood, Albert Worrall; Northern Rugby League- Billy Wood.

1930-31: Lancashire- Billy Wood.

1931-32: Lancashire- Albert Worrall; Tour trials- Ted Richardson.

1932-33: Lancashire- Billy Baxter.

1933-34: England- Fred Harris, Albert Worrall; Lancashire- Dicky Prescott; Rugby League XIII- Fred Harris, Albert Worrall.

1934-35: Lancashire- Fred Harris, Dicky Prescott; Northern Rugby League Tour of France- Ted Richardson.

1935-36: Lancashire- Dicky Prescott; Northern Rugby League Tour of France- Dicky Prescott.

1936-37: Northern Rugby League Tour of France- Fred Farrington.

1937-38: None.

1938-39: None.

1939-40: None.

1940-41: None.

1946-47: Lancashire- Peter Riley.

1947-48: Lancashire- Jimmy Rowe.

1948-49: Great Britain- Jimmy Ledgard; England- Jimmy Ledgard; Wales- Jack Bowen, Norman Harris; Lancashire- Ben Coffey, Ted Kerwick, Peter Riley, Jimmy Rowe. Yorkshire- Jimmy Ledgard.

1949-50: Great Britain tour of Australia and New Zealand (1950)- Jimmy Ledgard; England- Ted Kerwick, Jimmy Ledgard; Wales- Norman Harris; Lancashire- Ted Kerwick, Jimmy Rowe; Yorkshire- Jimmy Ledgard.

1950-51: England- Joe Egan; Other Nationalities- Trevor Allan; Empire XIII: Bill Kindon; Australasia: Trevor Allan; Lancashire- Joe Egan, Bill Kindon; Tourists- Joe Egan.

1951-52. Great Britain- Jimmy Ledgard; England- Jimmy Ledgard, Charlie Pawsey; Other Nationalities- Trevor Allan, Jeff Burke; Lancashire- Peter Foster, Ted Kerwick, Bill Kindon, Charlie Pawsey; Yorkshire- Jimmy Ledgard; Empire- Trevor Allan; Great Britain (non Test)- Charlie Pawsey.

1952-53: Great Britain- Charlie Pawsey; England- Jimmy Ledgard, Charlie Pawsey; Other Nationalities- Trevor Allan; Lancashire- Peter Foster, Frank Kitchen, Charlie Pawsey; Yorkshire- Jimmy Ledgard; Cumberland- Dick Breare; Great Britain (non Test)- Charlie Pawsey.

1953-54: Great Britain tour of Australia and New Zealand (1954)- Charlie Pawsey; Great Britain (non Test)- Charlie Pawsey; England- Jimmy Ledgard, Charlie Pawsey; Other Nationalities- Rex Mossop; Wales- Malcolm Davies; Lancashire- Peter Foster, Charlie Pawsey; Yorkshire- Jimmy Ledgard; Cumberland- Albert Moore; Tour trials: Charlie Pawsey.

1954-55: Great Britain 1954 World Cup (France)- Frank Kitchen, Jimmy Ledgard; Wales- Malcolm Davies, Stan Owen; Lancashire- Peter Foster, Frank Kitchen; Cumberland- Albert Moore.

1955-56: Great Britain- Peter Foster; England- Jimmy Ledgard; Lancashire- Peter Foster; Yorkshire- Jimmy Ledgard; Cumberland- Albert Moore; Great Britain (non Test)- Peter Foster.

1956-57: Lancashire- Peter Foster, Bill Kindon.

1957-58: Great Britain tour of Australia and New Zealand (1958)- Mick Martyn; Great Britain- Stan Owen; Lancashire- Peter Foster, Bill Kindon; Rugby League XIII- Stan Owen; Tour trials- Mick Martyn, Stan Owen.

1958-59: Wales- Gordon Lewis; Lancashire- Bill Kindon, Mick Martyn; Cumberland- Derek Hurt.

1959-60: Great Britain- Mick Martyn; Lancashire- Mick Martyn, Walt Tabern; Cumberland- Joe Hosking.

1960-61: Lancashire- Walt Tabern.

1961-62: Lancashire- Mick Martyn; Rugby League XIII- Ted Brophy, Danny Harris, Chris Landsberg, Bev Risman.

1962-63: Great Britain- Bill Robinson; Wales- Gordon Lewis, Stan Owen; Lancashire- Ian Hodgkiss.

1963-64: Great Britain- Bill Robinson; Lancashire- Bill Robinson; Cumberland- Derek Hurt.

1964-65: Great Britain Under-24s: Mick Collins, Rod Tickle.

1965-66: Great Britain: Gordon Lewis; Great Britain Under-24s- Colin Tyrer; Lancashire- Rod Tickle; Rugby League XIII- Gordon Lewis, Mick Martyn.

1966-67: Great Britain Under-24s- Colin Tyrer; Lancashire- Colin Tyrer.

1967-68: Great Britain 1968 World Cup (Australia and New Zealand)- Kevin Ashcroft.

1968-69: Great Britain: Kevin Ashcroft; Wales: Gordon Lewis; Lancashire- Rod Tickle, Bob Welding.

1969-70: Great Britain Tour of Australia and New Zealand (1970)- Dave Chisnall; England- Alex Murphy; Wales- Stuart Ferguson and Gordon Lewis; Lancashire- Kevin Ashcroft, Alex Murphy, Bob Welding.

1970-71: Great Britain 1970 World Cup (England)- Kevin Ashcroft, Dave Chisnall; Lancashire- Kevin Ashcroft, Dave Chisnall, Dave Eckersley, Alex Murphy, Joe Walsh.

1971-72: Great Britain- Joe Walsh; Lancashire- Jimmy Boylan, Dave Eckersley, Roy Lester, Joe Walsh.

1972-73: None.

1973-74: Lancashire- Jimmy Fiddler.

1974-75: Lancashire: Jimmy Fiddler, Tommy Martyn jnr.

1975-76: Wales- Clive Jones; Lancashire- John Davies.

131

Representative Honours

1976-77: Lancashire: Denis Boyd, Mick Hogan, Mick Stacey, Alf Wilkinson.

1977-78: Great Britain Under-24s- Alf Wilkinson, John Woods; Wales- Clive Jones, John Mantle; Lancashire- Dave Macko, Alf Wilkinson, John Woods.

1978-79: Great Britain tour of Australia and New Zealand (1979)- John Woods; England- John Woods; Great Britain Under-24s- John Woods.

1979-80: England- Des Drummond, John Woods; Great Britain Under-24s- Des Drummond, Alan Rathbone, Malcolm Swann, John Woods; Lancashire- John Woods; Cumbria- Eddie Bowman.

1980-81: Great Britain- Des Drummond, John Woods; Great Britain Under-24s- Des Drummond; England- Des Drummond, John Woods; Lancashire- Terry Bilsbury, Alan Fairhurst, Tommy Gittins, John Woods; Cumbria- Eddie Bowman.

1981-82: Great Britain- Des Drummond, John Woods; Great Britain Under-24s- Des Drummond, Ian Potter; England- Des Drummond, John Woods; Lancashire- Steve Donlan, Des Drummond, Ian Potter, Ray Tabern, Alf Wilkinson, John Woods.

1982-83: Great Britain- Des Drummond, John Woods; Great Britain (non Test)- Des Drummond, Ian Potter, Ray Tabern.

1983-84: Great Britain tour of Australia, New Zealand and Papua New Guinea (1984): Des Drummond, Steve Donlan; Great Britain- Des Drummond.

1004-85: Great Britain Ohris Johnson, England- Steve Donlan, Des Drummond.

1985-86: Great Britain- Des Drummond; Great Britain Under-21s- Gary Hughes, John Westhead.

1986-87: Great Britain Under-21s- Mike Ford; Lancashire- John Henderson, Derek Pyke.

1987-88: Lancashire- Tony Cottrell, John Henderson, Neil McCulloch, Derek Pyke.

1988-89: Great Britain Under-21s- Tim Street.

1989-90: None.

1990-91: None.

1991-92: Great Britain Under-21s- Jason Donohue; Lancashire- Paul Topping.

1992-93: Great Britain Under-21s- Jason Donohue; Wales- Mark Moran.

1993-94: Great Britain Under-21s- Scott Martin.

1994-95: None.

1995-96: None.

1996: None.

1997: None.

1998: Premiership Select- Anthony Murray, Paul Wingfield.

1999: None.

2000: World Cup (Great Britain, Ireland and France)- Ireland- Liam Bretherton; Wales- Dave Whittle.

2001: Ireland- Dave Bradbury, Liam Bretherton; Wales- Chris Morley; England Under-21s tour of South Africa- Neil Turley; Lancashire- Neil Turley.

2002: Wales- Gareth Price, Dave Whittle.

2003: Scotland- John Duffy; National League One- John Duffy, Alan Hadcroft, Danny Halliwell, Sean Richardson, Neil Turley. National League Under-21s- David Alstead, Lee Sanderson.

2004: Scotland- Dave McConnell; Cumbria- Oliver Wilkes.

2005: Scotland- Oliver Wilkes.

2006: Ireland- Scott Grix, Wales- Adam Hughes, Rob Roberts

2007: Ireland- Anthony Stewart; Scotland- Dave McConnell.

2008: World Cup (Australia 2008)- Ireland- Lee Doran; Scotland- Dave McConnell; Other internationals, Wales- Ian Watson.

2009: Scotland- Mick Nanyn; Wales- Ian Watson.

2010: None.

2011: Scotland- John Duffy.

2012: Ireland- Stuart Littler, Gregg McNally,

2013: World Cup (England, Wales, Ireland & France, 2013) Ireland- Bob Beswick, Simon Finnigan, Stuart Littler.

2014: Ireland- Bob Beswick, Stuart Littler, Michael Platt; Scotland- Jonny Walker.

2015: Ireland- Bob Beswick; Scotland- Jonny Walker.

2016: Scotland- Liam Hood; Wales- Sam Hopkins.

1878: Surveyor Fred Ulph became founder of the Leigh Club, playing at Buck's Farm.

1879: Leigh moved to the field behind Three Crowns public house in the Bedford area of town.

1886: Leigh went through the season undefeated.

1889: Leigh defeated the New Zealand Maoris, the first touring team to this country at Three Crowns Field. The crowd was 6,000. Leigh then moved to a new ground on Frog Hall Estate, later known as Mather Lane.

1892: Leigh fullback Tom Coop was chosen for the England RU side, playing against Scotland at Raeburn Place, Edinburgh.

1894: Leigh were suspended for a period of ten weeks by the Lancashire RFU for alleged professionalism.

1895: The Northern Union was formed after 22 clubs broke away from the Rugby Football Union. Leigh played Leeds in the first match under the new code on 7 September at Mather Lane, losing 3-6.

1896: The Northern Union Challenge Cup was inaugurated.

1897: Northern Union rules were amended from those adopted under rugby union. The line-out was abolished and replaced by a punt from touch. All goals were to be worth two points.

1898: Unrestricted professionalism was allowed in the Northern Union provided players followed legitimate employment at least three days per week.

1899: Centre Tom Anderton became the first player to complete one hundred consecutive appearances under both the auspices of the rugby union and Northern Union.

1901: Leigh's close rivals Tyldesley disbanded. Leigh won their first honour under Northern Union rules, being awarded the South West Lancashire and Border Towns Cup due to Warrington's default.

1902: Two divisions were introduced. The touch finding rule was introduced, with the ball having to bounce before entering touch. The working clause for players was abandoned, opening the door for full-time professionalism in some cases.

1905: Leigh Football Club became a limited liability company. Two divisions were scrapped. The Lancashire Cup competition was inaugurated and Leigh lost to Wigan in the first final after a replay at Broughton.

1906: Leigh were Champions of the Northern Union, securing the title with a scoreless draw at Barrow on the final day of the season. This was the last season of 15-a-side. After this season 13-a-side was introduced into Northern Union and a play-the-ball rule was introduced.

1907: Leigh defeated the first New Zealand tourists, known as the 'All Golds' 15-9 at Mather Lane before a crowd of 8,000.

1908: Leigh became the first side to defeat the first Australian tourists, known as the Kangaroos, winning 14-11 before 8,000 spectators at Mather Lane. Joseph Lavery, a New Zealander became the first overseas player to play for the Club.

1909: Kangaroo tourist Mick Bolewski became the first Australian to play for Leigh. The first Northern Union representative game was staged at Mather Lane, Lancashire losing 9-14 to the Australian tourists. The ground capacity was raised to 20,000 after extensions to the embankment on the popular side. International halfback James Jolley was recruited from Runcorn to become the Club's first official coach.

1910: Leigh forward Billy Winstanley was included in the first Northern Union tour party to Australia and New Zealand, soon later joining Wigan for a fee of £150 on his return.

1913: Only 300 spectators saw Leigh play Hull at Mather Lane, producing match receipts of £4.

1915: There was a ban on competitive football for the duration of the war. On 24 May A-Team forward Ernest Doorey was killed in action at Ypres, the first of 13 Leigh players to lose their lives serving in the Forces during World War One. The others were: Harry Bilsbury, Frank Ganley, Ben Lloyd, Ralph Makin, Paddy O'Neill, Ben Sumner, Jim Threlfall, James Tobin MM, Robert Topping, Billy Unsworth, Harry Ward and Sam Whittaker.

1919: Competitive football resumed in January.

1920: Joe Cartwright became Leigh's second tourist.

1921: Leigh beat Halifax 13-0 in the Challenge Cup Final at The Cliff, Broughton before a crowd of 25,000.

1922: The Mather Lane ground was purchased outright by the Club. A new covered grandstand was erected. The title of the Northern Rugby Football Union was changed to the Rugby Football League.

Key Dates in Leigh's History

1924: Walter Mooney and Joe Darwell were chosen to tour Australia and New Zealand, leaving for the seven-week journey by boat in April. Shaw's Brewery produced a souvenir brochure to mark the occasion, Darwell being licensee of one of their public houses. Winger Jimmy France set a new Club record with 30 tries, a record that stood for 31 years.

1926: In the year of the General Strike Leigh admitted miners free of charge to home games.

1927: Leigh signed former Wigan winger AJ Van Heerden, the first South African to play for the Club.

1928: The Grandstand at Mather Lane was doubled in size. An iron bridge over the canal was constructed to allow easier access for spectators. Fullback Tommy Clarkson became the first Leigh player to kick 50 goals in a season.

1930: A Mather Lane ground record attendance of 25,000 was recorded for a Challenge Cup semi-final between St Helens and Wigan, surpassing the crowd of 21,940 for the Wigan-St Helens Recs semi-final one year previously. Albert Worrall missed Leigh's game against Oldham due to injury, ending a run of 136 consecutive appearances.

1931: Leigh's first-team players went on strike for three weeks in protest at reduced terms. In three games Leigh fielded a team made up of reserve players.

1933: A public meeting was held on 15 June to outline the Club's financial difficulties. Liabilities of £5,600 were revealed. Financial support from 'an outside source' enabled the Club to continue.

1934: Leigh played under floodlights for the first time, losing 8-25 to London Highfield at the White City. The Duke of York was introduced to the Leigh team and officials during the half-time interval of the game at Broughton Rangers on 20 October.

1936: An Extraordinary General Meeting of the Club was held at the Rope and Anchor Hotel on 3 February at which the parlous financial situation was discussed.

1937: Two members of the RFL Management Committee were co-opted onto the board until the end of the season due to recurrent financial crises. The Club won only five games in the 1936-37 season. In November the Club directors resigned and the RFL was in control until a new Members' Club was formed on 21 February 1938. A crowd of only 200 (receipts: £8) saw Dewsbury win 46-6 at Leigh.

1938: Albert Worrall retired after completing a Club record 503 appearances.

1939: The Emergency League was formed due to the outbreak of war. Air Raid marshals were in attendance at all games and spectators were ordered to spread evenly around the terraces.

1940: The Club was without a home when Callenders Cable and Construction Company obtained a compulsory purchase order for the Mather Lane ground from the owners, Messrs George Shaw and Company Ltd of the Leigh Brewery. Leigh played all matches away in the 1940-41 season after being refused permission by the RFL to ground-share at Hindsford AFC. Leigh suffered a Club record 8-60 defeat at Salford in the short-lived Summer Competition.

1941: Leigh ceased playing after losing a Challenge Cup tie at Hunslet on 12 April. A total of 59 players turned out for Leigh in their 14 games, all of which were lost.

1946: The Leigh Club was reformed after a public meeting at Leigh Liberal Club. All home matches were to be played on the Leigh Harriers and Athletic Club Ground at Charles Street. Leigh's first match for over five years was at Rochdale Hornets on 31 August. Tries by Percy Aldred and Joe Farrell helped Leigh to a 6-5 win. Tommy Sale was one of only eleven players to play for the Club pre 1941 and post 1946 and was Leigh's first post war captain.

1947: Leigh moved to a new ground at Kirkhall Lane after purchasing the site (formerly used for allotments) for £2,500. The steel-framed stand from the old Mather Lane ground was dismantled and re-erected at the new ground. In June Leigh and Barrow were chosen by the RFL to play three promotional matches in Devon and Cornwall. A crowd of 17,000 saw Leigh's first match at the new ground in a Lancashire Cup-tie against St Helens, Saints winning 15-0. In October Jack Wood scored six tries and kicked eight goals in Leigh's 60-7 win over York.

1948: Fullback Jimmy Lodgard joined Leigh from Dewsbury for a fee of £2,650, a new RL record.

1949: French champions Roanne visited Leigh, Leigh winning 2-0.

1950: In May Leigh undertook a short tour of France, playing a Catalan XIII and Carcassonne. Leigh signed Wigan's international hooker Joe Egan for £5,000, another record RL fee and he became player-coach. In September Leigh paid £5,000 to capture Australian RU international centre Trevor Allan.

1952: Leigh won the Lancashire Cup for the first time, defeating St Helens 22-5 at Swinton. Jimmy Ledgard became the first Leigh player to kick one hundred goals in a season.

1953: Leigh became the second club in RL (after Bradford Northern) to install floodlights. These were completed in September at a cost of £4,100. There was a ground record attendance of 31,326 for a Challenge Cup-tie against St Helens. In July Leigh signed world sprint champion McDonald Bailey, then aged 32, but he was released from his contract in Feb 1954 after playing only one friendly game.

1955: Leigh beat Widnes 26-9 at Wigan to lift the Lancashire Cup for a second time; the following month they lost to Warrington in the final of the inaugural and only ITA Television Trophy competition staged at Queens Park Rangers' Loftus Road ground.

1956: The Pools got underway, producing valuable extra funding for the Club.

1958: Mick Martyn scored 23 tries for Great Britain on tour in Australia and New Zealand, a record for a forward on tour.

1959: The ground was renamed 'Hilton Park' in memory of former Chairman James Hilton who died in April.

1961: Leigh signed England RU international Bev Risman for a reported signing-on fee of £6,000.

1962: Two divisions were re-introduced and by finishing 17th in the one division table Leigh began the new era in Division Two.

1964: Two divisions were scrapped. Substitutes were allowed for injuries, but only up until half-time. Great Britain played France in the first-ever test match to be held at a Leigh ground. A crowd of 4,750 saw Great Britain's 39-0 victory.

1965: Substitutes were allowed for any reason, initially up until and including half-time. The BBC2 Floodlit Trophy competition began.

1966: The four tackle rule was introduced for Floodlit Trophy matches from October and for all matches from December. Former St Helens and Great Britain star Alex Murphy joined Leigh as coach in October, later becoming player-coach. Mick Martyn received a well deserved testimonial cheque of £910. Martyn scored 189 tries for Leigh, a club record.

1967: The first Sunday matches were played on 17 December. In one of two such fixtures Leigh entertained Dewsbury, winning 15-10 before a crowd of 6,000.

1968: Leigh played Wigan at St Helens in the BBC2 Floodlit Trophy semi-final, the first RL game to be televised in colour.

1969: Substitutes were allowed at any time. Leigh defeated Wigan 11-6 in the Floodlit Trophy Final at Central Park.

1970: Leigh remained undefeated at home in the league during 1969-70, for the first time in Club history. Leigh defeat St Helens 7-4 in the Lancashire Cup Final at Swinton.

1971: Leigh won the Challenge Cup for a second time, defeating Leeds 24-7 at Wembley. Alex Murphy won the Lance Todd Trophy as man of the match. The John Player Trophy was inaugurated. Stuart Ferguson played and scored in every one of Leigh's 48 games during the 1970-71 season, only the second player in RL history to achieve the feat.

1972: The six tackle rule was introduced.

1973: Two divisions were re-introduced. Leigh were relegated after the first season.

1974: Drop-goals were reduced in value to one point. On 7 December a crowd of 451 saw Leigh's home game against Hull, a post-war record low.

1976: The differential penalty rule was introduced for scrum offences. Leigh beat Doncaster 75-3, a new Club record win, on their way to promotion. Mick Stacey kicked 15 goals and scored 36pts in that game, both new Club records.

1977: John Woods set a new Club record of 38pts (4 tries, 13 goals) against Blackpool Borough.

1978: John Woods played and scored in every Leigh game during the 1977-78 season.

1981: Leigh defeated Widnes 8-3 in the Lancashire Cup Final at Wigan in a match televised live on BBC1.

1982: Leigh won the Championship for the second time in their history after defeating Whitehaven at the Recreation Ground in their final game of the season.

1983: The sin bin was introduced. The value of a try was increased to four points. The handover rule after the sixth tackle was introduced.

1984: Steve Donlan set a new Club record of 179 consecutive appearances.

1986: Leigh scored over one thousand points in the league for the first time in their history after winning the second division championship. Steve Halliwell scored a Club record 49 tries and Chris Johnson a club record 400 points. Leigh lost only one of their 34 league games in 1985-86. Leigh beat Keighley 92-2 at Hilton Park to set a new Club record.

1987: A new system for players' contracts was introduced.

1989: Leigh won 88-2 at Runcorn Highfield, a new Club record for an away game.

1990: John Woods became the Club record points-scorer. For the 1990–91 season the Club adopted the nickname the Bears, but this was dropped after less than a year.

1991: The Company went into administration and a new limited company was formed. Tony Cottrell became the club's first player-chairman. Three divisions were introduced. An Academy League was formed.

1992: Steve Simms became Leigh's first Australian coach. In November 1992, Leigh got a reprieve in the High Court following the threat of eviction from Hilton Park.

1993: Three divisions and the Lancashire Cup were scrapped. Two divisions were re-introduced. The ten-metre rule was introduced.

1994: The Club went into administration in July.

Key Dates in Leigh's History

1995: On 26 February Leigh suffered a Club record defeat, losing 4-94 at Workington Town. Horwich RMI FC made the decision to move from their ground at Grundy Hill to Hilton Park, changing their name to Leigh RMI FC for the 1995-96 season. As part of the deal a new company, Grundy Hill Estates Limited, was formed to take over the ownership of the ground. The first football game to be played at Hilton Park was a Northern Premier League fixture between Horwich RMI and Boston United on Saturday 4 March 1995, the visitors winning 4-0 before a crowd of 481. Meanwhile, Leigh adopted the title Leigh Centurions for the 1995-96 Centenary Season. The Cook Islands played Russia at Hilton Park in the Emerging Nations World Cup.

1996: Rugby League changed forever with the switch to summer and the formation of a European Super League after a multi-million pound contract with News Corporation and their UK subsidiary, broadcasters BSkyB. Leigh's first official summer fixture was a Challenge Cup-tie against Egremont on 14 January. Seven days later they played Bramley in the final league game of the Centenary Season. Leigh finished in second place in Division Two after the first summer season which ended on 25 August. Four substitutes were introduced.

1997: Leigh's hopes of a return to Wembley Stadium were ended with a home semi-final defeat against Hull KR in the short-lived Challenge Cup Plate.

1998: Leigh RMI lost 0-2 at home to Fulham in an FA Cup first round replay before a crowd of 7,125 at Hilton Park, a record for a football game at the ground.

2000: Leigh lost 12-13 to Dewsbury in the Premiership Grand Final at Gigg Lane, Bury.

2001: Neil Turley scored 55 tries in his first season with the Club, believed to be a world record for a fullback. Turley equalled Jack Wood's Club record by scoring six tries against Workington Town.

2002: Leigh lost to Huddersfield in the Premiership Grand Final.

2003: Leigh played a Russian side for the first time, hosting Locomotiv Moscow in the Challenge Cup. There was more last day agony as Leigh lost to Salford in what was now re-named the National League One Grand Final.

2004: Leigh won the National League Cup Final after beating Hull KR and then reached Super League after defeating Whitehaven after extra-time in the National League One Grand Final at Widnes. Neil Turley scored a Club record 468pts, and also kicked a Club record 187 goals. Turley set another Club record with 42pts against Chorley.

2005: Leigh finished bottom of Super League and were relegated back to the National Leagues.

2006: Tony Benson became Leigh's first coach from New Zealand. Leigh won the National League Cup Final, defeating Hull KR at Blackpool.

2008: The final season at Hilton Park. The final first-team game was an Elimination Play-Off against Whitehaven on 7 September, the visitors winning 30-24 before a crowd of 2,306. On 28 December Leigh played their first game at the Leigh Sports Village, entertaining Salford in a friendly.

2009: The first official game at Leigh Sports Village saw Leigh defeat London Skolars 74-6 on 15 February. On 21 May 2009, the Queen and Prince Phillip officially opened Leigh Sports Village.

2010: Now renamed Leigh Genesis, the football club left LSV to ground-share at Crilly Park and folded after the 2010-11 season.

2011: Leigh won the Northern Rail Cup after beating Halifax in the final at Blackpool. A ground record attendance of 10,377 saw England defeat Wales 42-4 in the Four Nations.

2013: Leigh won the Northern Rail Cup for the second time in three seasons after defeating Sheffield Eagles at The Shay. A ground record attendance of 10,544 was recorded for the World Cup game between Cook Islands and Tonga on 5 November.

2014: Leigh enjoyed the most successful season, results-wise in their history, lifting the Kingstone Press Championship League Leaders Shield and following up with a Grand Final victory over Featherstone Rovers. A Heritage Day commemorated past and current players who all received their unique Heritage Number.

2015: Leigh won the League Leaders Shield and reached the last eight of the Challenge Cup for a second successive season but failed to secure a place in Super League in the newly introduced Super 8s competition. The club was honoured at a civic ceremony at Leigh Town Hall when a star was unveiled in the town hall square alongside those celebrating Alex Murphy and musician Georgie Fame. Australian internationals Reni Maitua and Willie Tonga were among new recruits for the 2016 season, taking the club's tally of internationals on their playing roster to 12 players. A blue plaque was erected close to the site of the old Mather Lane ground in a ceremony attended by RFL and Club officials to mark the 120th anniversary of the first Northern Union game.

2016: Club President Tommy Sale MBE passed away on 3 January at the age of 97. The single most influential person in the history of the Club, his passing marked the end of an era. Leigh regained their place in Super League after a momentous year, winning the League Leaders' Shield for a third successive year and winning six games in the Qualifiers series. Neil Jukes replaced Paul Rowley as Head Coach on the eve of the season and steered his charges to 28 wins and one draw in 32 games. A new attendance record was set in the final home game of the season, 10,556 against Batley.

SUBSCRIBERS

Jerry Alderson
Paul Anderson
Keith Anderton
Kevin Ashcroft
Colin Ashley
David Ashley
Neil Barker
Derek Beaumont
Laura Beaumont
John Blackburn
Lewis Boardman
Brian Bowman
Michael Broome
Max Brown
Toby Bulcock
Jonathan Byrne
Eric W Carter
Tracey Carter
Terry Casey RIP
Matthew Chantler
Neil Cheetham
Les Cooke
Paul Cooke
Tony Cooke
Cliff Cunliffe
Matthew Arron Dawes
Allan Dickinson
Sharon Dillon
Ian Dodd
Joanne Durkin
Linda Duxbury
Chris Evans
Andrew Farr
John Farr
Martin Flannery
Joe Gormally
Graham Grimshaw
Mike Guest
Rebecca Hall
Steven Hall
Tony Hannan
Danny Hardman
Liam, Luke & Isabelle Harvey
Micky Higham
Harry Hulme
Adele Huyton
Amy Huyton
Jason Huyton
Gillian Jolley
Melissa Jones
Tom Jones
Neil Jukes
Bryan Kay
Christopher Kay
Fred Kenny
Liam Kenny
Janet Latham
Jennifer Latham

Mike Latham
Sarah Latham
Brian Leather
Amanda Lee
Dave Lewis
Gemma Lewis
Malcolm Lewis
Hayley Macdonald
Paul McCarthy
Chris Meadows
Eddie Minion
Thomas Minion
Alan Molyneux
Graham Morris
Paul Morris
Tom Morris
Alex Murphy OBE
Yvonne Murphy
Paul Joseph Naughton
Alan S Newsham
Michael Norris
Craig O'Donnell
Kevin O'Donnell
Steve Openshaw
Andrew Parkinson
Fred Parkinson
Colin & Joshua Pemberton
Jacqueline Phoenix
Gary Pratt
Vince Pritchard
Kieron Purtill
William Joseph Redford
Caroline Reynolds
Ken Reynolds
Eric Rowson
Karol Sanderson
Keeley Sandland
Bernadette Scotson
Tony Scotson
Andrew Seddon
Steve Seddon
Alan Smallshaw
David Smallshaw
Jordan Smith
Andy Speakman
Ian Speakman
Daniel Spencer
Andrew Stringer
John Stringer
Paul Sumner
Troy Sumner
Francis Taylor
Mark Taylor
Ian Thompson
Brian Wood
Simon Woodcock
John Woods

As 2016 came to a close, League Express handed out a number of fresh awards to Leigh Centurions staff and players.

Head Coach Neil Jukes was voted Kingstone Press Championship Coach of the Year and skipper Micky Higham as Kingstone Press Championship Player of the Year in the Readers' Polls.

And to cap off a hat-trick of awards, League Publications Managing Editor Martyn Sadler named Owner Derek Beaumont as his Man of the Year.

Responding, Derek Beaumont said:

"I would like to thank Martyn Sadler and League Express for their award of Man of the Year, along with Martyn's kind words towards myself and our club.

"I had no idea that I was even being considered for the title. I genuinely feel privileged to be named his Man of the Year in a sport that is littered with many great and influential figures, not least the coaches he mentions and many top quality players who have had fantastic contributions to their clubs.

"Interestingly Martyn has me spot on with his assessment and I, like I preach to my children, employees and friends, learn from experiences and mistakes which I think is a quality attribute found in any successful person. There have been times in my past when I have been too head strong with my drive, and this year I made a conscious effort to curb that and approach my goals with more respect and humanity.

"I am very protective of our club and it is correct that I have fallen out with people where I have felt our club hasn't been treated fairly, and that has included journalists from the League Express, but I have come to understand that it is part of the process and criticism and opinion will always be there and it isn't something you can control.

"Indeed the very fact that Martyn and League Express have chosen me given such situations is a clear example of that and a mark of how genuine the title is. As people know my motivator isn't for personal gratification but I must concede I

do feel rewarded for what has been a year that has been as incredibly difficult as it has been successful.

"I must also mention that my achievements were also greatly dependent on everyone involved at the club, in particular my fellow board members who are equally as driven and supportive, Neil Jukes whom I spoke to more than my wife in the first part of the season, along with all his coaching team and what emerged as a fantastic team representing our club.

"Ultimately it is with them that the responsibility and achievement lies, but I can say I will take this with pride and despite currently not drinking alcohol as part of my challenge with Marwan, will raise a glass of bubbly when I settle down to read my weekly pocket mags version of the League Express tonight.

"Thank you Martyn, and best wishes for 2017 to you and your team. I hope we can have some positive contributions to your publications throughout the year."